Apple Training Series

Mac OS X Server
Essentials

Edited by Schoun Regan

Apple
Certified

Apple Training Series: Mac OS X Server Essentials
Schoun Regan, Ed.
Copyright © 2006 by Apple Computer

Published by Peachpit Press. For information on Peachpit Press books, contact:

Peachpit Press
1249 Eighth Street
Berkeley, CA 94710
(510) 524-2178
Fax: (510) 524-2221
http://www.peachpit.com
To report errors, please send a note to errata@peachpit.com
Peachpit Press is a division of Pearson Education

Series Editor: Serena Herr
Developmental Editor: Cheryl England
Production Coordinator: Laurie Stewart, Happenstance, Type-O-Rama
Technical Editor: David Ekstrand
Technical Reviewers: Victor Gavenda and Owen Linzmayer
Copy Editors: Emily K. Wolman and Doug Adrianson
Compositors: Jeffrey Wilson and Craig Woods, Happenstance Type-O-Rama
Indexer: Joy Dean Lee
Interior Design: Frances Baca Design
Cover Design: Tolleson Design
Cover Illustration: Alicia Buelow; "Hand Holding Modem Plug" © Robert Daly/Getty Images
Cover Production: George Mattingly / GMD

ISBN 0-321-35758-2
9 8 7 6 5 4 3 2 1
Printed and bound in the United States of America

This book is dedicated to my wife Susan.
She is my center, and without her I would be lost.

Acknowledgments

Special thanks to Daniel Thomas.

Thanks also to David Ekstrand and to Cheryl England, who put in more hours than I do, if that's possible.

Thanks to the University of Michigan contingent. They make me miss Northeast Ohio even more.

I would also like to acknowledge several members of the Apple Consultant's Network (In no particular order); Pam Lefkowitz, Ben Greisler, Phil Goodman, Shelley Weiner, Benjamin Levy, Adam Schectner, Arek Dreyer, Steve Leebove, Doug Hanley, and Kok Yon Tan.

And a sad goodbye to Sing-Si Schwartz, an ACN of top caliber and a wonderful human being. You will be missed.

Contents at a Glance

Lesson 1 Getting Started 1
Lesson 2 Installing and Configuring Mac OS X Server 9
Lesson 3 Using Network Services 53
Lesson 4 Setting Up Gateway Services 103
Lesson 5 Authenticating and Authorizing Accounts 137
Lesson 6 Using Open Directory 201
Lesson 7 Understanding Print Service 247
Lesson 8 Using File Services 275
Lesson 9 Managing Accounts 353
Lesson 10 Implementing Deployment Solutions 439

Appendix A Introduction to Apple Remote Desktop 473
Appendix B Enterprise Solutions 503
Appendix C Additional Command-Line Interface Commands 523

Index 535

Table of Contents

Lesson 1 Getting Started 1
The Methodology 2
The CD Files 4
System Requirements 5
Certification 6
About the Apple Training Series 6

Lesson 2 Installing and Configuring Mac OS X Server 9
Installing Mac OS X Server 10
Configuring Mac OS X 11
Mac OS X Server Requirements 13
Planning Your Mac OS X Server Deployment 15
Installing Mac OS X Server 17
Initial Mac OS X Server Configuration 22
Tools 38
Troubleshooting 49
What You've Learned 49
Review Quiz 51

Lesson 3 Using Network Services 53
Understanding the Different Servers 54
Dynamic Host Configuration Protocol 54
Domain Name System 75
Software Update Server 96
What You've Learned 98
Review Quiz 100

Lesson 4   Setting Up Gateway Services 103

Protecting Your Network 104
Gateway Setup Assistant 105
Firewalls 114
Network Address Translation 124
Virtual Private Networking 129
What You've Learned 133
Review Quiz 134

Lesson 5   Authenticating and Authorizing Accounts 137

Managing Server Access 138
Creating and Administering User and
Administrator Server Accounts 138
Working With Group Accounts in Workgroup Manager . . . 151
Controlling Access Through Server Accounts 161
Setting ACLs With Workgroup Manager 168
What You've Learned 198
Review Quiz 199

Lesson 6   Using Open Directory 201

Directory Services Concepts 202
What Is Open Directory? 202
Overview of Open Directory Components 203
Configuring Open Directory 204
Network Users 212
Delivery of LDAP Server Information Over DHCP 216
Configuring an Open Directory Replica 223
Authentication Methods on Mac OS X Server 225
Backing Up Open Directory Files 237
Troubleshooting 240
What You've Learned 243
Review Quiz 245

Lesson 7   Understanding Print Service 247

Print Service Overview 248
Configuring Print Service 249

Configuring Client Computers 258
Managing Print Service 264
Monitoring Print Service 266
What You've Learned 271
Review Quiz 273

Lesson 8   **Using File Services** 275
Challenges of File Sharing 276
Different Protocols for Different Clients 276
Planning for File Services 278
Apple File Service 282
Windows File Service 306
NFS Share Point Access 320
FTP File Service 333
Troubleshooting File Services 345
What You've Learned 348
Review Quiz 350

Lesson 9   **Managing Accounts** 353
Concepts and Tools 354
Managing User, Group, and Computer List Accounts 357
Managing Preferences 368
Managing Network Browsing 414
Managing Mobile User Accounts 425
Troubleshooting 433
What You've Learned 434
Review Quiz 435

Lesson 10   **Implementing Deployment Solutions** 439
Deployment Issues 440
Managing Computers With NetBoot 441
Creating and Delivering Custom Packages 457
Deploying and Updating With Apple
Remote Desktop Admin 463
Creating Custom Packages 465
What You've Learned 469
Review Quiz 470

Appendix A   Introduction to Apple Remote Desktop 473
What Is Apple Remote Desktop? 474
Installation and Configuration 475
Apple Remote Desktop Capabilities 483
Getting the Best Performance 495
Security 496
What You've Learned 498
Review Quiz 500

Appendix B   Enterprise Solutions 503
iChat Server 504
QuickTime Streaming Server 505
Mail Services 509
Web Services 510
Xgrid 511
Xgrid Admin 513
Xsan 516
SANs Overview 518
What You've Learned 519
Review Quiz 521

Appendix C   Additional Command-Line Interface Commands . 523
Finding Files Using locate and find 524
Managing Processes From the Command Line 525
Monitoring System Usage 527
Managing Disks and Volumes 528
Working With the Command Line and the GUI 528
Searching Text Files Using pipe and grep 530
Additional Shell Filename Wildcards 531
Additional Mac OS X–Specific Commands 532
What You've Learned 532
Review Quiz 533

Index 535

1

Lesson Files   None

Time   This lesson takes approximately ½ hour to complete.

Goals   Understand the goal of this book

Gather the hardware required for this book

Install developer and server administration tools on your Mac OS X computer

Install the XSE_Materials folder on your Mac OS X computer

Getting Started

Welcome to the official Mac OS X Server Essentials training course offered by Apple Computer. This book serves as a self-paced guide and is designed to help you build the basic skills you need to effectively administer a Mac OS X server. *Mac OS X Server Essentials* details the graphical tools that Apple provides to configure system services.

The primary goal of this book is to prepare technical coordinators and entry-level system administrators for the tasks demanded of them by Mac OS X Server. To become truly proficient, you need to learn the theory behind the tools you will use. For example, not only will you learn how to use Workgroup Manager—the tool for configuring permissions—but you will also learn about the ideas behind permissions, how to think about permissions, and how to set up permissions to support your particular user environment.

This book assumes that you have some knowledge of Mac OS X, since Mac OS X Server is built on top of Mac OS X. Therefore basic navigation, troubleshooting of the system itself, and networking are all similar regardless of whether the system is Mac OS X or Mac OS X Server. The main differences you will encounter focus on the services provided with Mac OS X Server. For example, file sharing works very differently in Mac OS X Server than it does in Mac OS X. While DHCP and firewall services are included in Mac OS X, Mac OS X Server adds a rich interface to configure and monitor these services; as such, this book will concentrate on the features that are unique to Mac OS X Server.

Finally, you will learn to develop processes to help you understand and work with the complexity of your system as it grows. Even a single Mac OS X Server computer can grow into a very complicated system, and creating documentation and charts can help you develop processes so that additions and modifications can integrate harmoniously with your existing system.

The Methodology

Apple Training Series books emphasize hands-on training. The exercises contained within this book are designed so that you can explore and learn the tools necessary to manage Mac OS X Server. They move along in a predictable fashion, starting with the installation and setup of Mac OS X Server and moving to more advanced topics such as multiprotocol file sharing, using access control lists, and permitting Mac OS X Server to be a centralized storage center for user information and authentication via LDAP and Password Server, and to become a Kerberos key distribution center. If you already have a Mac OS X Server setup, you can simply skip ahead to some of the later exercises in the book, provided you understand the change in IP addressing from our examples to your server and are not running your server as a production server.

Course Structure

This book serves as an introduction to Mac OS X Server and is not meant to be a definitive reference. Because Mac OS X and Mac OS X Server contain several open-source initiatives, it is impossible to include all the possibilities and permutations here. First-time users of Mac OS X Server and users of AppleShare IP who are migrating over to Mac OS X Server have the most to gain from this book; still others who are upgrading from previous versions of Mac OS X Server will also find this book a valuable resource.

> **WARNING** ▶ The exercises in this book are designed to be nondestructive if followed correctly. However, some of the exercises are disruptive—for example, they may turn off or on certain network services suddenly; others, if performed incorrectly, could result in data loss or corruption to some basic services, possibly even erasing a disk or volume of a computer connected to the network on which the Mac OS X Server resides. Thus, it is recommended that you run through the exercises on a Mac OS X Server that is not critical to your work or connected to a production network. This is also true of the Mac OS X computer you will use in these exercises. Please back up all your data if you choose to use a production machine for either the Mac OS X Server and/or the Mac OS X computers. Instructions are given for restoring your services back to their preset state, but reasonable caution is recommended. Apple Computer and Peachpit Press are not responsible for any data loss or any damage to any equipment that occurs as a direct or indirect result of following the procedures described in this book.

Mac OS X Server is by no means difficult to set up and configure, but how you use Mac OS X Server should be planned out in advance. Accordingly, this book is divided into five sections:

▶ Lessons 2 through 4 cover installation, configuration, and network service options that enable Mac OS X Server to act as a firewall, VPN server, DHCP server, and gateway for other possible computers on your network.

▶ Lessons 5 and 6 define the differences between authentication and author-ization, and the various methods of providing each. Lesson 6 zeros in on Open Directory and the vast functionality it can provide.

▶ Lessons 7 and 8 cover the various file-sharing protocols—AFP, SMB, FTP, and NFS—and introduce the concept of sharing files and associating share points with users and groups. Lesson 7 demonstrates how to set up and manage print queues.

▶ Lessons 9 and 10 teach you to manage user preferences, create a network startup disk, and deploy disk images.

▶ The appendixes cover Apple Remote Desktop, which is Apple's remote management tool; enterprise services such as Web, Mail, QuickTime Streaming, Xgrid, iChat, and Xsan; and the command-line interface.

The CD Files

This book includes a CD that contains of all the files you need to complete the lessons. For each lesson of the book, there is a Lessons folder containing the applicable files. You will also need your Mac OS X Server Install DVD, since you will be installing the developer tools and Server Admin tools on your Mac OS X computer.

While installing these files on your computer, it's important to keep all of the numbered Lesson folders together in the main Lessons folder on your hard drive. You will, of course, complete this procedure after you have installed and configured your Mac OS X server for the first time.

Lesson files, reference files, and an Apple video tutorial on Kerberos are included. However, you'll also need to download certain updates from the Apple website at www.apple.com/support or, in some cases (such as Apple Remote Desktop), pur-chase the software from Apple.

Installing Files on the Client Computer

1 Put the XSE CD into your computer's CD-ROM/DVD-ROM drive.

2 Copy the XSE_Materials folder to the /Users/Shared directory.

3 Eject the CD.

4 Insert the Mac OS X Server Install DVD into your Mac OS X computer and install the DeveloperTools.pkg located in Other Installs/Xcode Tools/Packages.

5 While the Mac OS X Server Install DVD is still in the computer, install the ServerAdministrationSoftware.mpkg located in System/Installation/Packages.

6 When called for by the lesson, locate the appropriate files inside the XSE_Materials directory.

System Requirements

This book assumes a basic level of familiarity with the Macintosh operating environment. All references to Mac OS X refer to Mac OS X v10.4, which is the primary operating system assumed throughout the book.

Here's what you will need to complete the lessons in this book:

▶ Two Macintosh computers, one with Mac OS X 10.4 installed and one on which to install Mac OS X 10.4 Server

▶ One USB or FireWire storage device for transferring files from one Mac to the other

▶ An Ethernet switch to keep the two computers connected via a small private local network

▶ Two Ethernet network cables for connecting both computers to the switch

Certification

Apple Training Series: Mac OS X Server Essentials provides a thorough preparation for the Apple Mac OS X Server Essentials v10.4 certification exam (9L0-507), offered by Apple Computer. Before you take the test, you should review the lessons and ideas in this book, and spend time setting up, configuring, and troubleshooting Mac OS X Server.

You should also download and review the Skills Assessment Guide, which lists the exam objectives, the score required to pass the exam, and how to register for it. To download the Skills Assessment Guide, visit http://train.apple.com/certification.

Earning Apple technical certification shows employers that you have achieved a high level of technical proficiency with Apple products. You'll also join a growing community of skilled professionals. In fact, Apple Mac OS X certification programs are among the fastest growing certifications in the industry. In 2004 alone, these certifications showed an impressive 300 percent growth over the previous year.

Passing any of the Mac OS X certification exams for OS X v10.3 or higher also qualifies you to join the new Mac OS X Certification Alliance, a free program that recognizes and supports the thousands of Mac OS X experts worldwide.

For more information, visit http://train.apple.com/certification/macosx.

About the Apple Training Series

Apple Training Series: Mac OS X Server Essentials is part of the official training series for Apple products, which was developed by experts in the field and certified by Apple Computer. The lessons are designed to let you learn at your own pace.

For those who prefer to learn in an instructor-led setting, Apple also offers training courses at Apple Authorized Training Centers worldwide. These courses, which typically use the Apple Training Series books as their curriculum, are taught by Apple-certified trainers, and balance concepts and lectures with hands-on labs and exercises. Apple Authorized Training Centers have been carefully selected and have met Apple's highest standards in all areas, including facilities, instructors, course delivery, and infrastructure. The goal of the program is to offer Apple customers, from beginners to the most seasoned professionals, the highest quality training experience.

To find an Authorized Training Center near you, go to www.apple.com/training.

2

Lesson Files	None
Time	This lesson takes approximately 3 hours to complete.
Goals	Configure your Mac OS X computer for this book
	Install Mac OS X Server software
	Configure initial setup of Mac OS X Server
	Save your configuration settings

Lesson **2**

Installing and Configuring Mac OS X Server

You can break working with Mac OS X Server into three phases:

1. Planning and installation: Plan how the server will be set up, qualify and configure the hardware, and install the server software.

2. Initial configuration: Use Server Assistant to perform the initial Mac OS X Server configuration. You can also use the Network preferences pane to update the interface configurations, including increasing performance by combining multiple Ethernet interfaces to act as one.

3. Maintenance: After the server is running, use utilities such as Server Admin and Workgroup Manager to perform ongoing server and account maintenance.

This lesson begins with the first two phases, the initial installation and configuration. Then it introduces the tools that you will use throughout the rest of this book to manage your server.

Installing Mac OS X Server

Installation of Mac OS X Server should be done in two steps:

1   Before you install the software, take the time to evaluate the server needs of your organization and the Mac OS X Server hardware requirements.

2   Then, use the Mac OS X Server Install DVD to install the operating system, server applications, and utilities.

We will not be covering the upgrade process in this book. Upgrading from an existing version of Mac OS X Server is an option available to administrators. It is always best practice to back up any existing setup prior to running the upgrade. Then you can restore should anything go wrong.

> **NOTE** ▶ Updating the server software should be a planned event. Always run updates on a test system before rolling out into production. In some cases third-party solutions have not continued to operate smoothly with the new software. It is suggested that you preflight the update in isolation first and roll out the update once you have tested your implementation.

Mac OS X Server can be installed using either of two methods: locally, while you are sitting at the server, or remotely, from another computer on the network. Once the software is installed, configuration can take place. This can also be done either locally or remotely. Since a local installation and configuration does not force you to authenticate, you will be doing a remote installation in this lesson as if the server were in a server room or closet down the hall from you, without a video card to rely on. You should already have a Mac OS X computer running Mac OS X v10.4 and have downloaded and installed the latest software updates. You will also want to install the Mac OS X Server Admin Tools. These tools, which can be either downloaded from Apple's Support Web Site or obtained on the Mac OS X Server DVD, are what make the remote installation, configuration, and administration of Mac OS X Server possible (you should have already installed these tools in Lesson 1).

Configuring Mac OS X

After installing the Mac OS X Server Admin tools, you'll want to set a network location for the lessons so you can quickly refer back to them from any other location. You will also be changing your computer name to make it easier to follow the examples in this book. Make sure your Mac OS X computer is up and running and plugged in to an Ethernet switch. The computer that will be the Mac OS X server should also be plugged in to this switch.

1   Log in to your Mac OS X computer and open System Preferences.

2   Select the Sharing preferences pane and change the computer name to *XSE-CLIENT*. You can always change it back anytime you want.

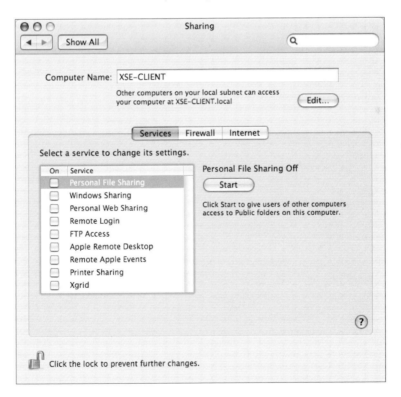

3   Click Show All and select the Network preferences pane.

4 Choose New Location from the Location drop-down menu and name the location *XSE Book*.

5 From the Show pop-up menu, choose Network Port Configurations and deselect all interfaces except Built-in Ethernet.

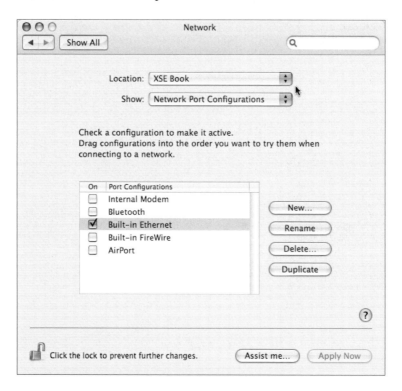

6 Select Built-in Ethernet from the Show pop-up menu. In the TCP/IP pane, choose Using DHCP from the Configure IPv4 pop-up menu.

You should not be getting an address at this point in time, since you will be configuring your Mac OS X server to provide those addresses in Lesson 3.

7 Click Show All and select the Accounts preferences pane.

8 Select Login Options, deselect "Automatically log in as" and click the option "Name and password" under "Display Login window as".

9 For these lessons you may also want to change your Energy Saver preferences pane settings to never have your Mac OS X computer go to sleep.

Mac OS X Server Requirements

Before installing Mac OS X Server, make sure the intended computer is qualified to run Mac OS X Server. All desktop Macintosh computers with built-in FireWire are supported by Mac OS X Server v10.4. Although Mac OS X Server can be installed on a portable computer, Apple does not support or recommend this configuration.

Minimum Hardware Requirements

The basic installation requirements are as follows:

▶ PowerPC G3, G4, or G5 processor

▶ Built-in FireWire

▶ 256 MB of RAM; at least 512 MB of RAM for high-demand servers running multiple services

▶ At least 4 GB of available disk space

You do not need a keyboard or display. As you will see later in this lesson, you can install Mac OS X Server using an administrator computer or another server.

> **NOTE** ▶ While the requirements are very similar, not all computers that could run Mac OS X Server v10.3 are supported by Mac OS X Server v10.4. Earlier computers that didn't have built-in FireWire, such as the Bondi Blue iMac computers, are no longer supported.

Additional Hardware Considerations

Typical considerations when choosing server systems include network and system performance, disk space, and RAM.

Networking

Be sure to consider the speed of the network interface when making a server hardware decision. Many of Apple's products support Gigabit Ethernet. You can also "combine" two Ethernet interfaces to act as one, to double network throughput.

Computer Speed

Although Mac OS X Server is supported on a wide variety of Macintosh computers, not all of them may be suitable for your needs. For a server that will only provide services for a few people, an iMac or eMac computer might meet your needs. For workgroups, you should use a Power Mac computer. For demanding server environments, you might consider using the Xserve. Xserve is a 1U rack-mount server that offers the ability to stack 48 Mac OS X Server systems in a typical server rack.

> **NOTE** ▶ Xserve, Power Mac G5, and any Macintosh Server G4 or Power Mac G4 released February 2000 or later include special hardware to detect an unexpected system shutdown and automatically restart the server machine. This feature works in conjunction with Mac OS X Server's ability to detect and restart an error in server service.

Those of you familiar with Mac OS X Server v10.3 may be familiar with the watchdog process used to launch server daemons. In Mac OS X Server v10.4 this process has changed. Mac OS X Server now uses launchd to handle automatic restarting of server processes. launchd is the Tiger process management daemon; more info can be viewed on the launchd man page by opening the Terminal application located in the /Applications/Utilities folder, typing man launchd, and pressing the Return key.

Planning Your Mac OS X Server Deployment

A server administrator should follow certain steps when setting up Mac OS X Server. The first step is to review your organization's server needs. Will the server be used mainly for web services, QuickTime streaming, file and print services, or something else? Will it be a dedicated server or will it have multiple uses?

After reviewing the intended uses of the server, fill out a server worksheet detailing the following information:

Server Worksheet

General information

Server/Xserve hardware serial number

MAC address(es)

Mac OS X Server software serial number

Administration account information

Administrator long name

Administrator short name

Password

Networking information

Computer name

Bonjour (local) name

Ethernet port information

Whether TCP/IP will be active on various interfaces

Whether AppleTalk will be active on one interface (AppleTalk can be active on only one interface)

IP address (for each interface to be used)

Subnet mask (for each interface to be used)

Router address (for each interface to be used)

DNS IP address (for each interface to be used)

DNS search domains (for each interface to be used)

Automatic or manual Ethernet connection speeds

IPv6 configuration

Directory information—how this server uses or provides directory information

Local only

Obtained from another server

Provided to other server

After completing the server worksheet, you can proceed with the installation.

Installing Mac OS X Server

When you start up from the Mac OS X Server Install DVD, you can open Disk Utility from the Utilities menu. Using this utility, you can divide the hard disk into one or more partitions and install Mac OS 9 drivers (although you should not run Classic on Mac OS X Server). You are given the following format options for your partitions:

► Mac OS X Extended (Journaled)

► Mac OS X Extended

► Mac OS X Extended (Case-sensitive/Journaled)

► Mac OS X Extended (Case-sensitive)

► UNIX File System (Not bootable)

► MS-DOS File System (Not bootable)

A single partition allows for simple installation. You can install Mac OS X Server over Mac OS 9 if needed without having to reformat the drive.

By using separate partitions you can segregate your data from the operating system. Having the operating system on its own partition conserves space by keeping user accounts from filling up the startup partition. In case you need to perform a clean install of Mac OS X Server, you can erase the entire partition and install the operating system without touching the data on the other partitions. Having multiple partitions does not increase speed, but installing multiple drives may increase server performance.

Installing the operating system on one drive and installing additional drives to store data can reduce access times to the operating system and to data. If you add the second drive on a separate bus, the server can read and write to each of those buses independently.

Another installation option is to install on mirrored drives. Mirroring provides redundancy and increases uptime if one of the drives fails.

You begin the installation of Mac OS X Server v10.4 from a DVD or CD by starting up directly from the Mac OS X Server Install Disc. If you've already started up your server from the internal drive, insert the Mac OS X Server

Install Disc and run the Install Mac OS X Server program. After you authenticate, the server reboots from the disc and proceeds with the installation process, starting with the selection of a language and then prompting you for initial information. It then proceeds uninterrupted until it completes the installation.

Local initial installation information that requires your input or response includes:

▶ Read Me information

▶ License agreement

▶ Destination drive for server software

▶ Installation type—Easy Install or Customize

From any Mac OS X v10.4 computer with Server Admin tools installed, you can use Server Assistant (located in the Server folder inside the Applications folder) to install Mac OS X Server v10.4 on a remote computer that is started up from the Install Disc. Running a remote installation does not give you all the options that are available locally. For example, you can't run Disk Utility or customize the installation options such as removing extra print drivers.

Server Assistant will search for and display all the computers on the local network that are started up from the Mac OS X Server Install Disc. You need to know the MAC address of your target computer to be able to choose it from the list of network computers should there be more than one computer started up from a Mac OS X Server Install Disc. When Server Assistant contacts the target computer, you are asked for a password. The password is the first eight digits of the computer's hardware serial number, or 12345678 if you are installing onto an older machine that doesn't have a serial number or possibly onto a computer whose motherboard has been replaced.

When you install Mac OS X Server v10.4 on Apple's Xserve systems, there are additional items to consider. For example, Xserve is designed to be run "headless" (with no monitor) and with multiple Xserve systems installed on a server rack. Performing a local installation in this situation would require attaching a monitor and keyboard, so a more convenient method may be remote installation using Server Assistant.

Another option for remote installation is to use command-line tools such as the installer command from Terminal in Mac OS X. Or, because Xserve is designed with a serial port, you can use command-line tools from an attached serial console, UNIX computer, or Windows computer. This book does not focus on command-line tools.

New in Mac OS X Server v10.4 is the ability to have the Install Disc in the remote machine and not at the server. In this scenario you do not need physical access to the server, nor is the server required to have an optical drive. You can, however, use other methods for remote installation. These include the following:

▶ Connect an external optical drive to the Xserve system via a FireWire cable.

▶ Use an optical drive on a computer connected to the Xserve system via a FireWire cable.

▶ Start the Xserve in Target Disk Mode and use another computer to install the server software on the Xserve system's mounted volume.

▶ Use another server with NetBoot services enabled to perform a network installation. As you will learn later, a server can be set up to install software onto other computers. This is extremely useful when you are setting up several servers—you can create one installation image and have it quickly replicated onto multiple computers.

Installing Mac OS X Server Remotely

Remote management and installation is often a headache for system administrators. Mac OS X Server is designed to be easy to install and configure in remote installations or headless environments. You will use your client computer to install Mac OS X Server on your server computer. You will want to have both your Mac OS X computer and your Mac OS X Server computer connected via Ethernet, not AirPort, to the same switch.

1 Write down the MAC address or addresses and hardware serial number (both can be found using System Profiler) of the computer on which Mac OS X Server is to be installed and start up the target computer from the Mac OS X Server Install Disc by holding down the C key, just as you would to do a local install.

2   Launch Server Assistant (/Applications/Server) on your Mac OS X computer.

Notice you did not have to worry about IP addresses. Bonjour takes care of that for you by automatically assigning 169.254.x.x addresses.

3   Choose "Install Software on a remote server" if not already selected and click Continue.

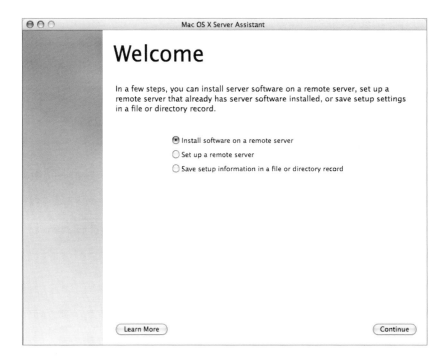

4 Select your intended server's computer from the Destination list and click Continue. Enter your server's serial number in the field when asked to authenticate.

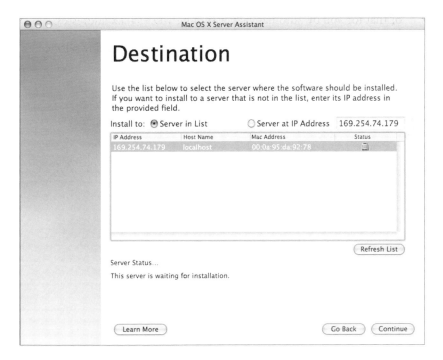

5 Choose the appropriate language for you.

6 Read the Important Information window.

7 Agree to the license agreement.

8   Select the disk or volume onto which Mac OS X Server will be installed. If you have another operating system on the disk or volume, you may be notified that the disk must be erased.

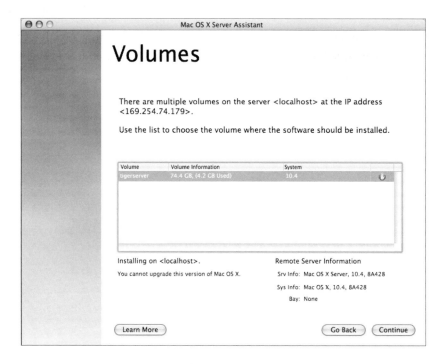

Your Mac OS X Server computer will now install the necessary software.

NOTE ▶ Never install Mac OS X Server without an active Ethernet connection.

Initial Mac OS X Server Configuration

If you did a local installation, upon completion of the installation a Welcome screen appears prompting you to create a valid server configuration. In Mac OS X Server v10.4, initial configuration is completed using Server Assistant, which runs both as an installation assistant and, following a successful installation of Mac OS X Server, as a separate application used to install and configure remote computers. In each case, Server Assistant uses slightly different steps. It is Server Assistant that is used to configure the administrator account, computer names, network interfaces, and directory usage. This makes the configuration process go quickly, provided you have already planned out the configuration of your server.

Mac OS X Server v10.4 can be configured automatically using a configuration file generated by the Server Assistant application, which is available from the Server Admin Tools CD, or inside the Server folder which is inside the Applications folder on an existing Mac OS X Server v10.4 installation. The generated configuration file can be stored on another mounted volume, such as an iPod, USB dongle or a CD-ROM, or as a record in directory services. The configuration files can be computer-specific, based on the MAC address, or they can be generic. If a configuration file is accessible to the newly installed server, Mac OS X Server will locate the file and automatically configure itself based on the settings in the configuration file.

Configuration Options

When using Server Assistant to set up a remote server, you are asked to select the destination computer and authenticate again using the first eight digits of the hardware serial number (or 12345678 if necessary). Local setup does not require these steps. At this point, both local and remote installations are similar. You select a language, choose a keyboard setting, set the serial number for the Mac OS X Server software, and then step through setting the following:

▶ Administrator account

▶ Network names

▶ Network interfaces

▶ TCP/IP connection

▶ Directory usage

▶ Services

▶ Date and time information

We will now take a brief look at the more important Server Assistant setup screens.

Administrator Account

After the serial number screen, you are asked to enter inital account information. The first account that is created on Mac OS X Server is an administrator account. However, the System Administrator account (root) is activated as well.

The password for root is the same as the password for the first administrator account, but they are not synchronized. If either the administrator or the system administrator's password is changed, the change does not affect the other account's password.

> **NOTE** ▶ Be aware that there can be multiple administrator accounts, but only one System Administrator account. Any administrator can enable or disable the System Administrator account with NetInfo Manager.

Network Names

After setting the initial administrator account, you are prompted to provide unique names for your computer.

▶   The *hostname* is a unique name for a server, historically referred to as the "UNIX hostname." The Mac OS X Server hostname is used primarily for client access to NFS home folders. In Mac OS X Server v10.4, you can no longer set the hostname in Server Assistant, as it is done automatically for you. Server Assistant sets the hostname to AUTOMATIC in the hostconfig file inside the hidden /etc folder at the root level of your server. This setting causes the server's hostname to be the first valid hostname or it follows the below path until it finds a name:

- The name specified in the /etc/hostconfig file (HOSTNAME=some-host-name)
- The name provided by the DHCP or BOOTP server for the primary IP address
- The first name returned by a reverse DNS (address-to-name) query for the primary IP address
- The local hostname
- The name "localhost"

▶ The *computer name* is used by clients who use the Apple Filing Protocol (AFP) to access AFP share points and print services on the server.

▶ The *local hostname* is the name Mac OS X users see for this server when viewing the computers listed in /Network/Local. Those computers on the same IP subnet can always access the server by entering the local hostname followed by .local.

NOTE ▶ The computer name can include spaces but the local hostname cannot.

Network Interfaces

The next step in configuration of your server is the network setup.

Apple servers can use multiple interfaces for network access. Examples include computers with AirPort cards installed, Xserve systems with dual Gigabit Ethernet, and Mac OS X Server computers with 4-interface Ethernet cards. Mac OS X Server can also use the FireWire interface for network access (IP over FireWire).

The Server Assistant displays any interfaces it finds so the administrator can select whether TCP/IP or AppleTalk should be enabled for each interface. You can enable TCP/IP on multiple interfaces, but you can enable AppleTalk only on a single interface. You are prompted for detailed configuration information for each selected interface on subsequent screens.

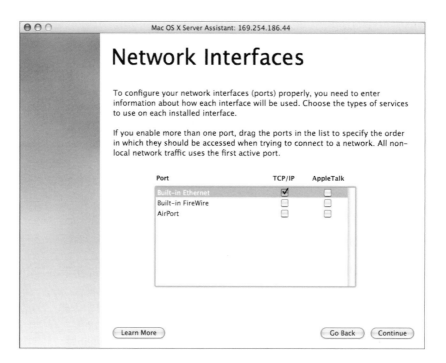

TCP/IP Connection

The screen shot below demonstrates how each Ethernet interface is displayed for configuration in the Server Assistant. Each interface has its own IP settings—for hosting different server services or dividing the amount of traffic supported over any one interface. You can also manually configure multiple interfaces or reconfigure network information later using the Network pane of System Preferences.

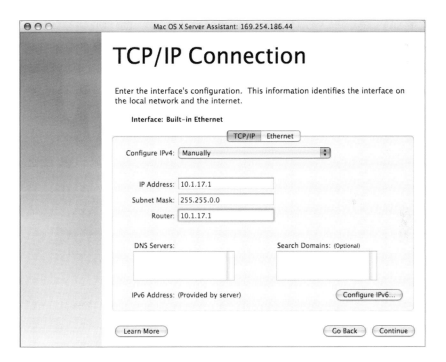

NOTE ▶ In the Network pane of System Preferences, you can also create multiple settings for a single interface. (To do so, you select the interface and then click the Duplicate button.) This option is useful for assigning multiple IP addresses to the same Ethernet interface. One use of this is to host multiple websites, with unique IP addresses and unique web pages, from a single server with only one Ethernet interface. This configuration may require modifying DNS entries.

Directory Usage

The Server Assistant then wants you to choose one of three directory configurations for your server: Standalone Server, Connected to a Directory System, or Open Directory Master. If you choose the second or third option, you will be prompted to provide further information.

User information is stored locally and can be accessed only by services on the local machine. Remote users can still connect to services via AFP, SMB, and so forth, but remote clients cannot sign in to user accounts via the login window on their local machines using account information stored on the server. This is a typical configuration for file servers.

If you already have a Lightweight Directory Access Protocol (LDAP) server or a NetInfo parent configured to give user information on your network, select Connected to a Directory System and click Continue. You are then prompted to select how you will access the directory system. This option makes the server a "child" to some higher authentication server. The default setting is to use a directory system specified by a DHCP server. This option allows you to use the directory system information delivered by the DHCP lease. You also have the option of configuring the server's connection to a specific Apple LDAP directory (such as another Mac OS X server) or a NetInfo directory (from a legacy system), or you can postpone connection to a third-party directory service.

> **NOTE** ▶ When setting up an Open Directory master server, it's best to set it up as a standalone server first. Test DNS and apply any operating system updates before you promote the server to Open Directory master.

If you choose to configure your server as an Open Directory master, user information is stored locally and can be accessed by remote machines. Remote users can connect to services via AFP, SMB, and so forth, and remote clients can sign in to user accounts via the login window on their local computers using account information stored on the server. The server provides access to the user information via LDAP by default. In the Server Assistant, you have the option to configure the Open Directory master as a primary domain controller (a server that provides authentication information for computers running Windows). Further configuration of the Open Directory master, including password services, is done using the Server Admin utility.

Services

Mac OS X Server provides a wide range of services. These services can be launched at startup time to make sure they are available without administrator intervention. However, if you do not need a service, leave it turned off to reduce overhead and increase security.

With an initial installation it is best to not enable any services during the installation process. Some services require proper supporting services, such as DNS or DHCP, to be running and configured correctly. None of the services will be configured by just turning them on. It is best practice to always configure your services before enabling them to start automatically.

After configuring directory usage, Server Assistant permits you to start any of the following services:

► Apple file service

► Apple Remote Desktop (ARD)

► FTP service

► iChat service

► Mail service

► NetBoot service

► Network Time service

► QuickTime Streaming service

▶ Software Update service

▶ Web service

▶ Windows file service

▶ Xgrid Agent service

▶ Xgrid Controller service

Date, Time, and Confirm Settings

Finally, initial configuration concludes by asking you to specify your time zone and choose whether or not this server will use a time server. At the Confirm Settings screen, you *can* apply the settings you have just configured, however, for this book we will be doing automatic configuration, so do *not* click the Apply button when finished with the following exercise.

Configuring Your Server Using Server Assistant

You can use the Server Assistant application to perform remote installations and configurations. You can do remote configuration by connecting to the server over the network and running the Server Assistant remotely.

1   Launch Server Assistant on your Mac OS X computer (located in the Applications/Server folder), choose the "Set up a remote server" option, and click Continue.

2   Place a checkmark next to your server in the Destination screen, double-click in the Password field, and again enter the first eight digits of the hardware serial number (or 12345678 if necessary) and click Continue.

3   On the following three screens, choose a language, choose a keyboard layout, and enter the Mac OS X Server software serial number, clicking Continue after each screen.

4 Set your name, short name, and password, and click Continue.

Use Server Admin as the long name, sadmin as the short name, and f00tba11 as the password (you are substituting zeros for the o's and ones for the l's in the password).

5 Use Server17 for the computer name, and the local hostname will appear automatically. Click Continue.

6   Choose only the Built-in Ethernet interface for TCP/IP and deselect any
other interfaces. Do not enable AppleTalk on any interface. Click Continue.

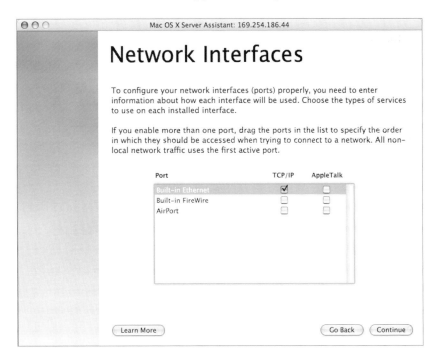

7   Depending on the computer on which Mac OS X Server is being configured you may see a different list of available interfaces. For this book, deselect all interfaces except the Built-in Ethernet interface and configure it by
first choosing Manually from the Configure IPv4 pop-up menu and then
entering the following information, after which you will click Continue:

▶   IP Address: *10.1.17.1*

▶   Subnet Mask: *255.255.0.0*

▶   Router: *10.1.17.1*

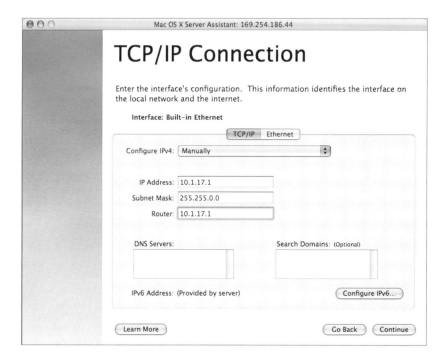

8   Choose the directory usage configuration—for this book, Standalone Server—and click Continue.

9 Do not start any of the services at this point. Click Continue.

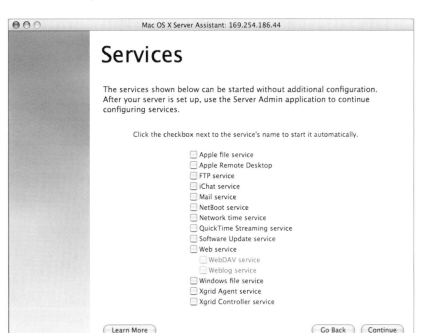

10 Enter the appropriate date and time information. Your server should not be connected to any outside network, therefore, do not allow your server to look for a Network Time server. Click Continue.

11 You are now at the Confirm Settings screen. Do NOT click the Apply button; rather leave your Mac OS X server unconfigured at this point. You will configure it in a later exercise.

Generating Configuration Data

You can also generate and save the configuration data for later use.

To create server configurations that can be used later, run Server Assistant and choose "Save setup information in a file or directory record." Then proceed to choose the configuration options for the target server in the subsequent screens.

You can create generic files or records to be used by any server, or you can create specific files or records, based on the Ethernet, or MAC, addresses of the target server. If you choose to create generic settings, you will need to leave the Network Names screen blank and configure TCP/IP to use generic settings, such as DHCP. After you have finished the configuration, you are given the option to save the configuration as an XML file, a text file (which can only be used as a description), or a directory record.

The XML file can be placed on any volume mounted on the target server. When the Server Assistant starts, it looks for such a file and automatically configures the server. If you choose to save a configuration as a directory record, you must save it to an existing and fully functional directory server. If you've done a generic configuration, use the record name "generic." Otherwise, use the MAC address of the target server as the record name. When the Server Assistant starts, if the target server is connected to a network that includes the directory server, the assistant will look for the directory entry and automatically configure the target server.

Since you have not configured your server yet, you will save this file for later use in case you want to try this lesson again. Saving the file enables you to install a fresh copy of Mac OS X Server and have it automatically configured based on the settings we have stated here.

Save Your Settings and Automatically Configure Your Server

You will now save all the settings from all the steps you just completed as a single file, enabling you to configure this server identically should you want to reformat or reinstall the server software.

1   From the Confirm Settings screen, click Save As.

2   Select the Configuration File option and deselect the "Save in Encrypted Format" checkbox. Click OK.

At the Save As dialog, you'll be creating a new folder called Auto Server Setup on your desktop. Since you are doing this remotely, you will be saving the configuration file to your local Mac OS X computer. Notice the name of the file is the 12-digit MAC address of your server, with "plist" as its extension.

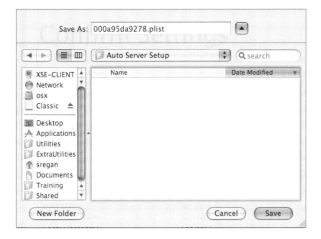

3   Save the file as the default name inside a newly-created folder on the Desktop called Auto Server Setup.

4   Quit Server Assistant without applying the settings.

5   Copy the Auto Server Setup folder from your desktop to a USB storage device or a FireWire device such as an iPod Shuffle or an iPod.

6   Plug in the USB or FireWire device to the Mac OS X server.

Automatic configuration should begin within 30 seconds.

Tools

After you have installed Mac OS X Server and performed the basic configuration, you will use a few utilities to perform additional configuration and maintenance of your server. This section introduces five key utilities:

▶   Network preferences pane

▶   Software Update

▶   Server Admin

▶   Workgroup Manager

▶   Apple Remote Desktop (a separate application purchased from Apple)

Later lessons will introduce additional utilities.

> **NOTE** ▶ You can run Mac OS X Server Admin tools only on Mac OS X v10.4 or later. You can administer earlier versions of the Mac OS X Server from the new tools, but the new tools rely upon features in Mac OS X v10.4 and will not run on earlier versions of the operating system.

Network Preferences Pane

When you are hosting a heavily used server, such as a high-demand file server, you may find that the amount of data that the server can send or receive is limited not by the speed of the server but by the speed of the network interface. Simply adding a second interface does not solve the problem, because the network traffic is targeted toward a specific network address, which is tied to a single interface.

Mac OS X v10.4 supports *link aggregate networking,* the ability to link two or more Ethernet interfaces together with the same IP address and have them appear as a single interface on the network. This allows network traffic to be shared between the two interfaces, in essence doubling the server's network throughput.

Link Aggregate Networking

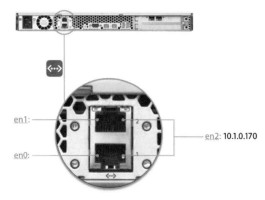

To take advantage of link aggregation, you must have two or more Ethernet interfaces installed on the server. Each of these interfaces must be connected to a network switch; if they are connected to a hub, the server will still be limited to the speed of one interface.

To combine the interfaces, create a new network port configuration in the Network pane of System Preferences. When you choose Link Aggregate for the port type, a sheet appears asking you to specify which interfaces should be combined. (In the illustrated example, the server is being configured to use the built-in Ethernet interface and one on a PCI card. After you create the link aggregate port configuration, you can configure the port as if it were a regular Ethernet interface.

As with any network interface, there will be times when you need to trouble-shoot issues related to the linked interfaces. To find out the status of the individual interfaces, choose the link aggregate configuration from the Show pop-up menu in the Network pane of System Preferences and then click the Status button. The Status pane lists each of the linked interfaces along with their speed, duplex setting, and status.

Software Update

After installation and setup are complete, run Software Update, located in System Preferences. Software Update uses the server's Internet connection to check for the latest software updates for the server. Software Update provides updates for both the base Mac OS X operating system and the Mac OS X server.

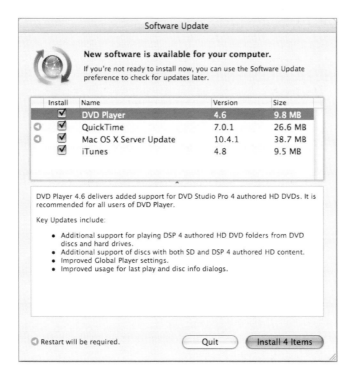

NOTE ▶ Plan for software updates. As updates to the server software become available from Apple, you will want to apply them to your servers. This should be done carefully. Your installation may contain third-party software or custom installations that have not been fully qualified with the updated software. Always preflight updates on nonproduction servers before rolling out the changes. Updates from Apple are important and will add value to your implementation. You need to evaluate the updates according to your customer's needs, and apply the updates when appropriate—not just because they are available.

Server Admin

With Server Admin you can configure and monitor services running on Mac OS X Server systems. To select a server to work with:

1   From your server, click the Server Admin icon in the Dock. Or, from your Mac OS X computer, launch Server Admin, which is located in the Applications/Server folder.

2   In the Address field, enter the IP address or use the existing local host-name (or DNS name if the network is set up for DNS in a production environment) of the server or click Browse to select from a list of servers on your local network.

    Use Server17.local for this book.

3   Authenticate as an authorized administrator. In this case use the user name and password you supplied earlier in the Server Assistant.

4   Click Connect.

    The Computers & Services list contains a list of all the servers you're connected to and the services available on each. To add a server to the window, click the Add Server icon in the toolbar and log in to the server. To remove a server from the list, select it and click Remove Server.

To work with the general settings for a server, select the server in the Computers & Services list and use the buttons at the bottom of the window:

1   Click Overview to view information about the server.

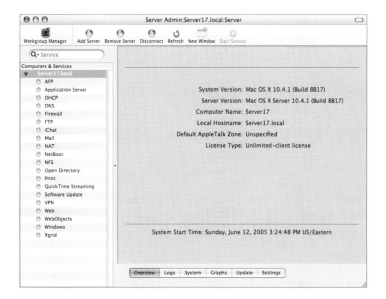

2   Click Logs to view the system log, software update log, and other logs.

3   Click System to view information about ports and volumes the server uses.

4   Click Graphs to view a graphical history of server CPU and network activity.

5   Click Update to use Software Update to update the server's software.

6   Click Settings to edit information such as the server's computer name and serial number, to configure certificate management, and to enable SNMP, NTP, ssh, and Macintosh Manager services.

> **NOTE ▶** You can enable Macintosh Manager only if an upgrade has taken place. Macintosh Manager is not installed unless you are upgrading from Mac OS X Server v10.3 to Mac OS X Server v10.4.

To work with a particular service on a server, click the disclosure triangle beside the server, then click the service. Use the buttons at the bottom of the window to manage the service's settings and display status information, including logs and graphs. To start or stop a service, select it in the Computers & Services list, then click the Start Service or Stop Service button in the toolbar. Server Admin can have several windows open at once by clicking the New Window icon in the toolbar, and you can be connected to several servers simultaneously by clicking the Add Server button in the toolbar.

Save Settings

The drag-and-drop icon (at the lower right of most settings windows) enables you to copy a service's settings to another server or to a property-list file. To copy service settings to another server you simply select the service in the server you want to copy to, click Settings to display the settings, and click the New Window icon in the toolbar. In the original window, select the server you want to copy from. Then select the service whose settings you want to copy, and click Settings to display the settings. Drag the drag-and-drop icon to the window displaying the same service settings on the other server, drop it in the Settings pane, and click Save.

To save the settings in a property-list file, drag the drag-and-drop icon to your desktop. To configure and save the AFP Service settings:

1   Click the AFP button in the Computers & Services list and then click the Settings tab at the bottom of the screen.

2   Make a change, such as adding a logon greeting, and click Save.

3   Drag the drag-and-drop icon to your Desktop.

The icon briefly changes to a miniature version of the Settings pane and it is automatically named AFP Config.plist.

4   Remove the logon greeting and click Save.

5   Drag the AFP Config.plist file back into the settings window.

Notice the login greeting is back.

Drag-and-drop icons provide an excellent way to quickly return to a set service state while you are configuring services.

NOTE ▶ To control the appearance of Server Admin lists, how often status data is refreshed, whether to use secure connections, and other behavior, choose Preferences from the Server Admin menu.

NOTE ▶ While using Server Admin, there is often more than one level/view for configuring a service. You may click the Settings button for one of the services and not see the primary configuration view for that service. Look for a Back button that will take you back to the primary configuration screen.

Workgroup Manager

With Workgroup Manager you can administer user, group, and computer accounts; manage share points; and perform client management functions for Mac OS X users. (Share points are folders or disks that are available for remote access when the server is running.) Account information can be entered individually or imported from a compatible file. There are two ways to use Workgroup

Manager, depending on whether you spend most of your time working with one server or several. If you work with a single server most of the time, authenticate when you open Workgroup Manager.

> **NOTE ▶** We cover Workgroup Manager only briefly in this lesson; it is covered in greater detail throughout the book.

To work with Workgroup Manager:

1   From your server, click the Workgroup Manager icon in the Dock. Or, from your Mac OS X computer, launch Workgroup Manager, which is located in the Applications/Server folder.

2   In the Address field, enter the IP address or use the existing local host-name (or DNS name if the network is set up for DNS in a production environment) of the server or click Browse to select from a list of servers on your local network.

> **NOTE ▶** If you administer several different servers and work with different directory domains (directories will be discussed in Lesson 6, "Using Open Directory"), open Workgroup Manager without authenticating. To do so, click Cancel in the Workgroup Manager Connect window and choose View Directories from the Server menu. You will have read-only access to information displayed in Workgroup Manager for directories you have access to. To make changes, click the lock icon to authenticate as an administrator.

3 After you authenticate, the user account window appears with lists of user, group, and computer accounts in the server's local directory domain. The following options are available:

▶ Click the Accounts icon in the toolbar to administer user, group, or computer accounts.

▶ Click the Preferences icon in the toolbar to work with preferences for managed user, group, or computer list accounts.

▶ Click the Sharing icon in the toolbar to work with share points.

▶ Click the Admin icon in the toolbar to launch Server Admin.

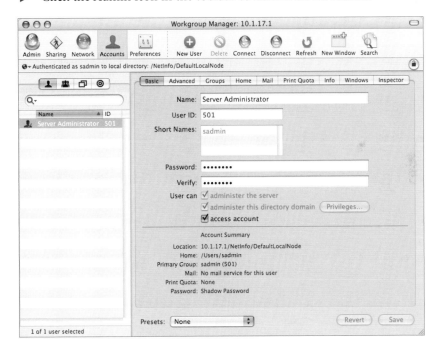

NOTE ▶ To control the way Workgroup Manager lists users and groups, whether it should use Secure Sockets Layer (SSL) transactions, and other behavior, choose Preferences from the Workgroup Manager menu.

Apple Remote Desktop

ARD is easy-to-use, powerful, open standards-based, desktop management software for all your networked Macintosh computers. IT professionals can remotely control and configure systems, install software, offer live online help to end users, and assemble detailed software and hardware reports for an entire Macintosh network.

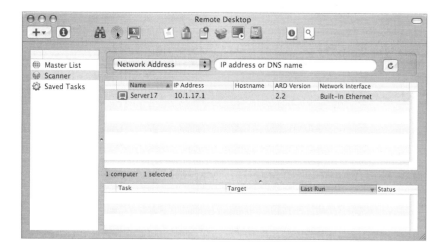

ARD is typically thought of as a client management tool, but it can also be used to remotely manage servers. While Server Admin and Workgroup Manager enable you to configure and manage services and accounts remotely, they don't do everything (change network settings, for example). With ARD you can remotely interact with and manage any Mac OS X computer, including one running Mac OS X Server, as if you were seated right in front of that computer. Additionally, ARD enables you to manage multiple computers simultaneously. For example, if you need to update multiple servers with the latest software from Apple, you can install the update package on all of your servers at the same time.

Although the ARD administration software (named Remote Desktop) is not included with Mac OS X Server and is not required for server administration, it can be very useful when administering a remote computer without a video display.

For more information about Apple Remote Desktop, see Appendix A, "Introduction to Apple Remote Desktop."

Troubleshooting

For troubleshooting during installation, you can display the installer log. This is most useful when an installation does not complete correctly. In that case, rerun the installation with the log file showing, so that you can identify where the problem occurred. To display the log, choose Installer Log from the Window menu while the installation is running. Another way to see the log file is to use the Terminal application, located under the Utilities menu when started up from the Mac OS X Server Install disc.

If you use Server Assistant to create an automatic configuration file, as we did in this lesson, be sure to delete the file from the drives attached to the server after the server has been set up. Otherwise, if you need to repurpose the server after you reinstall the server software, the server will be automatically configured using the old configuration data.

> **NOTE ▶** One common problem found in server installations is incompatibility with third-party hardware and software configurations. Many times bad third-party RAM has caused problems. Isolate the changes to your system when you run into problems. Keep the variables to a minimum.

What You've Learned

▶ Mac OS X Server requires a desktop computer with a PowerPC G3, G4, or G5 processor, built-in FireWire, at least 256 MB of RAM, and 4 GB of available disk space.

▶ The Installer and Mac OS X Server Assistant guide you through the initial configuration of your server.

▶ You can install and configure Mac OS X Server v10.4 remotely using a variety of tools such as Server Assistant and directory services.

▶ Link aggregation enables you to improve performance by combining two or more Ethernet ports and having them act as one.

▶ Apple provides updates to Mac OS X Server through the Software Update service. To ensure that your system is up-to-date, run Software Update on a regular basis.

▶ You use Server Admin to configure and monitor Mac OS X Server services.

▶ You use Workgroup Manager to manage user, group, and computer list accounts and share points.

References

The following documents provide more information about installing Mac OS X Server. (All of these and more are available at www.apple.com/server/documentation.)

Administration Guides

Mac OS X Server Getting Started (http://images.apple.com/server/pdfs/Getting_Started_v10.4.pdf)

Upgrading and Migrating to Mac OS X Server v10.4 Tiger (http://images.apple.com/server/pdfs/Migration_v10.4.pdf)

Apple Remote Desktop Administrator's Guide (http://images.apple.com/server/pdfs/Apple_Remote_Desktop_Admin_Guide.pdf)

Mac OS X Server Command-Line Administration (http://images.apple.com/server/pdfs/Command_Line_v10.4.pdf)

Apple Knowledge Base Documents

You can check for new and updated Knowledge Base documents at www.apple.com/support.

Document 301590, "Mac OS X Server: Admin Tools compatibility information"

URLs

Small Tree Communications White Papers: www.small-tree.com/whitepapers.htm

Review Quiz

1. What are the minimum hardware requirements for installing Mac OS X Server v10.4?

2. What information must you collect before installing Mac OS X Server?

3. What are three things that the Server Assistant application can be used to do?

4. In what formats can Server Assistant save setup information, and what is each format used for?

5. What tool should be used to keep Mac OS X Server up-to-date with the latest versions of software?

Answers

1. The minimum requirements are:

   ▶ A desktop Macintosh computer with a PowerPC G3, G4, or G5 processor

   ▶ 256 MB of RAM (at least 512 MB of RAM for high-demand servers running multiple services)

   ▶ 4 GB of available disk space

   ▶ Built-in FireWire

2. Serial number and MAC address of the computer, admin name and password, hostname, computer name, existing or proposed DNS configuration, TCP/IP configuration, and directory service usage

3. Server Assistant can be used to install Mac OS X Server v10.4 on a remote server, to set up a remote Mac OS X Server v10.4 system, and to save setup information for a Mac OS X Server v10.4 server in a file or directory record.

4. Server Assistant can save setup information in the following formats:

   ▶ Text file: Used as a description of the setup (just a reference).

   ▶ XML file: Can be placed on any volume mounted on the target server to automatically configure that server.

   ▶ Directory record: Can be saved in the directory service master to be discovered by a target server for automatic configuration of that server.

5. Software Update (in System Preferences)

3

Lesson Files	None
Time	This lesson takes approximately 2 hours to complete.
Goals	Use Server Admin to configure one or more valid DHCP subnets
	Use Server Admin to configure the DNS and LDAP information that a DHCP subnet will provide
	Use Server Admin to configure and monitor usage of DNS services on Mac OS X Server
	Use Network Utility to troubleshoot DNS record issues
	Set up Mac OS X Server to download software updates from Apple and then serve the updates to computers on the local network

Lesson **3**
Using Network Services

This lesson explains why you need a Dynamic Host Configuration Protocol (DHCP) server and a domain name system (DNS) server. You'll also learn how to configure DHCP services on Mac OS X Server to provide address, lease and renewal, and directory information. You will then change settings on the client computer to access Internet Protocol (IP) information via DHCP.

In addition, you'll learn how to use Mac OS X and Mac OS X Server tools to troubleshoot DHCP issues on the network. From the client computer, you will review what information can be gathered to assist you in troubleshooting. From the server computer, you will monitor DHCP activity and review log file entries.

For DNS, you will create a basic zone file allowing your server to provide DNS. You'll also learn about the various types of DNS issues, such as problems related to end users who misunderstand your DNS hierarchy and typographic problems within your DNS aliases. A system administrator must be able to determine authoritatively where a DNS entry is being resolved.

Understanding the Different Servers

Like any resource, network resources are limited. When an organization signs on with an Internet service provider (ISP), the ISP provides a limited number of IP addresses and a set bandwidth or maximum amount of network traffic allowed to the organization. To prevent extra charges, the organization must use the allocated addresses and bandwidth intelligently.

A company with unlimited resources could purchase an IP address for each computer on its network. However, this is inefficient because every company has intermittent network users, such as those who use portable computers and visitors. A more efficient approach is to purchase fewer IP addresses and allocate them dynamically as needed using a DHCP server.

Hosting an internal DNS server can reduce network demands and improve performance by locally caching hostname lookups. It can also be used to supplement and extend the domain name that the company purchased.

Another way to reduce bandwidth needs is to host a Software Update server. This allows updates to be served on the local network instead of each computer having to download the updates directly from Apple's website. This also enables a system administrator to make updates available only after they have been tested and qualified.

Dynamic Host Configuration Protocol

DHCP is a protocol for dynamically configuring a host machine. While most people associate DHCP with receiving an IP address, the configuration information provided to a machine can be much more than an IP address. Typically DHCP provides IP address assignment along with a valid subnet mask, router, DNS server, and domain name. DHCP can provide other host configuration information, such as the default information for connecting to a NetInfo directory. Mac OS X Server also provides a convenient way to configure the Lightweight Directory Access Protocol (LDAP) information to be sent to a requesting computer.

The process of the server granting an address to the client is well documented. In the illustration below, the interaction occurs in the following order:

1 A host iBook on the network is set to obtain network configuration information via DHCP. It sends a request to the network to see if a valid DHCP server is available.

2 A DHCP server receives the request from the iBook and responds with the appropriate information. In this case, the DHCP server responds with an IP address of 10.1.55.2, a subnet mask and router, a DNS server address of 10.1.0.1, and an LDAP server of ldap.example.com. The iBook then formally requests what the DHCP server offers. At this time, the iBook has a valid IP address and can start using the network.

3 As other devices come on the network and request configuration information via DHCP, they receive the appropriate information. In this case, the PowerBook receives the next available IP address of 10.1.55.3 as well as the same DNS and LDAP information.

4 As the eMac joins the network, it also receives appropriate DHCP information.

DHCP—Dynamic Host Configuration Protocol

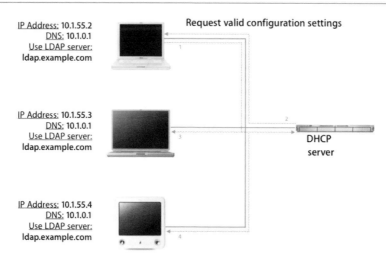

A key benefit that the DHCP server provides in this example is the assignment of configuration information to each host on the network. You do not have to manually enter this information from each machine under the "Manual" setting option. Use of the DHCP server also guarantees that users do not have network problems caused by incorrectly typed information, such as duplicate IP addresses, subnet, or DNS settings. If an organization has set up its network appropriately, a new user can take a new Macintosh computer out of the box, plug it into the network, and automatically be set up with appropriate IP, DNS, NetInfo, and LDAP information. This user can then authenticate against the company LDAP or NetInfo directory and access appropriate network services without doing any configuration. This capability provides an organization with an extremely simple way to set up and administer computers.

Configuring DHCP

Before you configure DHCP, you should know about the options available to you.

Server Admin is the tool that is used to configure DHCP on Mac OS X Server. You can configure multiple DHCP ranges, or *subnets* as they are called in Server Admin, as long as you don't allow the IP ranges to overlap. Use the Add Subnet button to set up DHCP ranges and enter all appropriate information.

To configure DHCP:

1   In Server Admin, select DHCP and click Settings to configure Mac OS X Server's DHCP service.

    The list of currently configured DHCP subnets appears.

2   Click the Add Subnet (+) button to set up a new subnet configuration. Either double-click a subnet or select it and click the Edit (pen) button to edit an existing subnet.

DHCP Subnet Information

You can configure multiple subnet ranges on Mac OS X Server in the Subnets pane. You could add an additional subnet range for a second range on an existing port, as shown below, or for a range on a different port. You might need to configure subnet ranges on multiple ports when using an Apple Xserve server with dual Ethernet ports or when using a computer that contains a four-port Ethernet card.

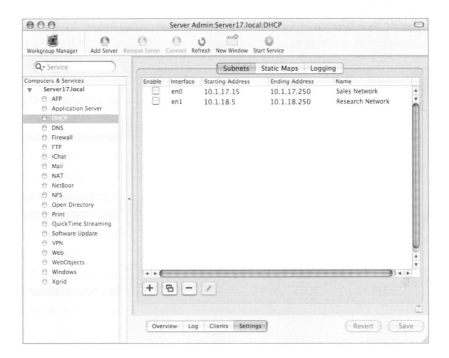

DHCP General Information

In the General pane, you can configure the IP settings that the DHCP server provides for a specific subnet. (You must be editing a subnet to see the General pane.) Enter an appropriate name for the subnet and select the network interface to be used for the range of addresses. Then enter the appropriate IP addresses to define the IP range in the Starting IP Address and Ending IP Address fields. This IP range must be unique and must not overlap with another DHCP subnet range being served. Next enter the appropriate subnet mask and router settings.

DHCP servers also use a range of IP addresses to lease an IP address to computers for a temporary period, known as the *lease time*. Leasing enables an organization to support a larger number of computers than there are available IP addresses by reusing IP addresses over time. For example, members of a sales force using portable computers may not all need IP addresses in the local sales office if many sales reps are not in the office each day. DCHP would be an ideal way to administer such an office: A host receives the IP address for the assigned lease time and relinquishes it when the network interface is no longer in use, such as when the machine shuts down. If a machine is still using the IP address, it can request an extended lease time.

Set the length of the lease time depending upon the needs of your organization.

NOTE ▶ Whenever you configure network information such as DHCP, verify that the service will not conflict with other services on the network. If the host configuration is not accurate, the DHCP server will cause problems for users trying to access network resources. To prevent this, you should provide only those DHCP addresses that are under your authority.

DHCP DNS Information

In addition to providing an IP address, DHCP can also provide additional network configuration information, such as the addresses for DNS servers. In the DNS pane, you set the DNS information that the DHCP server provides. DNS is discussed later in this lesson.

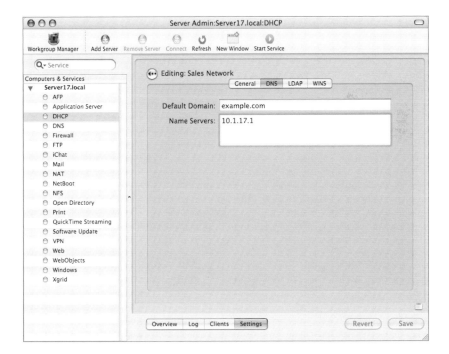

DHCP LDAP Information

LDAP is a network-based directory service designed to provide information to the client. The LDAP pane is where the administrator enters the LDAP configuration information that will be sent to clients. Clients that receive this information can connect to the LDAP server and be configured automatically to use that server's directory services. Mac OS X makes deploying LDAP easy by sending the configuration information to clients with the DHCP response over Option 95, which is the standard defined by the Internet Assigned Numbers Authority (IANA).

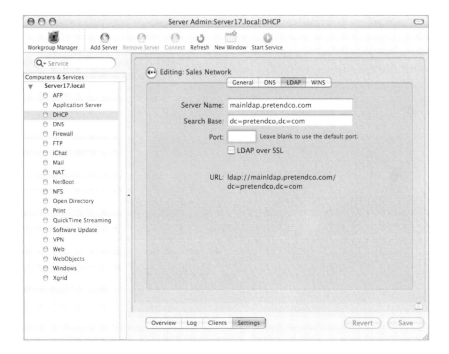

NOTE ▶ Apple's implementation of DHCP relies on BOOTP (Bootstrap Protocol), a protocol that was available before DHCP and is the basis for Apple's DHCP implementation.

DHCP Static Mapping

You can assign specific addresses to the computers on your network, if desired. This enables you to keep the ease of configuration of using DHCP while having some static servers or services. To assign an IP address to a computer, you will need the computer's Ethernet address (sometimes called its MAC address or hardware address). Each network interface has its own Ethernet address. If you have a computer that moves from being wired to the network to a wireless network, it uses two different Ethernet addresses—one for the wired connection and one for the wireless connection—so be sure to enter it twice if necessary.

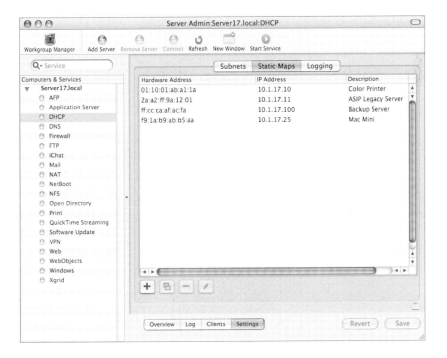

To assign static IP addresses:

1   Open the Static Maps pane for DHCP service and click the Add Static Map (+) button.

2   Enter the Ethernet address of the computer, which will receive a static address and the IP address you want to assign to it. If desired, you can write a description or note related to this mapping. Click OK.

DHCP Logging

Within the Settings pane of Server Admin for DHCP, you can set the level of detail for logs. Click the Logging button to access the Log Level pop-up menu, then set the level of detail that will be provided to the DHCP logs. The Medium setting lists general DHCP warnings and errors; the Low setting lists only more serious entries, such as a notice that the DHCP server did not start up as expected.

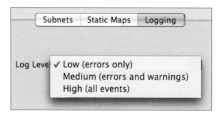

The DHCP log entries are contained in the main system log file. You can view the system log using other utilities such as Console or System Profiler, but if you use the Log pane for the DHCP service in Server Admin, only the DHCP entries will be displayed.

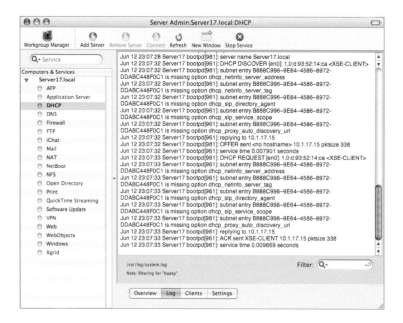

You can also look for specific DHCP events by entering them in the Filter field. Note the specific DHCP entries and the general flow of events for DHCP:

1. DHCP DISCOVER: A DHCP client sends a discover message to look for DHCP servers.

2. OFFER: A DHCP server responds to a client DHCP DISCOVER message.

3. DHCP REQUEST: A DHCP client requests DHCP configuration information from the DHCP server.

4. ACK: A DHCP server responds with DHCP configuration information for the DHCP client.

You can remember this chain of events with the acronym DORA: Discover, Offer, Request, Acknowledge.

Addresses that are assigned can of course be reused. The client sends a DHCP RELEASE message to the server when it is being shut down. This message notifies the server that the address can be reassigned to another client.

You can use Server Admin to view detailed information about the DHCP clients associated with a DHCP server. To view the DHCP client information, click the Clients button at the bottom of the screen.

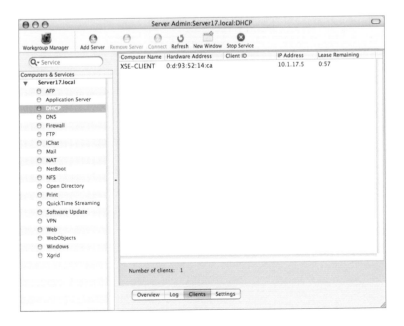

The DHCP Clients pane provides the following information:

▶ Computer name

▶ Hardware address (the MAC address associated with a specific DHCP client)

▶ DHCP client ID

▶ IP address assigned

▶ Lease time remaining

A DHCP client can have a client ID, which may provide an administrator more information about which host is assigned a specific IP address. Some service providers may require a valid client ID before providing an IP address from their DHCP server. Use the Network pane of System Preferences in Mac OS X to configure the client ID. In the DHCP server for Mac OS X Server, the client ID is simply a convenient way for the administrator to track specific clients. You can't actually change the behavior of the DHCP server based on the client ID.

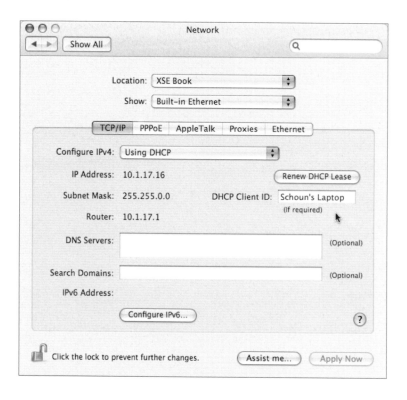

Create a DHCP Subnet

Follow these steps to create a DHCP subnet:

1 On your server, click the Server Admin icon in the Dock or from your Mac OS X computer, launch Server Admin (/Applications/Server).

2 If you have used Server Admin previously and added your information to your Keychain, your server will appear in the Computers & Services list on the left.

If this is the first time you are using Server Admin, enter the server's IP address, local hostname, or DNS name (if the network is set up for DNS), or click Browse to select from a list of servers on your local network. You should be using Server17.local for this book. You can also choose your server from the Connect Recent list under the Server menu.

3 Choose DHCP in the Computers & Services list, then click Settings at the bottom of the screen. You will use the Settings window to configure DHCP subnets (ranges) and determine how DHCP service messages will be logged.

4 Click the Add Subnet (+) button at the bottom of the pane to create a subnet for the en0 interface.

5 Enter the following values:

▶ Subnet Name: *Sales Network*

▶ Starting IP Address: *10.1.17.5*

▶ Ending IP Address: *10.1.17.5*

▶ Subnet Mask: *255.255.0.0*

▶ Router: *10.1.17.1*

NOTE ▶ Limiting your IP range ensures that your DHCP server does not send out IP addresses to other devices, should you be connected to a larger network. Only one device—in this case, your Mac OS X computer—should receive this single IP address.

6 Click the Lease Time pop-up menu to view the available options for lease time increments.

7   Leave the Lease Time value set to 1 and the Lease Time menu set to Hours, reflecting a lease time of 1 hour.

8   Click the DNS button adjacent to the General and LDAP buttons within the DHCP window. The Save Changes dialog appears. Click to save changes.

9   Enter the following DNS information in the appropriate fields:

▶   Default Domain: *pretendco.com*

▶   Name Servers: *10.1.17.1*

This pane provides the DHCP client computer with the correct DNS information via DHCP, even though you have yet to configure DNS on your server.

10   Click the LDAP button in the DHCP service pane.

The LDAP pane contains fields for LDAP information that will be delivered to DHCP clients.

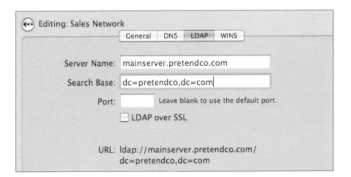

11 Enter the following values:

▶ Server Name: *mainserver.pretendco.com*

▶ Search Base: *dc=pretendco,dc=com*

The LDAP server has not been configured yet, but sending the information in the DHCP packet causes no harm at this point. The client will simply ignore it.

12 Click the Back button (the left arrow) to return to the Subnets pane.

13 Select the Enable checkbox for the subnet you just edited.

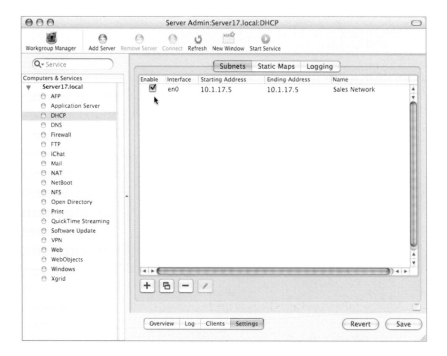

14 Click the Save button to save the new settings for this DHCP subnet name.

Note that you can drag the Preferences icon (located above the Save button) to the desktop to create a backup of these settings.

15 Click Start Service in the toolbar to start the DHCP service.

16 Click the Log button.

You can filter for specific entries in the log using the Filter field at the bottom right. For example, if you wanted to see whether your DHCP service was enabled, you could type *enabled* into the Filter field and see only the log entries that include that value.

17 Verify that the DHCP service is running.

If the indicator next to DHCP under Computers & Services is green, then the service is running.

Request a DHCP Address and Set a Client ID

Although DHCP is running, you'll want to check your Mac OS X computer to make sure it received the proper address.

1 On your Mac OS X computer, unplug the Ethernet cable, wait about 2 seconds, and plug it back in.

This enables your machine to do a Discover and look for the DHCP server.

2 Click the Refresh button in the Server Admin toolbar.

You should see in the log file that your Mac OS X computer now has the IP address of 10.1.17.5.

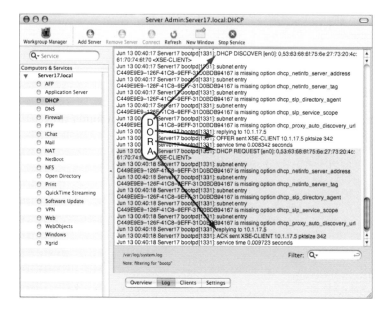

3 On your Mac OS X computer, open System Preferences and choose the Network preferences pane. Select Built-in Ethernet from the Show drop-down menu.

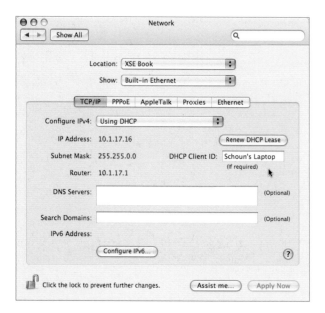

4   Enter your name in the DHCP Client ID field and click the Apply Now button.

5   Click the Refresh button in the Server Admin toolbar and then click the Clients tab at the bottom of the window.

You should see in the window that your Mac OS X computer now has a client ID associated with it.

The pane shows a list of all computers currently receiving a DHCP address from this server computer. Because you limited the DHCP range to provide only one IP address, there should be only one computer listed.

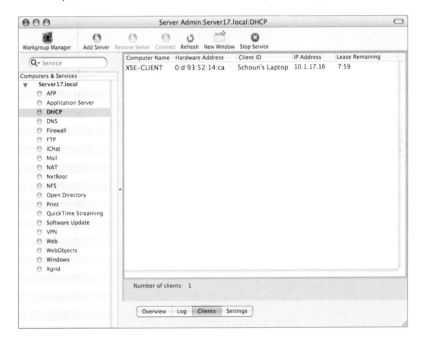

The DHCP Clients pane lists information about DHCP address recipients. This information includes the computer name, hardware address (Ethernet ID), DHCP client ID (if used), IP address, and lease remaining.

Note the Hardware Address column, which helps system administrators identify computers using the active network interface's Ethernet ID.

Troubleshooting DHCP

It is important to keep the DHCP service healthy, as computers cannot interact with each other over the Internet without IP addresses (although Bonjour allows Mac OS X 10.2 through 10.4 computers to communicate without a DHCP server on a local network).

When you are troubleshooting DHCP issues for Mac OS X, check the following:

▶ Is the machine configured correctly on the network? Check physical network issues, such as cabling, broken routers or hubs, and limitations of the physical subnet.

▶ Can you establish any network connection? Can you ping another host? Can you see another host over AppleTalk?

▶ Is the configuration set up properly? Are you using addresses assigned via DHCP or manually? If the problem is with DHCP, does a static address work?

▶ Is an IP address assigned via DHCP or is the address self-assigned (169.254.x.x range)? Can you ping another host via both IP address and hostname? Can you perform a DNS lookup?

From the client, you can see the DHCP packet information sent to it by using the Terminal application and typing *ipconfig getpacket en0* and pressing Return.

```
Terminal — bash — 92x27 — ⌘1
XSE-CLIENT:~ sregan$ ipconfig getpacket en0
op = BOOTREPLY
htype = 1
dp_flags = 0
hlen = 6
hops = 0
xid = 1539242971
secs = 0
ciaddr = 0.0.0.0
yiaddr = 10.1.17.16
siaddr = 10.1.17.1
giaddr = 0.0.0.0
chaddr = 0:d:93:52:14:ca
sname = Server17.local
file =
options:
Options count is 9
dhcp_message_type (uint8): ACK 0x5
server_identifier (ip): 10.1.17.1
lease_time (uint32): 0x6f60
subnet_mask (ip): 255.255.0.0
router (ip_mult): {10.1.17.1}
domain_name_server (ip_mult): {10.1.17.1}
domain_name (string): example.com
ldap_url (string): ldap://mainldap.pretendco.com/dc=pretendco,dc=com
end (none):
XSE-CLIENT:~ sregan$ ▮
```

When you are troubleshooting DHCP issues for Mac OS X Server, check the following:

▶ Is the DHCP server configured correctly on the local network? Is the server reachable on the network via ping? Is a static address properly assigned to the server?

▶ Is the DHCP service configured properly? Are the DHCP server subnet enabled and the DHCP service turned on?

▶ Does Server Admin show the expected DHCP client activity?

▶ Do the DHCP log entries match the expected activity for your server?

Turning Off DHCP Service

Now that you have tested DHCP, you must turn off DHCP service on your server and reconfigure your client computer to use a static IP address. You have already created a location for DHCP, so now you'll create a location for a static IP address.

1 Use Server Admin to stop the DHCP services by clicking the Stop Service button in the toolbar.

2 Click the Stop Now button on the confirmation dialog.

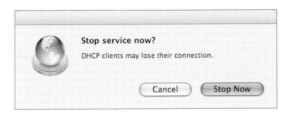

3 On your Mac OS X computer, open System Preferences and choose the Network preferences pane.

You will now configure the client machine to have a static IP address, since DHCP is now turned off on the server. Your current location is called XSE Book, so you will need to create a new location.

4 Choose Edit Locations from the Location pop-up menu, select XSE Book, and click Duplicate.

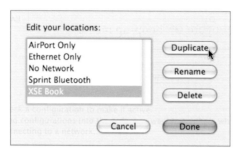

5 Rename the duplicated location *XSE Book Static* and click Done.

6 Choose XSE Book Static from the Location pop-up menu. Press Apply.

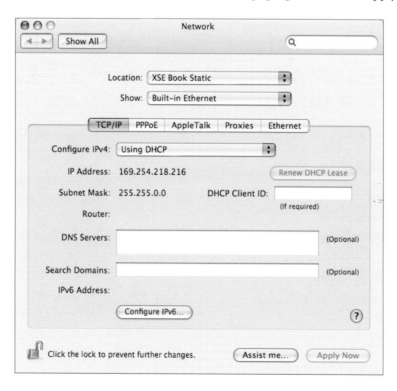

You may have already received a self-assigned address. These start with "169.254." and are created by Mac OS X, not given out by Mac OS X Server.

7 Choose Manually from the Configure IPv4 pop-up menu.

8 Enter the following IP configuration:

   ▶ IP Address: *10.1.17.2*

   ▶ Subnet Mask: *255.255.0.0*

   ▶ Router: *10.1.17.1*

   ▶ DNS Servers: *10.1.17.1*

   You will be configuring DNS services in the next section.

9 Click Apply Now and close System Preferences.

Domain Name System

DNS is the method Internet computers use to map IP addresses to domain names. Computers use IP addresses to locate one another, but they are not easy for people to commit to memory. Domain names, such as www.apple .com or train.apple.com, are much easier to remember, but they need to be translated into the IP addresses that computers use. DNS performs this translation.

DNS Basics

Here's a simple example for understanding DNS. Imagine a user who wants to access a website such as Apple's training site. That user is connected to the appropriate server for Apple's training department by entering *http://train.apple.com* in a browser. Behind the scenes, the graphic on the following page depicts what is actually happening on the Internet to make this connection occur.

Domain Name System (DNS)

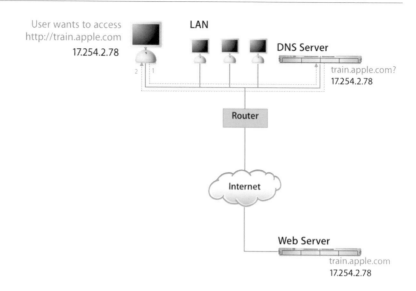

1. A user enters *http://train.apple.com*.

2. The user's computer checks with a DNS server to find the IP address associated with the domain name train.apple.com. The computer uses the DNS server configured in Network preferences to look up this information. This is referred to as a *forward lookup* or just *lookup*.

3. The DNS server determines the IP address that corresponds to the domain name requested in the lookup. It returns this information to the user's computer.

4. The user's computer then uses the IP address to request the training webpage by sending this IP address to its default Internet router.

This DNS scenario oversimplifies the true capabilities of DNS. The real power of DNS is that any valid Internet IP address in the world can be found quickly and easily, yet easily maintained. This is due to the global design of DNS.

DNS—How It Works

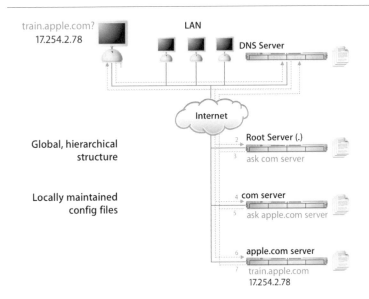

DNS combines a global search space with a local, relatively easy way to maintain this search space. It does this through a hierarchical structure in which each organization is responsible for maintaining its own DNS information.

Reviewing the previous request for a webpage, imagine that the request was coming from a computer at a company in Japan. The Japanese company may maintain its own DNS server but have no idea of how DNS is assigned for companies in the United States. In this case, the local DNS server would contact a parent DNS server, looking for the information on train.apple.com. If the parent DNS server does not have this information, it sends a request to a top-level "root" DNS server that can then contact appropriate servers to find the correct lookup information.

All valid DNS servers on the Internet can eventually find DNS information on any address by following the appropriate lookup through this top-level approach. In this case, the Japanese computer finds the appropriate DNS mapping by following the lookup process and eventually finding a DNS server in the United States that is responsible for mapping the address train.apple.com to the IP address 17.254.2.78.

This process highlights the other key aspect of DNS—locally maintained DNS servers. For example, Apple maintains a list of computers for various web services. Apple can reassign IP addresses internally to meet its server needs, as long as Apple maintains a correct set of DNS files on its local DNS servers and has these DNS servers configured appropriately to be available to higher-level DNS servers that contact them.

The key to these DNS servers is correctly configured files containing the DNS information. These files are typically referred to as *DNS configuration and zone files*.

DNS Setup

Mac OS X Server includes DNS server functionality based on the standard UNIX-based implementation BIND (Berkeley Internet Name Domain). BIND is the most common implementation of DNS in use on the Internet today, and Mac OS X and Mac OS X Server currently include BIND version 9.2.2.

Most companies that use Mac OS X Server for services such as file, print, and web serving have already established appropriate DNS service. This service could be provided by dedicated DNS departments in their organizations or by an ISP. Companies running their own mail services would also want to ensure DNS service to correctly map IP addresses to their mail domains. If a company has not established DNS service yet, the following steps are required to configure DNS for Mac OS X Server:

1   Register your domain name via any valid registrar, such as VeriSign.

2 Configure BIND on Mac OS X Server by modifying the DNS configuration and zone files.

3 Set up mail exchange (MX) records (optional).

4 Start DNS service.

With Mac OS X Server, you can configure DNS zone files with Server Admin.

NOTE ▶ This lesson covers the setup of basic DNS records. To find detailed information on configuring DNS files, refer to the Resources section at the end of this lesson.

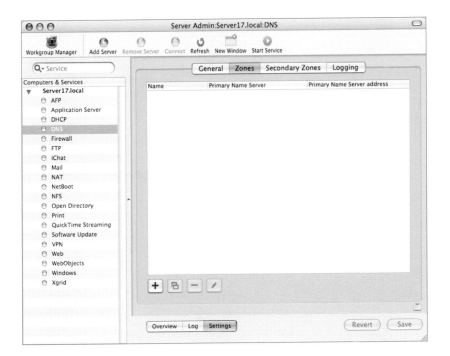

DNS Zones

Zones are the basic organizational unit of the DNS. Zones contain records, and are defined by how they acquire those records and how they respond to DNS requests. There are three kinds of zones:

▶ A *master zone* has the master copy of the zone's records and provides authoritative answers to lookup requests.

▶ A *slave zone* is a copy of a master zone stored on a slave or secondary name server. Each slave zone keeps a list of masters that it contacts to receive updates to records in the master zone. Slaves must be configured to request the copy of the master zone's data. Slave zones use zone transfers to get copies of the master zone data. Slave name servers can take lookup requests like master servers. By using several slave zones linked to one master, you can distribute DNS query loads across several computers and ensure that lookup requests are answered when the master name server is down.

Slave zones also have a refresh interval that determines how often slave zones check for changes from the master zone. You can change this interval by using the BIND configuration file. See the BIND documentation for more information.

▶ A *forward zone* directs all lookup requests for that zone to other DNS servers. Forward zones don't do zone transfers. Often, forward zone servers are used to provide DNS services to a private network behind a firewall. In this case, the DNS server must have access to the Internet and a DNS server outside the firewall. Finally, forward zones cache responses to the queries that they pass on. This can improve the performance of lookups by clients that use the forward zone.

To add a new DNS zone, go to the Settings pane and click the Zones button. In the Zones list, you see two zones that are created by default. To add more zones, use the Add Zone (+) button. You can delete, edit, or duplicate zones.

For each zone, you can add, edit, delete, and duplicate records. When you add
a record, you are prompted for the type of record you want to add. After you
add a record, it is displayed in the Records list for the zone.

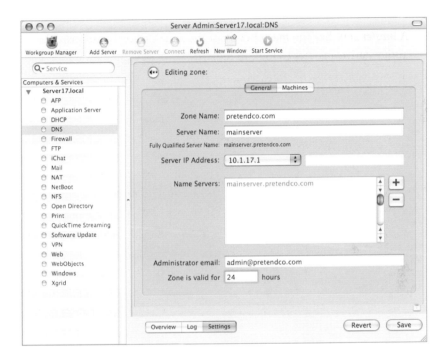

DNS Zone Records

Each zone contains a number of records. These records are requested when a
client computer needs to translate a domain name (like www.pretendco.com)
to an IP number. Web browsers, email clients, and other network applications
rely on zone records to contact the appropriate server. You create records by
adding machines to a zone in Server Admin.

Your master zone's records will be queried by others across the Internet so they can connect to your network services. There are several kinds of DNS records. Following are the records that are available for configuration by Server Admin's user interface:

▶ Address (A): Stores the IP address associated with a domain name. An A record is created for each machine entry added to a zone.

▶ Canonical Name (CNAME): Stores the "real name" of a server when given a nickname or alias. For example, mail.pretendco.com might have a canonical name of mailsrvr1.pretendco.com. A CNAME record is created for each entry in the Alias field when adding a machine to a zone.

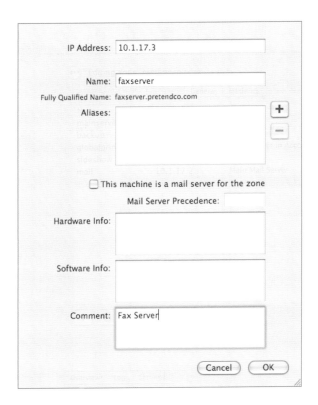

- ▶ Mail exchange (MX): Stores the domain name of the computer that is used for email in a zone. An MX record is created when you specify that a machine is a mail server.

- ▶ Pointer (PTR): Stores the domain name of a given IP address (reverse lookup). A PTR record maps an IP address to a computer's DNS name. The pointer record contains the four octets of the IP address in reverse order followed by in-addr.arpa. (For example, 10.1.0.1 becomes 1.0.1.10.in-addr.arpa.)

Mac OS X Server simplifies the creation of these records by focusing on the computer being added to the zone rather than the records themselves. As you add a computer record to a zone, Mac OS X Server creates the appropriate zone records that resolve to a certain computer address.

NOTE ▶ The term *fully qualified domain name (FQDN)* refers to the entire address of a host computer. For example, "sales.apple.com" is an FQDN, whereas "sales" is a relative domain name. To indicate that a domain name is fully qualified, add a trailing dot to it. For example, "sales.apple.com." indicates that this is not a relative domain name.

Add Records to a DNS Server

DNS is a complicated topic that covers a wide range of configuration options and settings. This lesson does not cover in-depth DNS configuration. You will add information to your DNS configuration that will enable you to associate a friendly name with your computer and see the effects of that change.

1   On your server computer, open the Terminal application located on the Dock.

If you are familiar with the Secure Shell (SSH) protocol, you can ssh into your server from your Mac OS X computer.

2   In the Terminal window, enter *cd /var/named* to navigate to /var/named.

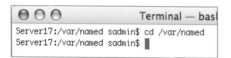

```
Server17:/var/named sadmin$ cd /var/named
Server17:/var/named sadmin$ ▊
```

3   List the contents of the ls -la folder.

```
Server17:/var/named sadmin$ ls -la
total 24
drwxr-xr-x    5 root   wheel    170 Jun 13 00:15 .
drwxr-xr-x   33 root   wheel   1122 Jun 12 23:52 ..
-rw-r--r--    1 root   wheel    195 Mar 20 15:23 localhost.zone
-rw-r--r--    1 root   wheel   2498 Mar 20 15:23 named.ca
-rw-r--r--    1 root   wheel    315 Jun 13 00:15 named.local
Server17:/var/named sadmin$ ▊
```

These are the default DNS configuration files.

4   Leave the Terminal window open.

5   Open Server Admin if it is not already open and connect to your
    server.

    NOTE ▶ You should always stop the DNS service before making changes
    to DNS configuration files.

6   Click the DNS service, click the Settings button, and click the Zones tab.

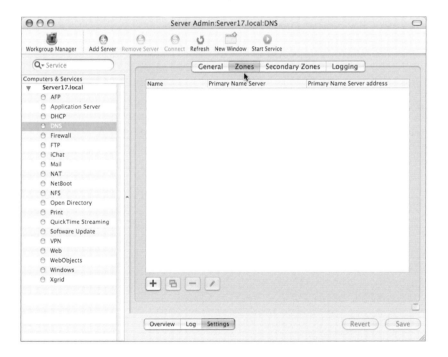

7 In the Settings pane, click the Add Zone (+) button to create a zone.

Enter the following settings:

▶ Zone Name: *pretendco.com.* (Make sure to enter the period at the end of the zone name.)

▶ Server Name: *server17*

▶ Administrator email: *admin@pretendco.com.* (Make sure to enter the period at the end of the address.)

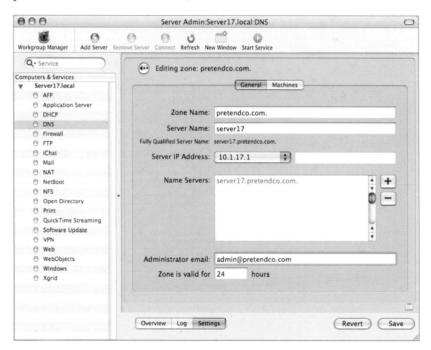

8 Click Save, and then click Start Service in the toolbar to start the DNS service.

9 Type *ls –la* in the Terminal window again, and note changes in the named folder.

```
Server17:/var/named sadmin$ ls -la
total 40
drwxr-xr-x    7 root  wheel    238 Jun 13 00:18 .
drwxr-xr-x   33 root  wheel   1122 Jun 12 23:52 ..
-rw-r--r--    1 root  wheel    323 Jun 13 00:18 db.10.1.17
-rw-r--r--    1 root  wheel    195 Mar 20 15:23 localhost.zone
-rw-r--r--    1 root  wheel   2498 Mar 20 15:23 named.ca
-rw-r--r--    1 root  wheel    320 Jun 13 00:18 named.local
-rw-r--r--    1 root  wheel    271 Jun 13 00:18 pretendco.com.zone
Server17:/var/named sadmin$
```

In this book, you will use Server Admin to make several changes that create and configure files on your disk. It's useful to be familiar with those file locations when troubleshooting. Review the contents of /var/named after you create the new zone.

Note that the list now includes multiple settings files for the default zone you created.

10 Now we will use the move comand to examine the content of the pretendco.com.zone file.

In the Terminal window, type *more pretendco.com.zone* and press Return.

This command displays the contents of your zone file. Entries with *A* to the left of the IP address are A records. You will see an A record for your server computer, created by default.

```
$TTL 86400
pretendco.com.                    IN   SOA   server17.pretendco.com. admin.pretendco.com.   (
                                        2005061302    ; serial
                                        3h      ; refresh
                                        1h      ; retry
                                        1w      ; expiry
                                        1h      ) ; minimum
pretendco.com.                    IN   NS    server17.pretendco.com.
server17                          IN   A     10.1.17.1
Server17:/var/named sadmin$
```

Enter the DNS Search Information

You now must enter DNS search information inside the Network preferences pane of both your Mac OS X Server and Mac OS X computers.

1 On your server, open System Preferences, navigate to the Network preferences pane, and click Configure to continue.

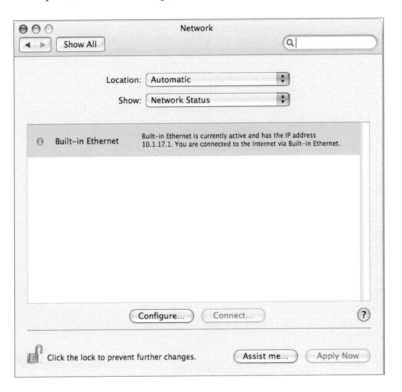

2 Enter the following values:

▶ DNS Servers: *10.1.17.1*

▶ Search Domains: *pretendco.com*

3 Click the Apply Now button and close System Preferences.

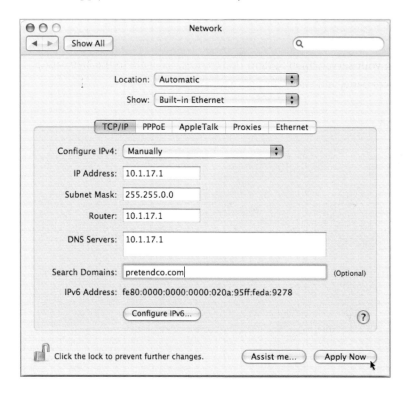

4 Repeat this process on the Mac OS X computer.

Create a DNS Alias for Your Client Computer

In a DNS hierarchy, there are explicit hostnames that resolve to IP addresses. However, a DNS server can maintain a number of different names for computers, which are called *aliases*. Aliases by themselves are simply friendly names that point to an IP address, and are often used to reduce typing or perform server redirection.

1 Return to Server Admin.

You will add a machine alias to your DNS entry and observe the result.

2 Select DNS and click the Stop Service button in the toolbar.

3 Click the Stop Now button in the dialog that appears to stop the DNS service.

4 Select the Settings tab of DNS and click the Machines button.

You will see a list with your server computer, entered by default.

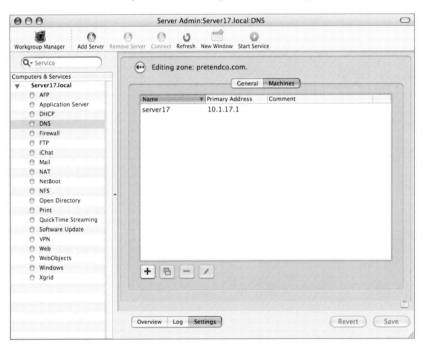

5 Click the Add Machine (+) button to add a new entry, and enter the following information:

▶ IP Address: *10.1.17.2*

▶ Name: *user17*

6 Click the Add Alias (+) button to add a new alias.

7 Type *client17* in the Aliases field and click OK.

8 Click the Save button and start the DNS service again.

9 Note changes in pretendco.com.zone by typing *more pretendco.com.zone* again in the Terminal.

> **NOTE** ▸ You can also use the up arrow to see the last command entered.

This command will refresh the display of your zone file. You will see a new entry, with your student name associated with the IP address and an alias that points to your A Record.

```
server17:/var/named sadmin$ more pretendco.com.zone
$TTL 86400
pretendco.com.                          IN    SOA    server17.pretendco.com. admin.pretendco.com.    (
                                               2005061304     ;  serial
                                               3h     ;   refresh
                                               1h     ;   retry
                                               1w     ;   expiry
                                               1h     )  ;   minimum
pretendco.com.                          IN    NS     server17.pretendco.com.
server17                         IN     A     10.1.17.1
user17                  IN     A     10.1.17.2
client17                         IN     CNAME   user17
server17:/var/named sadmin$ 
```

10 Check your pretendco.com.zone file to ensure that it reflects the changes you just made.

It is useful to understand how your zone files change over time.

Test the New Alias From Your Client Computer

The real test of any DNS change is when your DNS clients are able to use the new entry. Because of the limited number of services available, you will use ping from your client computer to see if its alias was configured properly.

1   On your client computer, open Network Utility and click the Ping button.

2   In the address field, type *client17* and click Ping.

The ping command should execute properly and resolve to 10.1.17.2.

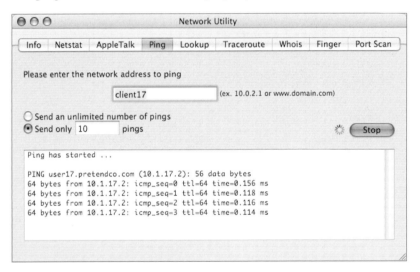

Monitoring DNS Activity

Within Server Admin, you can monitor DNS activity on Mac OS X Server using the Overview, Activity, and Log panes for DNS.

▶   The Overview pane displays information such as DNS server status (Running/Stopped), DNS version (BIND 9.2.2), number of zones allocated, and query logging status (Off/On).

▶ The Activity pane displays information on Source of Authority (SOA) queries and zone transfers.

▶ The Log pane displays current information about start time and DNS queries (lookups).

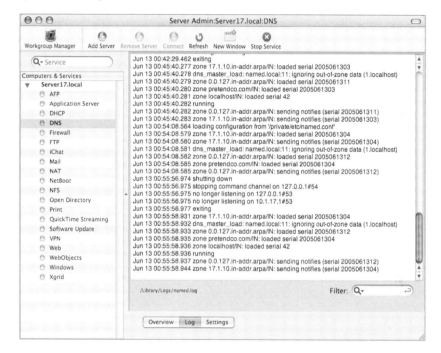

DNS is an essential function in any running version of Mac OS X. Many services look for DNS information to find critical information. Examples of these services are the login window, server administration tools, directory services, Internet communications, and any direct web access. Incorrectly configured DNS could result in a long delay in these services completing their associated tasks.

DNS is a complicated and subtle protocol. Its distributed nature often makes it difficult to discern where a problem lies: Is it the client, the local DNS server, or some remote DNS server on the Internet? Advanced DNS issues will likely require an experienced system administrator. However, there are few quick checks you can make easily.

Perform DNS Lookups

The best graphical tool for troubleshooting DNS issues is Network Utility's Lookup pane, where you can perform DNS lookups. Perform the following checks when you troubleshoot DNS problems:

▶   Check hardware and network issues.

▶   Verify that network settings are correct in the Network pane of System Preferences.

▶   Use Network Utility's Lookup pane to test your DNS server.

▶   Use Network Utility's Ping pane to test direct IP connectivity, bypassing DNS.

▶   Ping another computer on your subnet to test for basic IP connectivity, but also be sure to test the IP address that is listed as the DNS server in Network preferences.

▶   Check with a network administrator to ensure that DNS servers are con-figured properly.

> **NOTE** ▶ In most cases, DNS problems stem either from a local configura-tion issue (hardware, network, or software) or from an issue with a recently installed DNS server. DNS servers that have been in place for some time are typically not the source of problems.

Isolate and Resolve DNS Issues

DNS issues can take many forms. You may have problems that are related to end users who misunderstand your DNS hierarchy, or typographic problems within your DNS aliases. A system administrator must be able to determine authoritatively where a DNS entry is being resolved.

You have already tested your alias with a successful ping. You will now look up DNS information.

1   On your Mac OS X computer, in Network Utility, click Lookup.

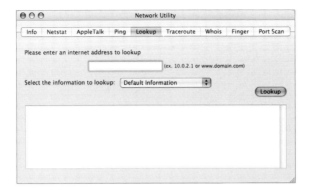

Lookup enables you to identify the server where DNS resolves for a particular value. You know that user17 and client17 were working, but now you should make sure you see how they resolve.

2   In the address field, type *client17.pretendco.com* and press Return.

Lookup requires an FQDN, which is why you must add "pretendco.com".

3   Scroll the response so that you can see the Authority Section information.

Your authority should be your server computer, server17.pretendco.com. This result shows that server17.pretendco.com. is resolved on your server computer, and the DNS service is working at that level.

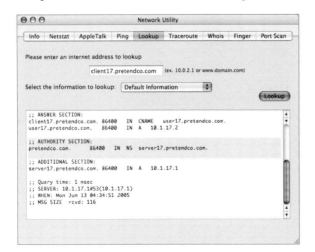

Software Update Server

A Software Update server enables you to manage Macintosh client updates on your network. In an uncontrolled environment, users may connect to the Apple Software Update servers at any time and update client computers with software that your IT group has not approved for use in your organization.

Using local Software Update servers, your client computers access only the software updates that you allow from software lists that you control, thus giving you more flexibility in managing computer software updates. For example, you can:

▶ Download software updates from the Apple Software Update servers to a local server for sharing with local network clients and reduce the amount of bandwidth used outside of your enterprise network.

▶ Direct users, groups, and computers to specific local Software Update servers using managed preferences.

▶ Manage the software-update packages users can access by enabling and disabling individual packages on the local server.

▶ Mirror updates automatically between Apple Software Update servers and your server to ensure that you have the most current updates available.

NOTE ▶ The Software Update service does not prevent client computers from accessing Apple's Software Update servers directly; it just mirrors updates provided by Apple. If you want to block users from accessing Apple's servers, then you must block client access to port 63000 on your network's main firewall.

Very little configuration is required to set up the Software Update server. The primary configuration you need to do is to determine if your server will automatically download all updates and provide them to your users. This is specified in Server Admin.

Before you set up Software Update service, you need to consider whether you want to provide all or only part of Apple's software updates. Your client computers may run application software that requires a specific version of Apple software in order for it to operate correctly. To prevent your users from installing updates that might be incompatible with your applications, you can configure your Software Update server with only the software-update packages that you approve. Restricting access to particular update packages might help prevent future maintenance and compatibility problems with your computers.

You can set client access to only specific update packages through Software Update Server by disabling automatic mirroring and enabling functions in the General pane. Regardless of the settings in the General pane, your server will automatically synchronize with the Apple Software Update server by requesting a catalog of available updates. If the "Automatically mirror updates from Apple" and "Automatically enable mirrored updates" options are not selected in the General pane, you can specify which updates to download (mirror) and which ones to enable in the Updates pane.

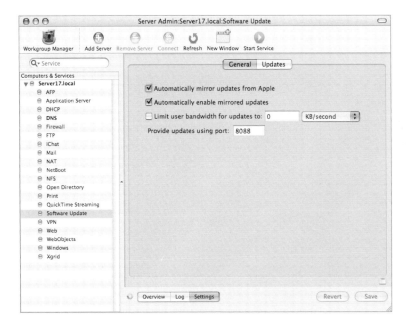

NOTE ► In your organization, you might identify individuals, groups, or groups of computers with common needs for only a few software update packages, whereas you may give others allow unrestricted access to all software updates. To provide varied access to software update packages, you'll need to set up multiple Software Update servers. Use Managed Preferences to configure these computers to access a specific Software Update server.

If your clients are having problems using your server to update their computers, check the Updates pane to make sure the updates are both mirrored and enabled. Also make sure required previous updates are installed. If you are not providing the full updates, note that if a client computer skips an earlier update, it will not install the most recent update until it has all of the previous updates installed.

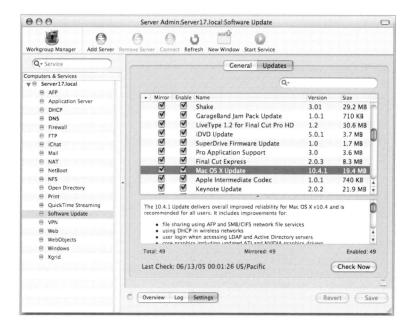

If you are experiencing poor response from a server, this may indicate a high load on the server. Try reducing the maximum user bandwidth in the General pane.

If your server is not receiving updates from Apple, make sure that your firewall is allowing your server access through port 63000.

What You've Learned

▶ Typically when one thinks of setting up a server, one thinks of configuring a file, mail, or web server. However, Mac OS X Server can provide even more fundamental network services, such as DHCP and DNS. It can also be used to mirror Apple's software updates.

▶ DHCP allows client computers to be assigned IP addresses dynamically without requiring manual assignment of permanent, static IP addresses. DHCP subnets are created using Server Admin. Each subnet contains a starting and ending IP address defining the range of addresses that can be assigned. The subnet entry also contains the subnet mask and router address that is provided to client computers. The entry can be configured to provide additional information, such as LDAP configuration information.

▶ DNS provides the ability for domain names to be converted to IP addresses. DNS is turned on in the General pane of Server Admin. Mac OS X Server provides tools for configuring the DNS zone files.

▶ Mac OS X Server also provides Software Update service, which downloads updates from Apple's Software Update server and serves them to computers on the local network. This provides more efficient use of limited bandwidth and gives over administrator control when updates are made available to local clients.

▶ If your clients are having problems using your server to update their computers, check the Updates pane to make sure the updates are both mirrored and enabled. Also, make sure required previous updates are installed.

▶ If you are experiencing poor response from an update server, this may indicate a high load on the server itself. Try reducing the maximum user bandwidth in the General pane.

▶ If your server is not receiving updates from Apple, make sure that your firewall is allowing your server access through port 63000.

References

The following documents provide more information about installing Mac OS X Server. (All of these and more are available at www.apple.com/server/documentation.)

Administration Guides

Mac OS X Server Getting Started (http://images.apple.com/server/pdfs/Getting_Started_v10.4.pdf)

Apple Remote Desktop Administrator's Guide (http://images.apple.com/server/pdfs/Apple_Remote_Desktop_Admin_Guide.pdf)

Mac OS X Server Command-Line Administration (http://images.apple.com/
server/pdfs/Command_Line_v10.4.pdf)

Books

Albitz, Paul, and Liu, Cricket. *DNS and BIND* (O'Reilly, 2001).

Apple Knowledge Base Documents

You can check for new and updated Knowledge Base documents at
www.apple.com/support.

Document 107684, "Mac OS X Server 10.3: Tested and theoretical maximums
(limits)"

URLs

The International Software Consortium website: www.isc.org

Review Quiz

1. How does DHCP differ from manual configuration of network settings?

2. What DHCP configuration information can be delivered via Mac OS X Server?

3. How do lease times affect DHCP address assignment?

4. Why might a client fail to receive a DHCP address, including renewal issues?

5. What are the global and local aspects of DNS architecture?

6. What three possible steps can you take when investigating a DNS problem?

7. What are two benefits of setting up a Software Update server?

Answers

1. DHCP is a way to provide an entire network of computers with IP addresses
    by means of a central server. Manually configuring network settings requires
    that an administrator (or user) type proper IP address information for each
    and every computer on the network.

2. IP address, subnet mask, router, DNS server, default domain, WINS server, and LDAP server.

3. The lease time is the minimum amount of time for which a client has use of an IP address without explicitly releasing the address. If a lease has not expired and the client has not released the address, the DHCP server does not reassign that address. Thus, if you set lease time to a year, and a client computer permanently leaves the network, that computer's IP address is potentially unavailable for up to a year.

4. Reasons could include a misconfigured DHCP server, network problems that prevent the DORA exchange, and the DHCP server and client being on different subnets. If the DHCP server becomes unavailable after the client obtains an address, the client will be fine throughout the lease time. If the DHCP server is still unavailable at the end of the lease time, the client should stop using that IP address, either by shutting down IP altogether or by using a private, nonroutable address.

5. DNS is a distributed system. It is local in that each separate domain is responsible for its own configuration, so that domain configuration files are located on multiple DNS servers across the Internet. It is global in that all the separate domains are integrated into one unified system in which queries are handled by the responsible name server and all clients can obtain correct name resolution from anywhere on the Internet.

6. You can:

   a. Verify network settings.

   b. Use Network Utility to test for forward and reverse lookups.

   c. Use Network Utility to ping the DNS server.

   d. Use Network Utility to test for basic IP connectivity by pinging another device on the subnet.

7. By setting up a Software Update server, you can control which updates are available to clients on your local network. It also reduces bandwidth demands to the Internet, as updates are downloaded from Apple once and then re-served across the local network as often as needed.

4

Lesson Files	None
Time	This lesson takes approximately 1 hour to complete.
Goals	Use Gateway Setup Assistant to configure firewall, NAT, and VPN services
	User Server Admin to enable, configure, and monitor firewall service
	Given a set of firewall rules, determine which rule is applied to a given packet
	Use Server Admin to filter IP traffic based on destination IP port and originating address
	Use Server Admin to enable, configure, and monitor NAT service
	Describe the relationship between IP ports and services on an IP host
	Understand and configure VPN services

Setting Up Gateway Services

When setting up any server, you must consider security. This chapter introduces you to several services that permit you to run Mac OS X Server as a gateway to the Internet, while providing secure pathways for users to access information and a wall behind which users can hide, protecting them from the potential hazards of Internet traffic, and stopping unwanted intruders from accessing your server.

Mac OS X Server has a single method of handling these options, but this lesson will delve into why these services are necessary and how to manage them for better performance and security.

The focus is on four main areas:

▶ *Gateway Setup Assistant* configures basic firewall, virtual private network (VPN), network address translation (NAT), and domain name system (DNS) services on Mac OS X Server.

▶ A *firewall* keeps unwanted requests from coming in while insuring only selected requests go out.

▶   Network Address Translation allows one public Internet Protocol (IP) address to act on behalf of your entire network.

▶   Virtual Private Networking lets computers connect to your Mac OS X server's network securely.

Protecting Your Network

Providing secure services in today's environment can be a challenging proposition. Here are some of the issues facing network administrators:

▶   Access to services from outside the local network must be limited or controlled.

▶   Remote clients need access to internal network resources via the Internet.

▶   Internal clients need to share a single external Internet address.

Mac OS X Server provides solutions to each of these challenges. Using the tools available, administrators can customize the security of the services they provide.

For example, attackers can sniff network traffic and possibly obtain your email address and password. Or they can grab information and not allow it to go to the proper destination until they have modified it to suit their needs. Or possibly they knock on a few of the over 65,530 ports on your computer, looking for a way inside. These methods of exploitation and intrusion must be dealt with *before* they happen.

Depending on the type of attack you are trying to prevent or level of security service you want to have, you can implement specific combinations of services:

▶   Firewalls give you control over the types of data that can enter or leave the network.

▶   VPN allows trusted users to access your network from outside the firewall.

▶   NAT provides a range of IP addresses internally, with only one externally accessible address.

When combined, these services often make a powerful team against the potential threats to your Mac OS X server and your network that exist on the Internet today. While each of these can seem very complicated to set up, they can be implemented quite easily and still retain a high level of security. If further configuration is needed, all three of these services can be expanded, customized, and adapted to fit any need.

Protecting Your Network

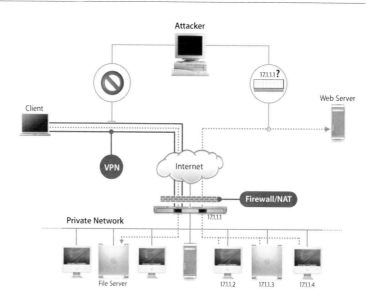

Gateway Setup Assistant

The Gateway Setup Assistant is a basic configuration tool that you can use to set up the firewall, NAT, and VPN services that provide gateway functionality. You enter the pertinent data in the assistant screens, and the assistant configures and enables the services for you in a highly integrated way. The Gateway Setup Assistant also configures services such as Dynamic Host Configuration Protocol (DHCP) and DNS. These are required for the firewall, NAT, and VPN services to function properly.

The Gateway Setup Assistant is designed to help you create a basic configuration of these services; you'll need to use Server Admin, however, to customize your configuration or implement advanced services. The Gateway Setup Assistant should not be used on top of already configured server settings.

NOTE ▶ Gateway Setup Assistant will overwrite existing DHCP, DNS, NAT, firewall, and VPN settings. It will also change TCP/IP port data, which other services such as directory service may rely upon. Use Gateway Setup Assistant before configuring these other services.

When you are finished with the Gateway Setup Assistant, you can either print the configuration information or save it to a file so that you can refer to it later.

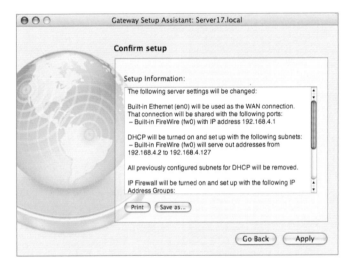

Gateway Setup Assistant will do the following:

1. Assign the "internal" interfaces on the server an address that falls in the 192.168.x.1 range.

2. Set aside addresses in the 192.168.x.x range for DHCP (and optionally VPN).

    The 192.168.x.x range is hard-coded in the tool. Gateway Setup Assistant writes over the port information each time it executes.

3. Enable DHCP Server and configure it to provide the addresses set aside to computers on the internal network.

4. Optionally start the VPN server and set aside a range of addresses for VPN clients.

5. Enable NAT to allow machines on the internal network to share the server's Internet connection.

6. Enable firewall and block all traffic coming from the Internet (except information required for connections and responses to queries from the server) while allowing all traffic from internal clients to go out.

7. Enable the DNS server, which is configured by default as a caching server, to improve performance of named services for internal clients.

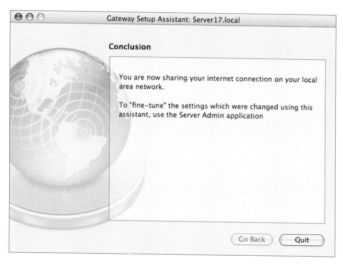

Configuring Gateway Setup Assistant

In this lesson, you'll work with both of your computers to create two separate networks and configure your server to act as a gateway that connects them. You will connect your Mac OS X computer to your server via a FireWire cable, simulating a second network.

> **NOTE** ▶ Do *not* run the Gateway Setup Assistant on a network that is connected to the Internet or any other computers, other than your Mac OS X computer that has been used for previous lessons. The Gateway Setup Assistant automatically modifies and edits network settings that could have a negative impact on your network.

1 Save the DHCP and DNS settings on the Mac OS X server.

Setting up the gateway server will change the DHCP settings on the server. After you complete this exercise, you'll need to reestablish the DHCP settings you created in Lesson 3, "Using Network Services." Save the DHCP settings so you can use them later.

2 Open Server Admin on your server, click DHCP in the Computers & Services list, and then click Settings.

3 Drag the Tear Off icon in the lower-right corner to the desktop.

Notice that a file is created called DHCP Config.plist.

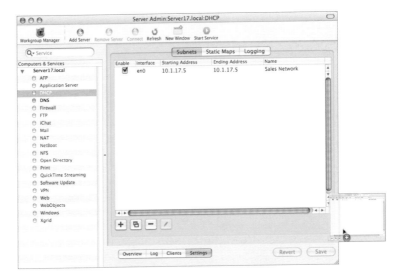

4 Repeat this process with the DNS service, firewall service, NAT service, and VPN service.

5 Quit Server Admin.

6 Create a folder on your desktop called *Service Backup Configurations* and drag all five files into that folder for later use.

7 While still working on the server, open System Preferences and click on the Network pane. Choose "Network Port Configurations" from the Show pop-up menu and check the Built-in FireWire checkbox. Click Apply Now.

8 On your Mac OS X computer, create and choose a new location and call it *NAT*. Enable only the FireWire interface.

9 On your Mac OS X computer, disconnect the Ethernet cable from the switch and connect the FireWire cable between both computers.

10 Open Gateway Setup Assistant, located in /Applications/Server on your server, and authenticate as the server administrator.

11   Click Continue at the introduction window and select the wide area network (WAN) interface in the WAN window (in this case, your built-in Ethernet interface). Click Continue.

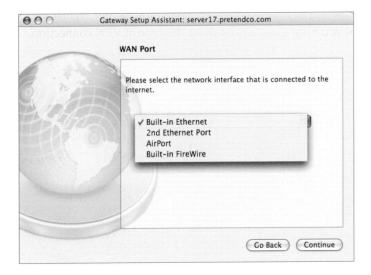

12   Select the built-in FireWire interface for the local area network (LAN; in this case, the interface that provides the connection to the WAN) and click Continue.

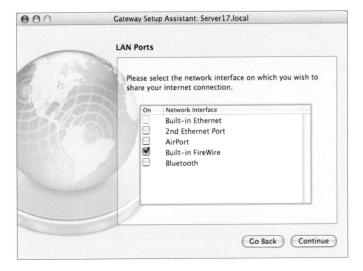

13 Place a checkmark in the "Enable VPN for this server" checkbox, enter a shared secret of your choosing, and click Continue.

A *shared secret* (eight or more alphanumeric characters with punctuation is a good idea) is another passphrase, in addition to your regular password, that you must enter before using this type of VPN connection.

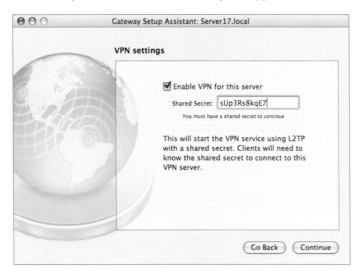

14 Click Save As to save your settings to a text file or Print to print them so you'll have them for later use. Then click Apply.

Your server is now configured for DHCP, DNS (if not already configured), firewall, NAT, and VPN.

Verifying Gateway Setup and Resetting Server Services

Although you have a very small network, you can still check to ensure that the Gateway Setup Assistant configured settings correctly.

1 Verify that the services have started by opening Server Admin on your server and checking each service.

In the last procedure, you changed settings on four (or possibly five, if DNS is not already configured) services simultaneously.

2 Verify that your Mac OS X computer has an IP address over FireWire by opening the Network preferences pane.

Because of the limited setup of this small network, you cannot test all the possible gateway settings further.

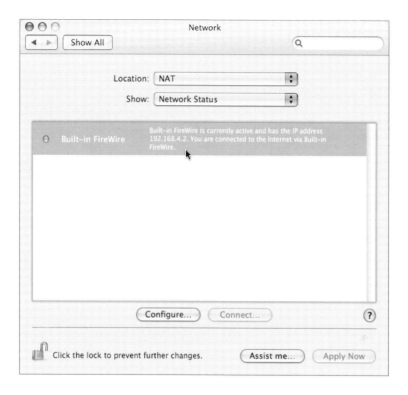

3 Reset your network location back to XSE Book Static on your Mac OS X
computer and unplug the FireWire cable from both computers. Reconnect
the Ethernet cable.

4 On your server, open the Network preferences pane and deselect Built-in
FireWire. Apply the change.

5 Launch Server Admin on your server and turn off the following services:

▶ DHCP

▶ Firewall

▶ NAT

▶ VPN

Click Stop Now in any alerts that appear.

6 Open the Service Backup Configurations folder on your desktop, drag the appropriate PLIST files into their respective settings windows, and save the changes.

This returns all the services to their preconfigured states.

Firewalls

Mac OS X Server includes a firewall service that you can use to restrict access to your server based on a requesting machine's IP address.

When the firewall is enabled, each IP service request that Mac OS X Server receives is first checked against a list of firewall rules that define which IP addresses have access to specific port numbers. The port numbers are used to identify specific services, such as Apple File Service (AFS; port 548) and web service (port 80). With the firewall enabled, a Mac OS X Server can allow one machine to access a service while blocking requests from another machine for the same service.

Mac OS X Server Firewall

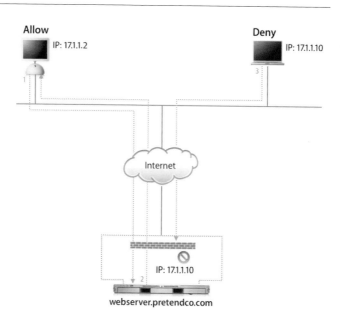

Access through a firewall is based on the requesting machine's IP address. If the IP address of the requesting machine is within a specified range of addresses, the request is denied or allowed, depending on the exact rule applied. For example, pretendco.com can use the firewall service to allow any request from an internal address but deny any request from an external address, except for those belonging to trade partners.

Since the firewall service essentially determines which machines are allowed to access services on a given server, it is a good tool to consider when security is important.

NOTE ▶ If the firewall does not find a specific rule that applies to the request, it applies the default general rule, which denies all Transport Control Protocol (TCP) connections.

Basic Firewall Configuration

By default, firewall service blocks all incoming TCP connections. Before you turn on firewall service, make sure you've set up rules allowing access from IP addresses you choose. Otherwise, no one will have access to your server.

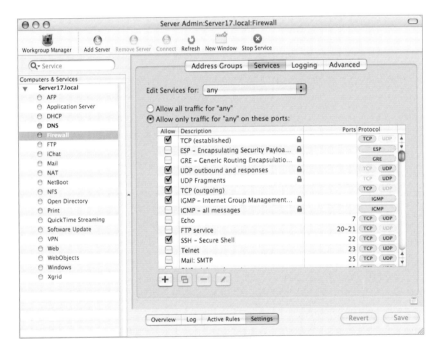

To start or stop the firewall service, click Firewall in the Computers & Services list in Server Admin and click Start Service or Stop Service.

When you start firewall service for the first time, most TCP packets are denied until you change the rules to allow access. By default, only the ports essential to remote administration are available. These include but are not limited to the ports for Remote Directory Access (625), server administration via Server

Admin (687), and Secure Shell (22). For any other network service, you must create rules, or configure existing rules, to allow access to your server. If you turn off firewall service, all addresses are allowed access to your server.

You can easily allow standard services—such as Apple Filing Protocol (AFP), File Transfer Protocol (FTP), print, web, and Windows—to access your server through the firewall.

To open the firewall for standard services:

1 Open Server Admin, click Firewall, and click General.

2 Select the "any" address group from the IP Address Groups list.

3 Select the services you want to allow and click Save.

The "any" group lets you open the firewall to any IP address. But if you want, you can define other groups of IP addresses for your firewall rules and can configure them separately. You can use these groups to organize and target the rules.

Addresses can be listed as individual addresses (for example, 192.168.2.2) or as IP addresses with a Classless Inter-Domain Routing (CIDR) netmask format (for example, 192.168.2.0/24). CIDR consists of the IP address followed by a slash (/) and the IP prefix, a number from 1 to 32 that specifies the number of significant bits used to identify a network. For example, 192.168.2.1/16 means the first 16 bits (the first two numbers separated by periods) are used to represent the network (every machine on the network begins with 192.168), and the remaining 16 bits (the last two numbers separated by periods) are used to identify hosts (each machine has a unique set of trailing numbers). The subnet mask that corresponds to CIDR 16 is 255.255.0.0.

To create an address group, click the Add (+) button in the IP Address Groups pane. Enter the group name, enter the addresses and subnet mask you want the rules to affect, and then click OK. To edit an existing group, select the group and click Edit.

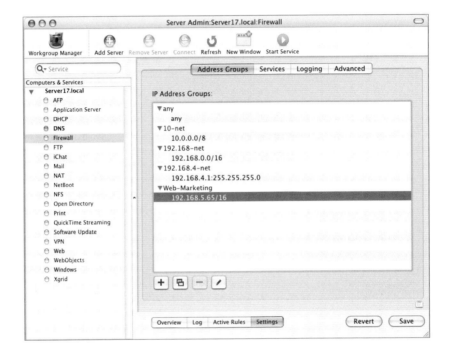

Firewall-Service Monitoring

A firewall is a network's first line of defense against malicious intruders. One way to maintain security is to monitor your firewall to make sure that it's working properly and to detect patterns of access attempts that might indicate a serious threat.

To monitor the logs, enable logging in the Logging tab of the firewall settings in Server Admin. You can view the log using the Log pane of the firewall service.

Each rule you create in Server Admin corresponds to one or more rules in the underlying firewall software. Log entries show you the rule applied, the IP addresses of the client and server, and other information.

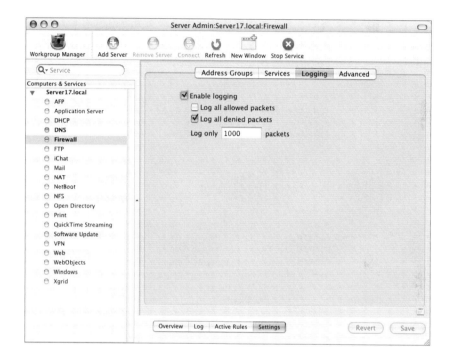

For example, the following log entry shows that the firewall service used rule 65000 to deny (unreach) the remote client at 10.221.41.33:2190 from accessing server 192.168.12.12 on web port 80 via Ethernet port 0:

Dec 12 13:08:16 ballch5 mach_kernel: ipfw: 65000 Unreach TCP 10.221.41.33:2190
192.168.12.12:80 in via en0

The following log entry shows that the firewall service used rule 100 to allow the remote client at 10.221.41.33:721 to access the server 192.168.12.12 on the LPR printing port 515 via Ethernet port 0:

Dec 12 13:20:15 mayalu6 mach_kernel: ipfw: 100 Accept TCP 10.221.41.33:721

192.168.12.12:515 in via en0

The Overview pane shows a simple summary of the firewall service: whether the service is running and which rules are active.

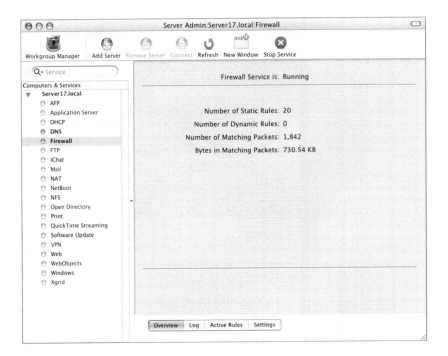

Advanced Firewall Configuration

You can use the Advanced pane of the firewall's Settings tab to configure very specific rules for TCP ports. You can apply a rule to all IP addresses, a specific IP address, or a range of IP addresses.

Test the Firewall

1 Launch Server Admin on your server and select the AFP service from the Computers & Services list, and start the service. Make sure the only other service that is running is DNS.

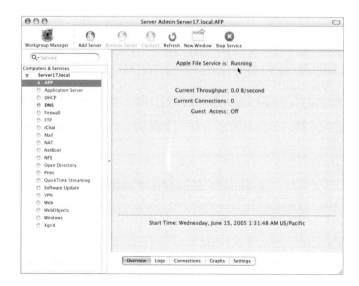

2   Verify that the AFP service is running.

3   From your Mac OS X computer, choose Connect to Server from the Go
menu. Enter *10.1.17.1* in the Address field and click Connect.

The "Connect to Server" dialog appears, showing the server over port
548—the AFP port to which the Connect to Server dialog defaults when
you type in an IP address or domain name. You do *not* need to enter a
user name or password here. The dialog simply provides verification that
the port is open.

4   Click Connect, choose a volume to mount, and close the Connect to
Server dialog.

5   Launch Server Admin on your server and select the Firewall service from
the Computers & Services list. Click the Settings tab if it is not already
open and then click the Services button.

6   Verify that "any" is selected in the "Edit Services for" drop-down menu.
Select "Allow only traffic for 'any' on these ports," and then choose the
ports that you want "any" to be able to access.

7 Scroll down to make sure port 548 (Apple File Service) does *not* have a check mark next to it.

Having it selected once the firewall is turned on will still allow connections from any IP address to that port on your server.

8 Turn on the firewall service and verify that it is running by selecting the Log tab at the bottom of the window.

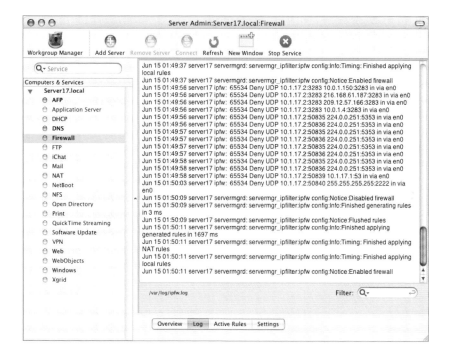

9 From your Mac OS X computer, attempt to connect again like you did in step 3.

10 View the dialogs as they attempt to connect to your server.

Your attempt at a connection will eventually will time out and you will not be connected.

11 From Server Admin, enter *548* in the Firewall Log window's search box and press Return.

You can see the deny rules in effect when you attempted to contact your AFP server with the firewall active and blocking access to port 548.

12 Turn off the Firewall in Server Admin on your server. Confirm that you can now connect over port 548 again by repeating step 3.

This shows just a fragment of what is capable with the firewall service.

Network Address Translation

Network Address Translation (NAT), which is sometimes referred to as *IP masquerading* or *IP aliasing*, is a technique that lets an entire group of network devices in a private network use a single IP address to communicate with devices on other networks. NAT both circumvents the shortage of IP addresses and provides some security to private networks since hosts inside the private network are not directly addressable from the Internet.

Network Address Translation (NAT)

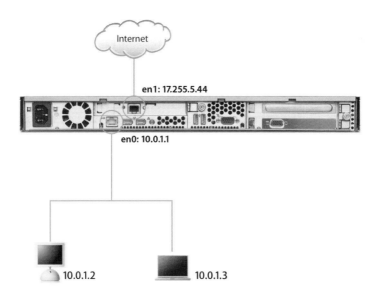

NAT has several forms, including the following:

- ▶ *Static NAT* maps a private IP address to a public one (one-to-one mapping).

- ▶ *Dynamic NAT* maps a private IP address to the first available address from a list of public addresses.

- ▶ *Port Address Translation (PAT)* maps multiple private IP addresses to a single public one using different ports. This is also known as *port overloading, single address NAT,* and *port-level multiplexed NAT.*

With Mac OS X Server, you can take advantage of NAT to protect private networks. For example, you can connect an Xserve computer to your private network using one of its Ethernet interfaces, and connect it to the Internet (over a T1 line or other fast connection) using the second Ethernet interface. With this setup, you can use the NAT service to shield the private network at pretendco.com behind the Xserve computer's IP address. This allows the other pretendco.com computers to access the Internet by sharing the Xserve computer's T1 line and IP address while still remaining private—that is, they are not directly accessible from other computers on the Internet.

How NAT Works

A Mac OS X Server system running NAT takes all the traffic from your private network and remembers which internal address made the request. When the NAT router receives the response to the request, it forwards the response to the originating computer. Traffic that originates from the Internet does not reach any of the computers behind the NAT system unless port forwarding is enabled. Port forwarding lets you reroute packets sent to specific ports on the NAT system to other hosts in the private network.

In the illustration below, the PowerBook user requests a page on the Internet—in this case, the Apple home page. The request goes to the default router address (10.0.1.1), which is the address of the en0 Ethernet interface of an Xserve computer running NAT.

The NAT router running on the Xserve computer notes the IP address of the PowerBook that sent this request (10.0.1.3) and an internal port number (6509) to associate with this specific request. The NAT router then forwards this request to the appropriate host on the Internet using the address of the Xserve computer's en1 Ethernet interface (17.255.5.44), which is connected to the Internet, as the new source (the "from" address). The Xserve computer also supplies its own port number (8668) for this request.

The web server receives a request for a page and returns the page requested. In this case, the server returns the page to the requesting address 17.255.5.44 at port 8668.

The Xserve computer receives the response page from www.apple.com and forwards the response to the appropriate host on the private network by changing the destination address to match the host that requested the page. In this case, the port number 8668 informs the Xserve computer that this request is to be sent to address 10.0.1.3 at port 6509. The PowerBook then displays the resulting webpage from www.apple.com.

NAT—How It Works

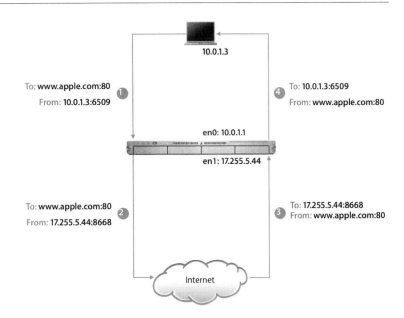

Basic NAT Configuration

You use Server Admin to start NAT service. In the Computers & Services list, click NAT, and then click Settings. In the "Network connection to share" pop-up menu, choose the network interface that connects to the Internet or the external network. Save your settings, and then click Start Service.

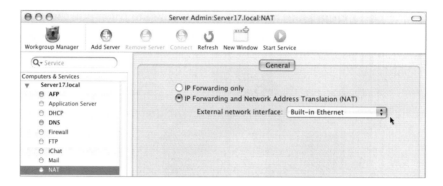

NAT automatically adds a divert firewall rule to transfer incoming packets to the NAT process. In order for the divert rule to function, the firewall service must be turned on. Because the default "deny everything" rule is also activated, all incoming and outgoing connections are blocked. Thus, you need additional firewall rules to allow traffic through the server.

> **NOTE** ▶ The only form of NAT that you can start in Server Admin is PAT.

NAT-Service Monitoring

The NAT Overview pane in Server Admin enables you to monitor your NAT service for troubleshooting and security purposes. You can see if the service is running and how many TCP, User Datagram Protocol (UDP), and Internet Control Message Protocol (ICMP) links are active.

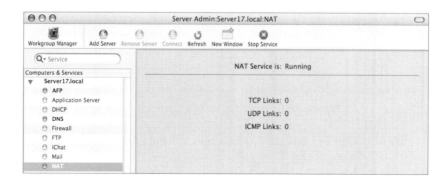

In addition to monitoring active protocol links in the Overview pane, you might want to view NAT packet divert events, which the firewall service logs.

Virtual Private Networking

A virtual private network (VPN) provides a solution for encrypting transactions. VPN is a way to use an unsecure network, such as the Internet, as the transit for private network traffic. This traffic remains private because the transactions are encrypted. The result is that you can remotely connect to a private network as if the remote computer were attached directly to that private network.

Virtual Private Network

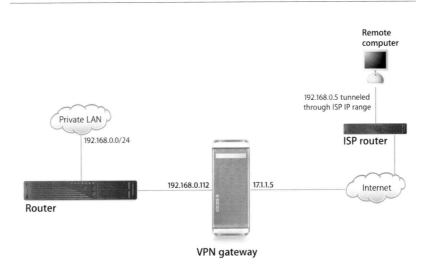

With a VPN, your organization can securely connect branch offices over the Internet, allow verified remote mobile users to access private resources from any connection on the Internet, and link multiple LANs together over great distances.

Once the VPN service is configured, users create the tunnel by opening a connection. In Mac OS X, this is usually done with Internet Connect with the

VPN client configured to contact the VPN server. Once a connection is made to the server over an unsecure connection, the user is prompted to authenticate. After the user authenticates properly, the VPN server issues the client a new IP address within the range of the secure network. At that point, all further private network transactions are routed through the tunnel using the new IP address.

Basic VPN Configuration

Before configuring VPN, you need to decide on the authentication method you will use. The MS-CHAPv2 authentication is a fairly simple user name/ password authentication model using a hash of the user's password. However, this challenge/response means of authenticating may not provide the level of security your organization requires.

As an additional measure of security, you can use other authentication methods that provide a more robust level of security, such as two-factor authentication, where the password is a combination of something the user has (a token) and something the user knows (a personal identification number, or PIN), or Kerberos authentication if your Mac OS X server is acting as a Kerberos Key Distribution Center (KDC).

If you choose to use an authentication method other than the default MS-CHAPv2 method, you will need to follow the configuration instructions from the author of the method. Typically this involves copying configuration or preference files from the server running the method, then manually chang- ing the VPN settings to use the files to read information from the server (AuthenticatorEAPPlugins and AuthenticatorProtocols keys). If you plan to use the default authentication method, you can skip this process and proceed to enable the transport protocols.

NOTE ▶ See http://rsasecurity.agora.com/rsasecured/guides/ imp_pdfs/ MacOSX_ACE_51.pdf for an example of the type of configuration necessary to enable alternate authentication methods for VPN.

To enable and configure VPN service, choose VPN from the Computers & Services list in Server Admin and click Settings. You'll see two tabs representing your two choices for a transport protocol: Layer Two Tunneling Protocol (L2TP) and Point-to-Point Tunneling Protocol (PPTP). Your choice of transport protocols depends on the client operating systems you want to support. Although PPTP is more compatible, L2TP has more robust security. The configuration for VPN is stored in /Library/Preferences/SystemConfiguration/com.apple. RemoteAccessServers.plist.

Each of these tabs permits the entry of an IP address range. The L2TP has the stronger authentication scheme, the ability to define a shared secret (eight or more alphanumeric characters with punctuation), and the ability to allocate a range of IP addresses that will be given to VPN clients.

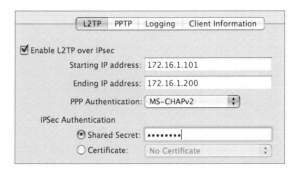

Under PPTP, you select the encryption key and allocate a range of IP addresses.

NOTE ▶ If the IP address range that you define is not already served by a DHCP server, you will need to go to the Client Information pane and define the network mask and DNS server that will be given out with the IP address by the VPN service. Furthermore, if both L2TP and PPTP are used, make sure that both protocols use separate, nonoverlapping IP address ranges.

VPN Client Information Configuration

In the Client Information pane, you need to create network routing definitions if you want the users connecting to you to have access to various networks. In the image below, the first two definitions specify that connections to the 172.16.1.0 range and the 192.168.1.0 range will be routed to the private network, and the private DNS server will handle DNS requests. The third definition specifies that connections to the 17.1.1.0 range will be public and the VPN server, which in this case is also the public DNS server, will handle DNS requests.

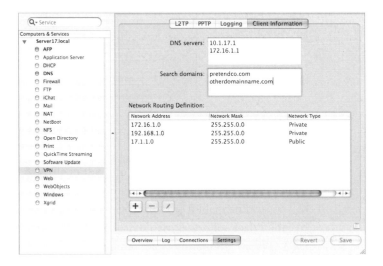

Troubleshooting VPN

Once you have configured the VPN service in Server Admin, you use netstat to verify that the routing tables were built accurately. On the command line, type *netstat -rn* to view the routing tables and verify custom network routing definitions. You can also type *netstat -an* to view the state of all sockets and verify that UDP port 500 is listening for requests.

In Mac OS X running the VPN client, you can review the state of the pppd process to verify that you are receiving the correct parameters from the server. For example, typing *ps -auxww | grep pppd* will show you the specific configuration used by the VPN session. You can also use tcpdump to view the packets before and after they are encrypted.

The VPN logs provide a good starting point for troubleshooting; you can view them in Server Admin. You can set the detail level for the logs in the Logging pane as either nonverbose (indicate only conditions that require immediate attention) or verbose (indicate all activity). You can also customize the schedule to archive the logs.

What You've Learned

▶ Gateway Setup Assistant is an installation tool that configures basic DHCP, NAT, firewall, and VPN services in an integrated fashion.

▶ When firewall service is enabled, each IP service request that Mac OS X Server receives is first checked against a list of firewall rules that define which IP addresses have access to specific port numbers. You use Server Admin to configure firewall service in Mac OS X Server.

▶ Server Admin lets you enable the PAT (port overloading) form of NAT, which maps multiple private IP addresses to a single public one using different ports.

▶ VPN services let you encrypt transactions. VPN allows you to use the Internet for private network traffic. There are two protocols supported, L2TP and PPTP.

References
The following documents provide more information about installing Mac OS X Server. (All of these and more are available at www.apple.com/server/documentation.)

Administration Guides

Mac OS X Server Getting Started (http://images.apple.com/server/pdfs/
Getting_Started_v10.4.pdf)

Network Services Administration (http://images.apple.com/server/pdfs/
Network_Services_v10.4.pdf)

Upgrading and Migrating to Mac OS X Server v10.4 Tiger
(http://images.apple.com/server/pdfs/Migration_v10.4.pdf)

Mac OS X Server Command-Line Administration (http://images.apple.com/
server/pdfs/Command_Line_v10.4.pdf)

Apple Knowledge Base Documents

You can check for new and updated Knowledge Base documents at
www.apple.com/support.

Document 107699, "Offering SecurID authentication with VPN Server"

URLs

FreeBSD Racoon configuration: www.freebsd.org/doc/en_US.ISO8859-1/
articles/checkpoint/racoon.html

Review Quiz

1. How does firewall service in Mac OS X Server prevent unwanted visitors
   from accessing the server?

2. What are firewall address groups used for?

3. If you have multiple firewall rules that could potentially apply to a given
   IP address, what determines which rule is applied first?

4. Describe NAT. What does it do? What purpose does it serve? What are its
   drawbacks?

5. Which form of NAT is supported in Server Admin?

6. Which tool can you run to view the routing tables after a VPN setup?

7. Name the two transport protocols used in VPN.

Answers

1. The firewall service checks the IP address of any request for service before allowing access. This prevents requests from unwanted guests from reaching any server services, if the firewall is configured correctly.

2. You can use these groups to organize and target the firewall rules. Groups allow you to apply rules to a predefined set of IP addresses.

3. The most specific rule applies. A rule applied to a single IP address is the most specific, and smaller IP ranges are more specific than larger IP ranges.

4. NAT is a way to provide Internet access to multiple IP clients using only a single IP address that is valid on the Internet. It is used to give a small workgroup of machines access to the Internet without needing an Internet IP address for every client. Its primary drawbacks are that it makes it difficult for computers on the Internet to find computers on the NAT network, since the NAT computers don't have valid Internet IP addresses (although this can be interpreted as a security-enhancing feature).

5. Server Admin supports Port Address Translation (PAT), which maps multiple private IP addresses to a single public one using different ports. PAT is also known as port overloading, single address NAT, and port-level multiplexed NAT.

6. netstat

7. Layer Two Tunneling Protocol (L2TP) and Point-to-Point Tunneling Protocol (PPTP).

5

Lesson Files	Lesson_5/employees
Time	This lesson takes approximately 2 hours to complete.
Goals	Configure Mac OS X Server to control access to an account
	Configure Mac OS X Server to control access to files and folders based on user and group accounts
	Define authentication and authorization as they are used in Mac OS X Server
	Use Workgroup Manager to configure share points and permissions
	Use Workgroup Manager to create local user accounts and groups
	Understand and implement ACLs in Mac OS X Server

Lesson **5**

Authenticating and Authorizing Accounts

Authentication is the process by which a person identifies which user account he or she will use on the system. This is similar to, but slightly different from, saying that authentication is how a person proves his or her identity to a system. This distinction is useful because multiple people may share the same user name and password, or one person may have multiple user accounts on the same system. In each case, the name and password identify which user account the person wants to use, assuming the name and password are entered correctly. While there are other methods of authenticating a user account, such as smart card or voice print, a name and password are the most common (and are assumed for this lesson).

Authorization is the process that determines what a person with an authenticated user account can do on the system. Authorization is associated with user account file-access permissions that are set through Mac OS X or through Mac OS X Server administration tools for service access across permissions.

This lesson will cover creating and maintaining user and group accounts on your server. You'll learn how to configure user and group accounts as well as how these accounts are used for controlling access to both server files and services. Access is based on authentication, therefore it is important that you understand how authorization is handled.

Managing Server Access

When configuring any server for access by users, you'll need to determine what services the server will provide and what levels of user access to assign. So far, we have discussed only network services, which do not require any specific user access to the server once the service is enabled. For many of the other services this book will cover, such as file sharing, you will need to create specific user accounts on your server.

When considering the creation of user accounts, you'll want to determine how to best set up your users, how to organize them into groups that match the needs of your organization, and how to best maintain this information over time. As with any service or IT task, the best approach is to thoroughly plan out your requirements and approach before starting to implement a solution.

Creating and Administering User and Administrator Server Accounts

Authentication occurs in many different contexts in Mac OS X and Mac OS X Server, but it most commonly involves using a login window. For example, when you start up a Mac OS X computer, you may have to enter a user name and password in an initial login window before being allowed to use the system at all. (By default, Mac OS X is set to automatically log in the first account that was set up on the system, without asking for a password. Unless you change this default setting using the Accounts pane of System Preferences, you will not see the initial login window when you start up the system.) While the login example might seem to apply only to Mac OS X, it could be that you are authenticating to a user account that lives across the network on Mac OS X Server.

Another example occurs when you connect to a network server, whether via Apple Filing Protocol (AFP) or Server Message Block (SMB). A user must authenticate before accessing these services, even if logging in just as a guest user. If a login name and password are not correctly entered, a "Login failed" alert appears, indicating a failed attempt at authentication.

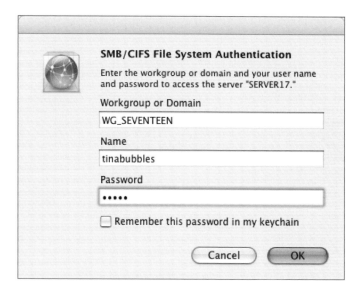

To administer a server through Server Admin or Workgroup Manager, an administrator must use a valid administrator account for authentication. This is required whether the server is being administered locally or remotely.

Using Workgroup Manager for User Accounts

Workgroup Manager is the primary tool for configuring user accounts on Mac OS X Server. To grant a person specific permissions on Mac OS X Server, you must set up a user account. User accounts on Mac OS X Server are the same as on Mac OS X, although accounts created with Workgroup Manager provide more complex options and settings. They also enable you to create *network-visible accounts,* accounts that can be used to log in remotely.

On Mac OS X Server you can have local user accounts and network accounts. Standard user accounts on Mac OS X enable a person to access files and applications local to that machine. Similarly, user accounts on Mac OS X Server permit users who log in locally to access files or services (such as mail and print services) that are located on the server, but they also give remote users access to server volumes and associated files if the users are created in a network-visible directory service. Local users can connect to servers remotely, but can log in only locally.

Here are some examples of Mac OS X Server user account settings:

▶ Name

▶ User ID (UID)

▶ Short names

▶ User password type

▶ Home folder location

▶ User address information

▶ Mail settings

▶ Print settings

When using Workgroup Manager with Mac OS X Server, you can assign multiple short names to a single user account. The first short name cannot be longer than 31 characters, but additional short names can contain up to 255 characters. This could allow a user to have a different email name, without having to change the previous short-name entry. The initial short name is the one used to create the home directory for that particular user.

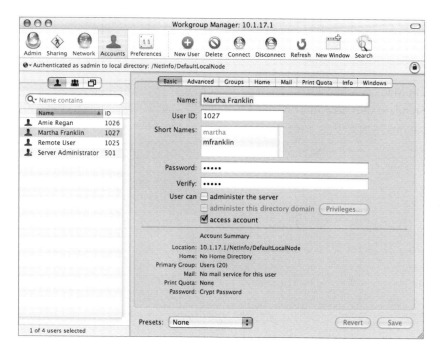

In the Basic pane, the user ID is a numerical value that the system uses to differentiate one user from another. Though users gain access to the system with a user name, each name is associated with a UID, and that's what the computer primarily cares about.

Note that when two users with different names and passwords but with the same UID access documents and folders, the system will consider them to be the same owner. And yes, you can create two users with the same UID in Workgroup Manager without getting an error message.

Using Workgroup Manager for Administrator Accounts

An administrator account is a special type of user account on Mac OS X Server that enables the user to administer the server. A user with an administrator account can create, edit, and delete user accounts, as well as modify the settings of various running services on the Mac OS X server where the administrator account exists. The administrator uses the Server Admin application to configure most service settings, and Workgroup Manager to edit user account preferences and share points.

To give a user an administrator account, select the "User can administer the server" checkbox in the Basic pane in Workgroup Manager.

There are two administrator options, "User can administer the server" and "User can administer this directory domain." Setting the server option permits the user to manipulate file access on the server, while the directory administration option pertains to the directory data only. This means that a *server* administrator can add a user directory but cannot add a user account to the directory, and a *directory* administrator can add a user account to the directory but cannot set file permissions for the user.

> **NOTE** ▶ If your computer is an Open Directory server and the "User can administer this directory domain" checkbox is selected, the selected user is allowed to administer the directory domain. Open Directory and management of directory domains is covered in Lesson 6, "Using Open Directory."

Configuring Local User Accounts

Mac OS X Server creates a list of local accounts for accessing resources, such as files when running as an AppleShare file server. You will use the Workgroup Manager utility to add two sample local users to your server computer and then import a file containing additional users.

> **NOTE** ▶ During this entire lesson, you will be using your Mac OS X computer to configure your Mac OS X Server computer. This demonstrates that you can perform server configuration from any Mac OS X computer that has network access to your server computer. You will also be authenticating Workgroup Manager as your Server Admin account.

Add Users

Follow these steps to add two users to your Mac OS X server:

1 On your Mac OS X client computer, open Workgroup Manager and connect to your Mac OS X server as Server Admin.

Because you have not configured your computer to share account information, you will be notified that your directory node is not visible on the
network. You will learn about directory services in Lesson 6.

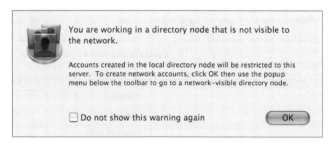

2 Click OK.

3 Make sure that the Accounts button is selected in the toolbar, the list of
users is displayed, and the current administrator account is selected and
visible.

4 Click the New User button in the toolbar.

If the button is dimmed, click in the list of users to activate the button.

5 In the Basic pane, enter the following information for the first new user:

▶ Name: *Tina Bubbles*

▶ Short Names: *tinabubbles*

▶ Password: *tina*

▶ Verify: *tina*

6   Leave the other settings at their default values (including leaving Presets, at the bottom of the window, set to None), and be sure you don't select "User can administer the server."

7   Double-click the second line (the empty one below "tinabubbles") in the Short Names field to add another short name.

8   Type *bubbles* and then click Save.

The new user name appears in the list of users on the left side of Workgroup Manager window. You should also see that the first short name is now dimmed, indicating that it cannot be changed. Notice that the name and alternate short names can be edited after this point.

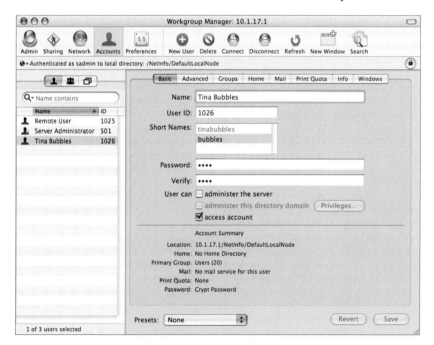

9   Add a second user, Warren Peece, by clicking the New User button and
entering the following values:

▶   Name: *Warren Peece*

▶   Short Names: *warren*

▶   Password: *warren*

▶   Verify: *warren*

Leave the other settings at their default values.

10   Click Save.

11   Select the existing Server Admin account from the list of current users.

Notice that the administrator account has the "User can administer the
server" option selected.

Now compare the two new accounts with the administrator account. What are
the differences between the three accounts? The "User can administer the
server" and "User can administer this directory domain" options are selected
on Server Admin and not on the others. When you create new users, they are
not automatically administrators. You must check the appropriate boxes to
allow them to be administrators.

Configure Comments and Keywords

During the setup of accounts, you can configure advanced features such
as comments and keywords in each account. These features are useful for
organizing users or searching for particular users based on something other
than name or user ID. This provides for a more realistic search pattern
should you need to specify a range of users without actually adding them
to a specific group.

1   Select Tina Bubbles from the users list.

2   Click the Advanced button.

3   In the Comment field, type *Employee#:408081*.

4   Click the Add Keyword (+) button next to the Keywords field.

5   In the sheet that appears, click Edit Keywords.

6   In the "Manage available keywords" sheet that appears next, click the Add Keyword (+) button.

7   In the text field, type *Manager*.

8   Click the Add Keyword (+) button again.

9   In the second text field, type *Marketing*.

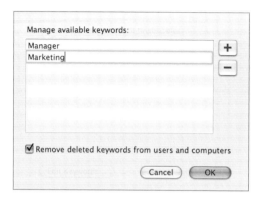

10 Click the Add Keyword (+) button again to add a third keyword: *Engineering*.

11 Click OK to save the new keywords and return to the "Select the keywords to add to tinabubbles" sheet.

12 Select Manager and click OK to add the Manager keyword to Tina's user account.

13 Click Save.

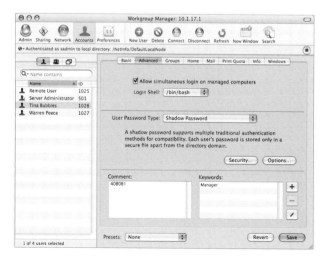

14 Click the Add (+) button again and add the Marketing keyword to Tina's account. Click Save.

15 Select Warren from the user list, click the Add (+) button, and add the Manager and Engineering keywords to Warren Peece's user account.

16 Add Employee#: 410103 to the Comment field for Warren's user account, and click Save.

17 In the search field above the Users list, choose "Keyword contains" from the menu next to the magnifying glass icon and type *Manager*.

Only Tina Bubbles and Warren Peece's accounts should appear in the user list.

18 In the search field above the Users list, choose "Keyword contains" and type *Eng*.

Warren Peece is now the only user listed, because you added the Engineering keyword to only Warren's account.

19 In the search field, choose Comment Contains and type *41*.

Only Warren Peece should be listed in the user list because his account's comment contains "41" in his employee number.

Exporting and Importing Users and Groups

You can create user accounts individually, or you can import them from a properly formatted file. The file could be created on your own, created with a third-party tool, restored from another server, or restored from a backup of the current server. To back up and restore user and group accounts (discussed in the next section) from a Mac OS X Server computer, use the Export and Import commands in Workgroup Manager.

To back up user and group accounts defined in Workgroup Manager, select the accounts, choose the Export command from the Server menu, and specify a name and location for the resulting file.

To restore user or group accounts using Workgroup Manager, use the Import command from the Server menu. In the Import dialog, choose "Ignore new record" from the Duplicate Handling pop-up menu.

> **TIP** You can import files containing user and group accounts using the Import command.

When you are setting up a new server and will be supporting more than just a few users, you will probably import the users from a configured text file instead of adding each of them individually. In this section, another system administrator has provided you with a file containing formatted user records for you to use with your server.

> **TIP** When importing user and group accounts with the Import command, try to limit the number of accounts in each file to 10,000 users. Although importing a larger number of accounts for a single file is supported, you will find that keeping the number of accounts smaller is more manageable.

1 In Workgroup Manager on your Mac OS X computer, choose Server > Import.

2 In the Import Users sheet, navigate to and select the /Users/Shared/ Student_Materials/Lesson_05/employees file.

Leave all the settings at their default values.

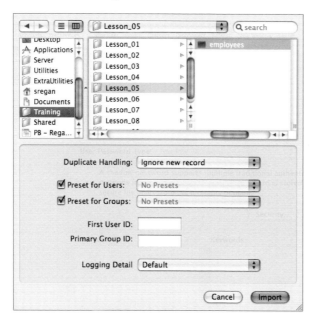

3   Click Import.

An additional eight users are imported. Because passwords are not
included in the users' import files, you need to set a password for each
new account. For now, you will set all or the accounts to use the same
password, changeme.

4   In the Users list, select all of the newly imported accounts.

5   In the Advanced pane, choose Shadow Password from the User Password
Type pop-up menu.

This option appears if multiple accounts are selected.

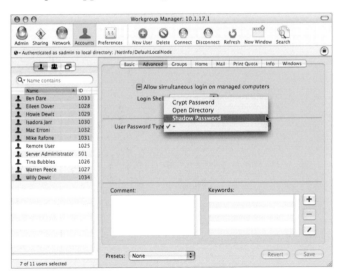

6   In the dialog that appears after selecting Shadow Password, in both the Password and Verify fields, type *changeme*. Click OK.

7   Click Save.

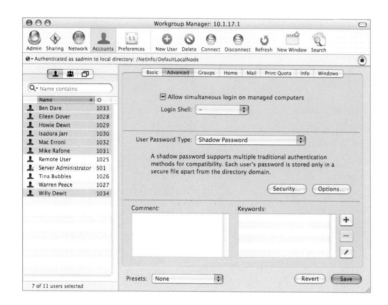

You have set all the new accounts to use the same password. In Lesson 6, you will learn how to use Workgroup Manager's password policies to force users to set a new password.

Working With Group Accounts in Workgroup Manager

Group accounts are closely associated with user accounts on Mac OS X Server. Group accounts enable administrators to quickly assign a set of permissions to multiple users. While Mac OS X allows an easy way to change group assignments and permissions through the Get Info command, it does not provide a way to easily create groups or assign users to groups. Because most Mac OS X computers deal with at most a few users, the ability to create groups is not a big issue. With servers, however, the ability to easily create and modify groups is critical.

To create a group, simply click the New Group button in the Workgroup Manager toolbar and enter a name for the group. There are additional options for the group, but they are not required for the group to be functional.

Long user and group names can contain non-Roman characters. Depending on the character set, you may have as few as 85 characters available for the long name. If you are using exclusively Roman characters in your user names, you can safely use 255 characters. Short user and group names must consist of no more than 255 Roman characters.

Mac OS X Server v10.4 addressed a number of limitations with how groups were used in previous versions of Mac OS X Server. For example, the restriction of users having membership in only up to 16 groups has been removed. Groups can also be nested in other groups, which allows a more natural way to represent users in an organization.

User Accounts and Group IDs

Every user has a single primary group ID (GID). The system stores the user's primary GID in the underlying user account record. All other group membership information is stored in the underlying group records. When a user creates a file, the default group is used for read permissions.

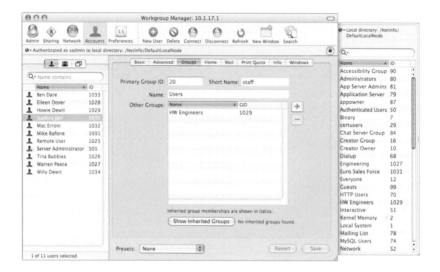

Using Workgroup Manager, you can remove a user from a group either by editing the Other Groups field in the user account or by editing the group account. However, you cannot change a user's primary group ID by these methods. Users who are members of a group by virtue of their primary group ID appear in italics in the group membership list. This is your indication that you can't remove them from the group account as you normally would—by selecting the user and clicking Remove. Instead, you have to edit the primary group ID in the user account.

Creating Groups With Workgroup Manager

You'll use Workgroup Manager to create and manage local groups.

1   In Workgroup Manager on your Mac OS X computer, click Accounts in the toolbar.

2   In the left pane of the window, click the Groups button.

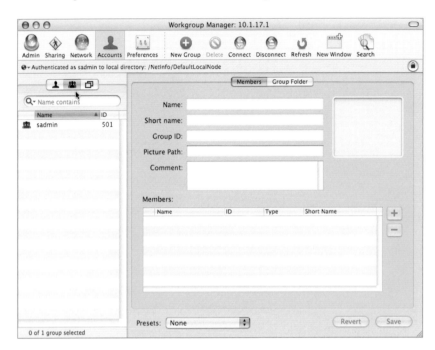

3   In the toolbar, click the New Group button to create a new group.

4   Enter the following information for the first new group:

▶   Name: *Engineering*

▶   Short name: *engr*

5   Leave all other fields at their default values and click Save.

6   Create a second group:

▶   Name: *Marketing*

▶   Short name: *mktg*

7   Leave all other fields at their default values and click Save.

8   Now create two more groups: Project X and Project Y.

9   Create a group for the Project X team:

▶   Name: *Project X*

▶   Short name: *projectx*

10   Leave all other fields at their default values and click Save.

11   Create another group for the Project Y team:

▶   Name: *Project Y*

▶   Short name: *projecty*

12   Leave all other fields at their default values and click Save.

Associating Users With Groups

Now that you have created four groups, you need to assign the users that you previously created to them. You will do this using two different methods: adding users to a group and adding group membership to a user account.

Add Users to Groups

The most common approach for populating groups with users is to select a group and then add one or more users to it. On your server, you will select a group and then add users to the group based on keywords.

1   Select the Marketing group from the Groups list.

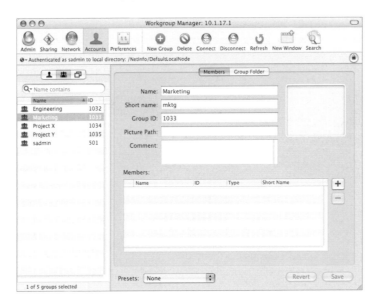

2   In the Members pane, click the Add Group Members (+) button to the right of the Members list.

The Users & Groups drawer appears.

3   From the pop-up menu in the search field in the Users & Groups drawer, choose Keyword Contains and type *Mar*.

This locates all of the users with the Marketing keyword.

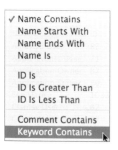

NOTE ▶ Searches are case-sensitive, and they look at long names, not short names.

4   Select all of the displayed users and drag them to the Members list.

You should now see the users listed in the Members area for the Marketing group.

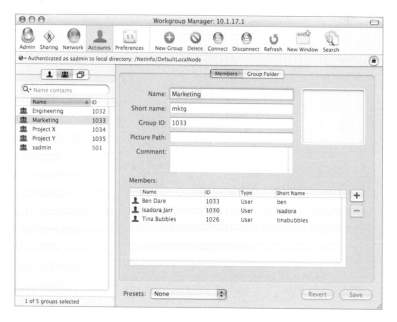

5   Click Save.

Add Group Membership to a User Account

While you could easily use the process in the previous section to add Warren
to the Project X and Project Y groups, try an alternate approach by adding the
groups to Warren's account.

1   Click the Users button on the left side of the Workgroup Manager window
and select Warren Peece from the Users list.

2   Click the Groups button.

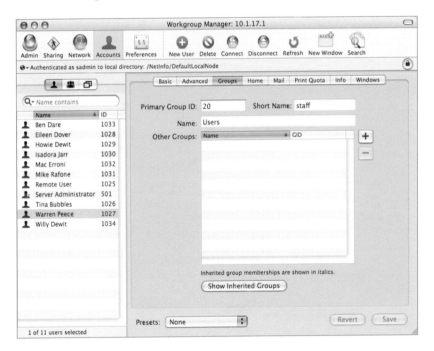

3   Click the Add Groups (+) button.

The Groups drawer appears, displaying the list of groups that are currently
defined on the system. This list includes both the groups that you created

and the system-defined groups that Mac OS X Server created during installation.

4   Select the Project X group and drag it from the Groups drawer to the Other Groups text field.

Notice that as you drag the group, the pointer changes to a plus sign. This means that you are adding this group to the text field.

5   Click Save.

You have now successfully added the Project X group membership to Warren's account. However, Warren also needs access to Project Y.

6   Repeat steps 3, 4, and 5 to add the Project Y group to Warren's user account.

You have just added multiple groups—Project X and Project Y—to Warren's user account.

Adding Groups to Groups

Let's say that you need a group that enables you to control permissions for the entire Engineering department, which consists of two divisions, Project X and Project Y. You could populate the Engineering group with all of the individual engineering user accounts. However, an easier approach is to simply add the two project groups to the Engineering group. This effectively adds all members of those groups to the main group, which is a much more efficient way to manage groups than in previous versions of Mac OS X Server.

1   Click the Groups button on the left side of the Workgroup Manager window and select the Engineering group from the Groups list.

2   In the Members pane, click the Add Group Members (+) button to the right of the Members list to open the Users & Groups drawer.

3   In the Users & Groups drawer, click the Groups button.

4   Drag the Project X and Project Y groups to the Members list.

All members of the Project X and Project Y groups now have access to
anything that the Engineering group does.

5   Click Save.

You have now added both users and groups to your server, as well as
groups to groups.

Controlling Access Through Server Accounts

Authorization is used throughout Mac OS X and Mac OS X Server. The most common example is usually transparent to the user: Every time a user accesses a file, the
computer checks file permissions against the user's account information to see if
the user is authorized to use the file. In Mac OS X and Mac OS X Server, owner
and group permissions are associated with every file, folder, and application.

When accessing a file server, you typically have to authenticate and then you see a choice of valid share points available to mount. When you navigate inside a mounted share point, folders' badges (small icons displayed on or under the folder icon) show whether you are authorized for read-write, read-only, write-only, or no access for that folder.

Authorization and Mac OS X Server v10.4

POSIX permissions are the permissions that have been used on Mac OS X and Mac OS X Server since day one. They are still used both on Mac OS X and Mac OS X Server, and they exist for every file system file or folder on the file system. POSIX permission are the traditional UNIX-style permissions that enable you to apply read, write, and execute permission for three groups of users: the owner, the group, and all other users. The permissions that you set in the Get Info window of Mac OS X are POSIX permissions.

Before Mac OS X v10.4, POSIX permissions were the only way to control file access on Mac OS X Server. Mac OS X Server v10.4 builds on the Mac OS X heritage of using POSIX permissions, but it adds the ability to define complex access rules that are not possible with standard POSIX permissions. This is done with *access control lists (ACLs)*. ACLs are supported on disks formatted as Mac OS Extended volumes. They are stored in the file system itself, using extended attributes that have always existed in Mac OS Extended file systems, but have been unused. This is how ACLs are supported without reformatting the volume to a new file-system format.

For users accessing the server over the network, ACLs are supported for AFP and SMB connections. ACLs are also compatible with ACLs from the Windows world, thus providing a better user experience when accessing Mac OS X Server from Windows clients, since users expect a more granular level of permissions settings than were previously available with Mac OS X Server. These access permissions can be set to support a rich organizational workflow where user permissions need to vary widely as a document gets passed among different authors and reviewers.

In addition to file-system ACLs, Mac OS X Server also supports *service ACLs*, which are separate from file-system ACLs in implementation and purpose, despite the similar name. Service ACLs enable you to define who has access to specific services on Mac OS X Server. You could use service ACLs to allow all users to log in via AFP connection, but restrict SSH (Secure Shell) connections to administrators.

> **NOTE ▶** While file-system ACLs are covered in the remainder of this lesson, service ACLs will be covered in the specific service lessons.

It is important to understand that ACLs are familiar to Windows administrators yet are something of a new concept to Macintosh administrators. This makes the introduction of Mac OS X Server v10.4 into a Windows environment easier to implement.

Review of POSIX Permissions

Every file and folder in Mac OS X has set ownership and permissions information that define the privileges available for that file or folder. Ownership includes configuring both an owner and a group, while permissions includes setting specific access settings for the owner, the group, and everyone else, commonly referred to as "other." When set from Finder, these permissions can be Read & Write, Read Only, Write Only, and No Access. When set from the command line, there are a few more possibilities, but the main configurations involve toggling bits for read, write, and execute permission. When you change the ownership or permissions of an item using a command-line interface, the changes are reflected in the Info (or Inspector) window for that item. Likewise, when you change the permissions in the Info window, the changes can be seen when displaying the item in a command-line interface.

In POSIX, the user ID associated with the file or folder defines permissions ownership. If the numeric UID of the file or folder matches the UID defined in the user account, then that user is considered the owner of the file or folder.

Group access is determined similarly: Each file or folder has a group ID associated with it. Each group account has a numeric GID. If the user is a member of a group with a GID that matches the GID of the file or folder, then the user has access as defined in the group permissions settings.

In the example above, the *d* in front of the permissions indicates that the file is a folder (*d* for *directory*). The permissions for the owner, rwx, correspond to Read & Write in the Info window for that folder. The x, or execute, permission on a file identifies a program that can be run. For a folder, the execute permission determines whether or not the folder can be searched. To access a file in a folder, you must have search permission for each folder from the root folder down to and including the folder containing the file. The execute bit cannot be set using the GetInfo command from the Finder under the File menu.

POSIX Permissions Limitations

As a simple example of setting access permissions, suppose you have a school district that is configuring a shared math folder (named Math Files) on its server. The district's administrators want to allow math teachers to read, write, and delete math files, and to allow any math student to read the same files. Ideally they would like to set the Math Files folder so only math students, not all students, are allowed to see it. This simple example would be difficult to support with standard POSIX privileges, as you would be limited to a single group to control privileges.

There are a couple of approaches to this problem, yet each has its limitations. In the first method, you assign the Math_Teachers group to the folder and give the Math_Teachers group read and write access. Then you prevent math students from writing by assigning read-only access to Everyone. The problem with this scenario is that you have granted read access to everyone in the school for the Math Files folder.

Another approach is to consolidate the math users—teachers and students—into a consolidated group called Math Department. You can give this group access, and deny access to everyone else. This solves the problem of the entire school accessing the Math Files folder, but you have introduced a new problem: Since the students and teachers are combined into a single group, Math Department, students and teachers have identical access privileges, and you want students to read only, not to write. You've lost that granularity. You could probably create two subfolders with different group access permissions for math students and math teachers, but what if you wanted even finer control? Maybe non-math teachers should have read-only access similar to math students.

You get the point: You must work around limitations in the permissions system rather than using the permission system to naturally express the access and workflow that exists in the organization. Luckily, the access-control system in Mac OS X Server v10.4 helps you find a natural way—ACLs—to set up and enforce access permissions.

Setting POSIX Permissions With Workgroup Manager

To modify the POSIX permissions for a folder:

1   In Workgroup Manager on your Mac OS X computer, click Sharing in the toolbar and select a folder in the file system for which to apply settings. Click the Access button.

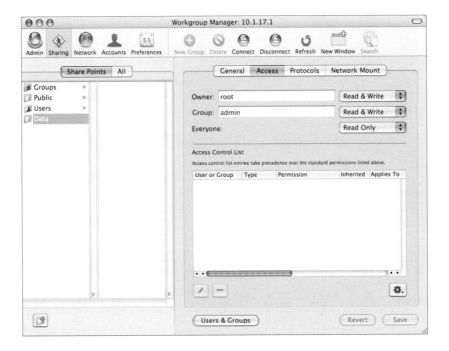

2   Click the Users & Groups button to open the Users & Groups drawer.

3   Individually drag a specific user and group to the Owner and Group fields, respectively, to change the current settings, and then click Save.

4   Use the pop-up menus to assign permissions for owner, group, and everyone.

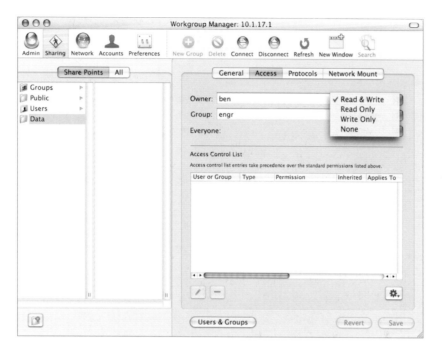

As in Mac OS X, when a user attempts to access a file or folder, the user account is compared with the file or folder's owner and group. If the user account is the owner, then the permissions assigned to the owner are enforced, and the permissions for the group and everyone are ignored for that account. If the user account is not the owner but is a member of the group, then group permissions are enforced. If the account is neither the owner nor a member of the group, everyone's permissions are enforced. In an "owner-only delete" scenario, an authorized user has read-write access to the file but only the owner can delete it. This option, known as the *sticky bit,* can be set only at the command line via chmod +t.

Setting ACLs With Workgroup Manager

You must enable ACLs for the volume before you can edit them on a shared item. Select the volume from Workgroup Manager and, under the General pane, click the "Enable Access Control Lists on this volume" checkbox.

Once you have enabled ACLs, use Workgroup Manager to assign users to groups and permissions to the ACL. Here's where to update the file-system access-control entries in the ACL (this is similar to POSIX permissions management, except for the location where you drag the users and groups from the Users & Groups drawer):

1   Select a location in the file system for which to apply settings. Click the Access button.

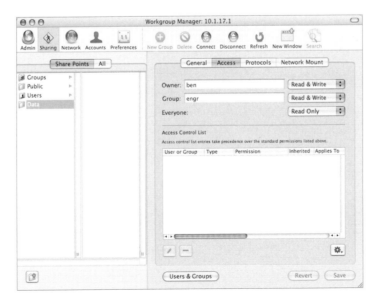

2   Click the Users & Groups button to open the Users & Groups drawer.

3   Drag a specific user or group to the Access Control List box.

4   Use the pop-up menus on a user or group entry to select permissions from standard predefined sets. Alternatively, click the Edit (pencil) button to configure custom settings.

5   Configure additional users or groups as required.

6   If desired, use the pop-up menus by the Owner or Group field to propagate settings to enclosed files or folders.

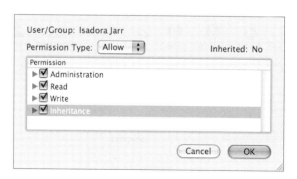

ACLs can grow complex in a large organization. Judicious use of group membership should help clarify which users have access to which items, but you may still find yourself unsure of who has access to a given folder. The Effective Permissions Inspector will tell you exactly what access a particular user has to the selected folder. To use this tool, choose Show Effective Permissions Inspector from the Action menu. Once the inspector window opens, drag a user or group to the window; the inspector will display the precise access permissions for the given user or group and the selected file, folder, or volume.

You have learned that POSIX owners and groups are determined by user and group IDs. Since UIDs and GIDs are simple integers, it is possible that users can have duplicate user IDs. Usually this is an error, but sometimes an administrator will want the POSIX UID to be identical on two separate users.

ACLs are much more complex and require a unique identification of a user or group. For this purpose, every user and group has a globally unique ID (GUID). This is not exposed in the user interface (the GUI), since there should be no reason to change it. Every time a user is created, a new 128-bit number is generated, based upon the clock time when the user is created. In this way, users and groups are virtually guaranteed of unique identification in ACLs.

> **TIP** ▶ "I can't see the files I should see" can be a common complaint from users who access a complex server. Next time you hear this, use the Effective Permissions Inspector to investigate the permissions that user has.

ACL Workflow Examples

When working with ACLs, it is important that you plan your setup properly to avoid conflicting permission settings, such as having a user be a member of two groups, one with read permissions on a folder and one with no access permissions on the same folder. These types of conflicts can occur if you do not plan your ACL permissions models well.

Multiple Groups

The POSIX permissions work well in a single desktop mode such as Mac OS X client. Yet when the system becomes more complex, such as in a corporate or enterprise environments, the POSIX model does not scale as well.

Complex workflows might require more than just the Owner, Group, and Everyone classes available with POSIX. In particular, having a single group is very limiting. The POSIX owner must be an individual user account (it can't be a group), and granting permission to Everyone usually opens up the files to a wider audience than you want. ACLs permit multiple groups assigned to a folder, each with a unique permissions setting. This is a common requirement in any environment that has multiple groups collaborating on a single project. Imagine a production environment that has writers, graphics editors, copy editors, and production editors. Different groups work on the same file at different points during the project.

Each group would have specific permissions for each folder. For instance, a user in the Writers group can put a document in the Submissions folder and can read and write to that file while in that folder. However, the Copy Editors group can only read the files in the folder. Those users in the Production Staff and Graphics Editors groups are specifically denied any read or write access to the Submissions folder.

Also, users in the Writers group are allowed to move the document into the Editors folder, but are denied permission to read what is in the folder. Users in the Copy Editors group have read permissions and are allowed the specific write permissions of creating folders or files within the Editors folder, so they can make a copy of the document within the folder. Users in the Graphics Editors group have read permissions as well, but are allowed only write attributes to the document; they cannot create new files within the Editors folder. Users in the Production Staff group can read the files.

Finally, users in the Production Staff group can copy the document into the Production folder, and can read and modify any documents in that folder. Users in the Writers group are specifically denied permission to read or write to the folder or any documents in the folder. Users in the two editor groups have all the read permissions, but can write only extended attributes.

Nested Groups

In addition to assigning multiple groups to a single folder, Mac OS X Server v10.4 allows groups to contain *other groups*. Your Writers group may be broken down further into yet other groups based on the types of article they write, such as features or columns.

If ACLs permit multiple groups assigned to a folder, you might wonder why nesting groups are required. For example, why assign the Writers to the Submissions folder instead of directly assigning access to the three groups (Feature Writers, Staff Writers, Ad Copy Writers)? The effect would be the same.

Breaking groups down into subgroups can make your access easier to understand as an administrator. If you need to come back to your server a month later and give all your writers access to a new folder, you would have to recall the organizational details of your groups. Are you going to remember that to grant all writers access, you need to assign the Feature Writers, Staff Writers, and Ad Copy Writers groups to the new folder? With an all-inclusive group such as Writers, your job is simpler.

Nested groups can be used to reflect the structure of your organization. A publishing example is used above, but another example is a school: a grade level could be a group, which contains the individual classes of students.

While powerful, nested groups should be used with care. If you build a deep, complex hierarchy, you may find that access is harder—rather than easier—to understand. Mirroring your organizational structure is usually safe and useful. Be wary of ad-hoc groups. It may be a quick way to give access to some users, but later on may make understanding your access more difficult.

Inheritance

Another feature of ACLs is *inheritance:* items inside a folder acquiring the ACLs of the folder. Users will normally be dealing with inherited permissions for files. As users create files on the server, the tools they use do not set any explicit ACLs on the item being copied. This includes the Finder in Mac OS X v10.4. In this case, the permissions on the file are the permissions on the enclosing folder.

Inheritance is another tool you can use to enable your workflow. The workflow example above of multiple groups is fairly simplistic in that a user either has full read-write access to a folder and its contents, or can't see anything inside that folder. With inheritance, your actual permissions can be subtler. You may want the Editors group to have read-only access to the Submissions folder, but still allow only the Writers group to be able to make changes to files or add new files. Inheritance allows this. Give the Editors read access on the Submissions folder, and by inheritance they also have read-only access to all files in the Submissions folder.

POSIX Permissions Versus Access Settings

Mac OS X Server v10.4 added the ability to set a finer grain of control over access settings using ACLs that are compatible with the Windows environment. Seventeen additional settings can be made on a folder (or share point) from inside Workgroup Manager. This allows a richer set of capabilities to be defined for read and write access as well as for administrative control (such as who can change permissions on or ownership of a folder). In Workgroup Manager, these settings are enabled on folders, not individual files, although files can obtain these permissions through inheritance. This folder-level control allows a finer level of management, without having to worry about administering permissions for thousands or millions of files individually.

The following dialog displays the settings available from the Finder.

NOTE ▶ Access-control settings are made on a container basis for either folders or share points, not on individual files themselves. Individual files obtain their respective ACL settings from their containing folder.

The inheritance configuration determines where the ACL settings get propagated to, such as to the folder itself, any files or folders one level down, or to files or folders descendant from this folder. While the initial inheritance setting applies only for files and folders created afterward, you can propagate these settings manually to apply them to enclosed files or folders.

How File-System ACLs Work

When you use Workgroup Manager to define ACLs, you are creating individual *access control list entries (ACEs)*. These entries and lists are specific to a file-system location and are set on container objects—either share points or folders. Each ACE contains the following information:

▶ User or group associated with this entry

▶ Type of entry (Allow or Deny)

▶ Permissions (Full Control, Read & Write, Read, Write, or Custom, along with inheritance settings)

The order of entries is important, as lists are evaluated top to bottom by Mac OS X Server.

Allow and Deny matches work differently for ACLs. Allow matches are cumulative for all matches that apply to a user, whether from user or group matches. Deny matches apply on first match.

ACLs on a file do not change when you use the move command to move a file from one folder to another on the same volume. In this situation, the file is not copied and deleted. Instead, there is a change to the pointer to where the file is located. If you move between volumes, a copy and delete does occur and the file inherits the ACLs from the new enclosing folder.

Allow Access Is Cumulative

In the diagram below, assume that algebra tutors are algebra students, and that all algebra students are students. The folder has three entries in the ACL:

▶ All students can read the contents of the folder (inherited from the parent).

▶ Algebra students can write to the folder.

▶ Algebra tutors can administer the folder.

All students in the school can see the selected folder and files inside that folder. Algebra students have write access by virtue of their membership in the Algebra Students group, but they also have read access by virtue of their membership in the All Students group. Thus, Algebra Students have read-write access. Algebra tutors, who are algebra students, can read, write, and make administrative changes, such as change permissions or ownership.

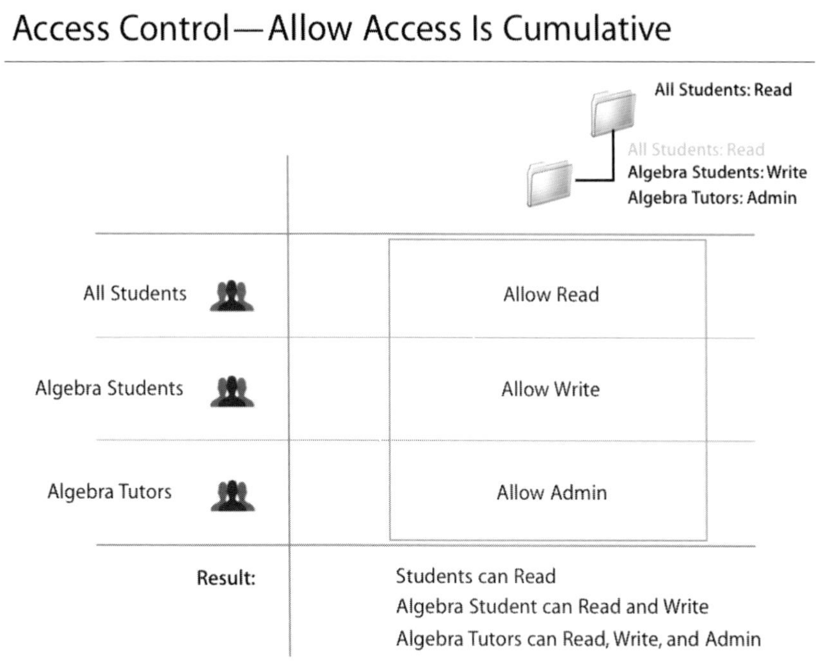

Access Control—Allow Access Is Cumulative

All Students: Read

All Students: Read
Algebra Students: Write
Algebra Tutors: Admin

All Students	Allow Read
Algebra Students	Allow Write
Algebra Tutors	Allow Admin

Result:
Students can Read
Algebra Student can Read and Write
Algebra Tutors can Read, Write, and Admin

Notice that inherited permissions have to be considered for the cumulative Allow access. Algebra students and algebra tutors can read by virtue of being in the All Students group. If that is not what you intended, you could remove inherited privileges from the folder using Workgroup Manager.

Deny Access Is First Match

Now suppose that inside the Math folder is a folder containing student evaluations. It is important that no student gain access to this folder or its contents. Notice that because of inheritance, students would normally have read access to the folder. In order to keep students out of this folder, you can place a Deny access control on the folder for the All Students group.

The Deny access overrides all other access controls on the folder for the specified group. Even though algebra tutors have a read access ACE (from their membership in the Student group), a write access ACE (from their membership in the Algebra Student group), and an admin access ACE (from their membership in the Algebra Tutors group), the Deny access—which applies to all students—overrides all of these ACEs, and no student can access this folder.

Group Membership and ACLs

Using ACLs to control access to server resources can be extremely valuable, as long as care is taken up front to organize your user and group accounts appropriately. The recommended way to approach this management is to take advantage of using smaller groups to correctly mimic the needs of your organization, including nesting groups within groups. Use these group accounts to manage access on a more granular basis.

You could address your classroom situation by creating a single group for all teachers, which is made up of two groups: Staff Teachers and Student Teachers. You could then manage staff and student teachers independently and assign access rights as needed. Over time, if a student teacher becomes a full-time teacher, you can simply move her account into the Staff Teachers group. This enables you to continue managing access on a group/organizational basis, instead of dealing with access entries for individual teachers, which can get quite unwieldy.

Configuring Access Control

In this section, you will create a folder hierarchy and a means of controlling access to facilitate the workflow of the users and groups on your server. Using only file-system ACLs, you will follow the path of an example project from development. You will discover that the ability to manipulate a file can be determined by where the file is located in the system, rather than by who created or "owns" the specific file.

It is important to note that changes take effect only when you save. It is good practice to save your work frequently.

To properly configure your server, you will need to understand the intended workflow of your users. You have set up two groups, Engineering and Marketing, and each group needs different access to files at different times during a project. For this exercise, you will be adding new groups to this equation: a Projects group and a Contractors group.

Create the Folder Structure

In the example being used in this lesson, the folder structure is project-based, not department-based. As a document meets a particular milestone, it will be moved from one location to another. You will create project folders and assign ACLs for those folders to control workflow. This may be different from the way you managed documents with POSIX permissions.

The first step is to turn on ACLs on the file-server volume. Then you will create a project folder hierarchy. You can create the folders in the Finder, but you can also use Workgroup Manager, which enables you to create folders on your server remotely without having physical access to it.

1 On your client computer, open Workgroup Manager and connect to your server.

2 Click the Sharing button in Workgroup Manager's toolbar.

The main window displays the Sharing settings, the current share point, and the owner and groups assigned to it, as well as their access permissions.

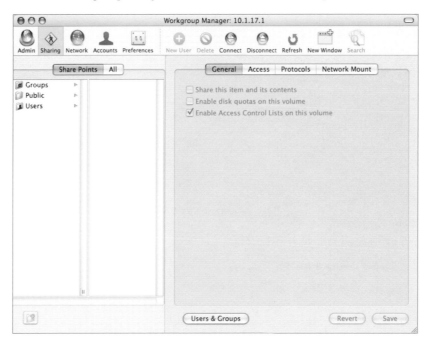

3 Click the All button.

This view enables you to navigate the local hard drive and set permissions on folders not contained within a share point.

4 In the left column, click the startup volume.

In this example, the name of the volume is tigerserver.

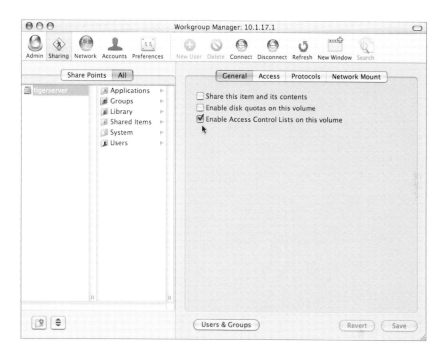

5 Verify that "Enable Access Control Lists on this volume" is selected and click Save if necessary.

This allows ACLs to be utilized on all folders and the volume itself. You must enable ACLs at the volume level.

6 Select Shared Items in the second column of the window.

7 Click the Create New Folder button in the lower-left corner of the window.

This creates a new folder within the Shared Items folder.

8 In the Name field, enter *Project Phantom*.

This folder will be used for the development product.

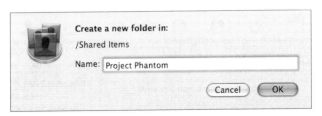

9 Inside the new folder create three subfolders: Development, Pre_Release, and Release.

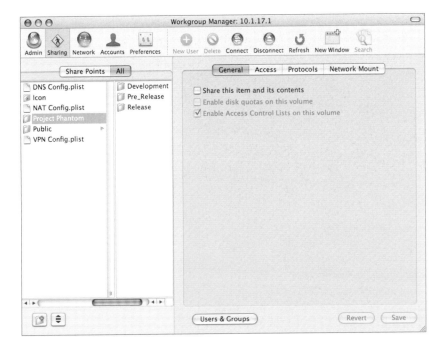

10 Click the General button and select the "Share this item and its contents" checkbox for the Project Phantom folder.

This turns the Project Phantom folder into a share point that will be mountable by your users.

Create Additional Groups and Remove a Member From a Group

As mentioned above, in addition to using the existing Marketing and Engineering groups, you need to create two additional groups for this exercise: Projects and Contractors. These will represent project management and temporary employees. Also, to demonstrate changing access, you must make sure that the user Warren is part of the Engineering group only, not part of the Marketing group.

1 Click the Accounts button in the toolbar, click the Groups icon, and create two new groups, Projects and Contractors.

These groups are empty now; you will add users later.

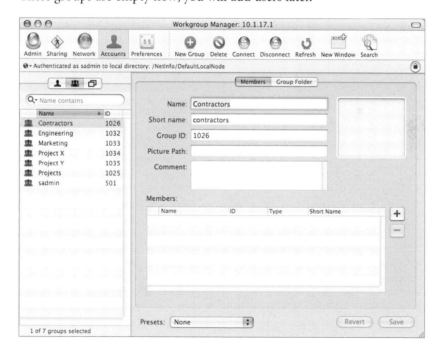

2 From the Accounts section of Workgroup Manager, select the Marketing group.

3   Remove Warren from the Marketing group if he is a member by selecting him and clicking the Delete (-) button, and then click Save.

Set Ownership and Permissions for the Development Folders

Now that you have created the folder structure, you need to assign group ownership and permissions of each of the folders.

1   Click the Sharing button in the toolbar, select the Development folder, and click the Access button.

The fields in the Access pane show that the Development folder is currently owned by the sadmin, and admin is the group assigned to this folder.

The admin group is a reserved group account that is created when Mac OS X Server is installed. The root account, also known as the System Administrator or superuser account, is also created when Mac OS X Server is installed. Because it is a system-level account, it is not listed in the Users

Accounts list in the Accounts pane, but it is listed in the Users list in the Users & Groups drawer.

This window shows that the owner, sadmin, has read-write access to this folder, as do members of the admin group. The Everyone permissions are set to Read Only.

The Development folder will be left with POSIX permissions for the first phase of the exercise to illustrate the power of using ACLs. Remember, there will be a Contractors group and associated users.

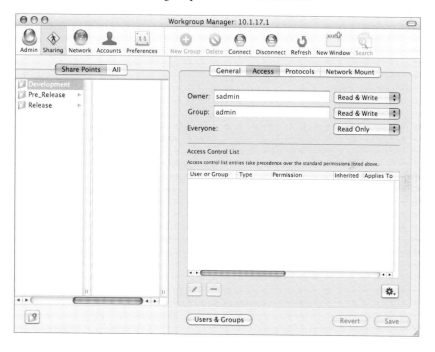

2   Click the Users & Groups button to open the Users & Groups drawer.

Now drag users and groups to the Access pane to change permissions.

▶ Set the Owner permissions for the Development folder to warren.

▶ Set the Group permissions for the Development folder to Engineering.

▶ Set the Everyone permissions for the Development folder to None.

3 Click Save.

Will members of the Contractors group be able to access the Development folder that is owned by Warren Peece with a group of Engineering and Everyone No Access? No. They would need to be made part of the Engineering group or Everyone would have to have some type of access. What POSIX permissions would you need to set to allow them access? Everyone would need to have Read and Write access.

Set the Access Control for the Pre_Release Folder
You will use an ACL instead of POSIX permissions for the Pre_Release folder.

1 If not already selected, click the Sharing button in the toolbar and select the Pre_Release folder, then click the Access button.

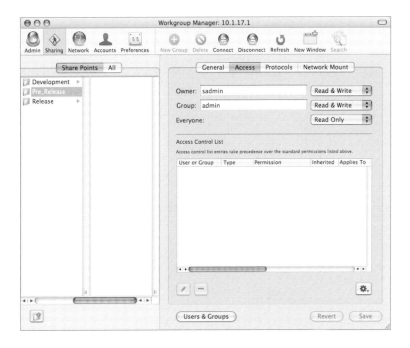

2   Click the Users & Groups button to open the Users & Groups drawer, select the Group list icon, and drag the Marketing group to the Access Control List box.

3   Select the Marketing entry in the Access Control List box and, in the Permission column, give the Marketing group full control.

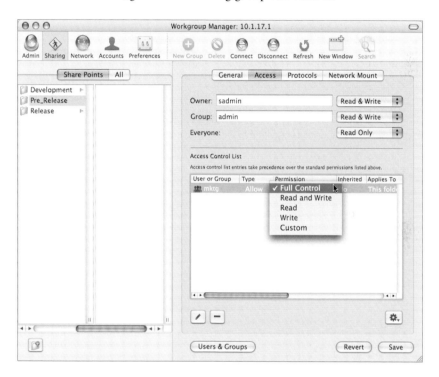

4   From the Groups list, drag the Engineering group into the Access Control List box.

5   Select the Engineering group in the Access Control List box and give it Custom access that permits reading and writing but does not let them delete files or folders. Click OK.

Effectively you have allowed the Engineering group full edit control, but group members cannot remove items.

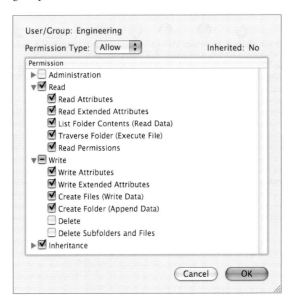

6   Click OK, then click Save.

Set the Access and Permissions for the Release Folder
Just as you did for the Pre_Release folder, you must set the access controls for the Release folder. The group for the Release folder will be Projects. You do not need to assign members in that group to establish access; all access will be determined by the ACLs, as with the Pre_Release folder. If later you want to grant access to this folder, you can add users or groups to the folder ACLs.

1   If not already selected, click the Sharing button in the toolbar and select the Release folder, then click the Access button.

2   Click the Groups button in the drawer and drag the Projects group to the Access Control List box.

3   Select the Projects entry in the Access Control List box and give the Projects group full control.

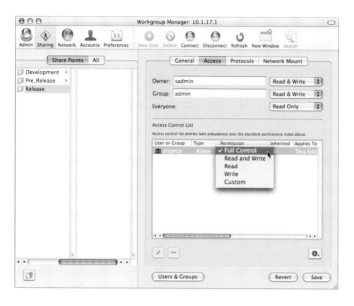

4   Drag the Marketing group to the Access Control List box.

5   Select the Marketing entry in the Access Control List box and give them custom access that permits reading and writing but does not let them delete files or folders.

6 Drag the Engineering group to the Access Control List box.

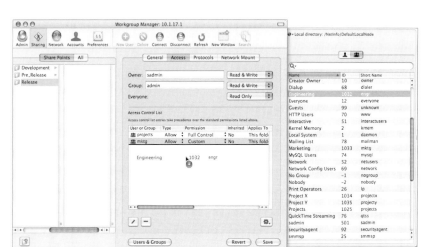

7 Double-click the Engineering entry in the Access Control List box and click OK to give the Engineering group read-only access.

8 Click Save.

Add New Users

Now that you have created the folder structure, create two additional users and assign them to groups, as you learned earlier in this lesson, "Configuring Local User Accounts":

▶ Project manager Pamela Clarke, short name pclarke, password pclarke, in the Projects group

▶ Contractor Mike Smith, short name msmith, password msmith, in the Contractors group

Watch the Workflow

You have now configured the server with the proper project folders and appropriate users and groups. You will now create a document and watch the access during a normal workflow.

1 From the client machine, connect to the server machine as Warren.

2 Select the Project Phantom share point. Click OK.

3 Using TextEdit, create two text files, one named Engineering Spec and one named First Source, and place them in the Development folder.

Warren has full access to the Development folder.

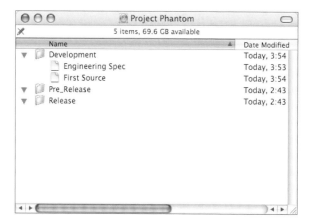

4   Create a subfolder inside Development called Code and move the First
Source file into that subfolder.

5   Option-drag the folder from Development to Pre_Release.

This copies the folder and its contents instead of moving it.

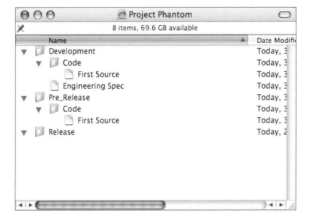

6   Disconnect as Warren and connect as Tina Bubbles.

7   Attempt to view the permissions on the files in the Development folder.

As a member of the Marketing group, Tina does not currently have access to the Development folder. Since there are no ACLs on the Development folder and Tina isn't a member of the Engineering group, she cannot see the files in that folder.

8   View the files in the Pre_Release folder.

9   Edit the First Source file by adding some text to the file and save it in a new folder called Reviewed.

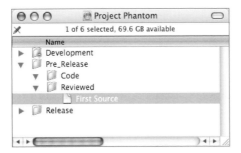

10   Move the Reviewed folder from Pre_Release to the Release folder.

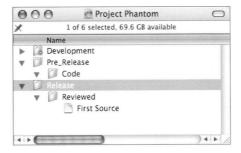

This indicates a project ready for production.

11   Disconnect as Tina and connect as Pamela Clark.

12   View and attempt to view the documents in the other folders.

13   Create a new folder inside Release named Ready and move the file First Source into it.

The other groups should still have read access to the Ready folder. View the file and folder info in the Finder using the Get Info command.

Add Groups to the Access Path

Now that you have configured a basic set of access to the program folders and viewed how the access changes when a document or folder is moved from one container to another, you will add groups to groups and see how that impacts the access.

1 Disconnect as Pamela and connect as the contractor Mike Smith.

2 Verify that you can access the data in the Pre_Release and Release folders.

3 Disconnect as Mike Smith.

4 Open Workgroup Manager, click Sharing, and navigate to the
    Development folder in the Share Points list on the left.

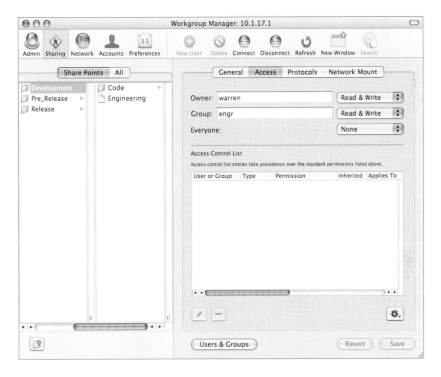

5 Click the Users & Groups button and click the Groups button in the drawer.

6 Drag the Engineering group to the ACL pane and give it full control.

    You have added ACLs to the Development folder. You will now give the
    Contractors group access to the Development folder.

7 Drag the Contractors group to the ACL pane and give them read and write access without allowing them to delete files or folders.

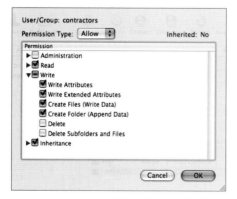

8 Click Save.

Add Deny Type Access

You just gave the Contractors group access to the Development folder. (The Marketing and Projects groups still do not have access.) An easy way to do that would have been to add the Contractors group to the Engineering group once you set the Development ACLs, but that would have given the contractors additional access that you don't want them to have. With Deny access, you can limit users and groups to better narrow down the permissions model you are seeking.

1   Click Accounts and click the Groups button in Workgroup Manager on your Mac OS X computer.

2   Add the Contractors group to the Engineering group and click Save.

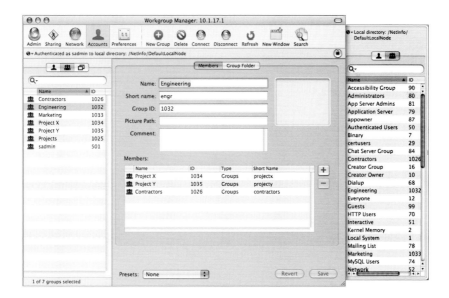

3   Click Sharing and navigate to the Pre_Release folder.

4   Click the Users & Groups button and click the Groups button in the drawer.

5 Drag the Contractors group into the Access Control List box.

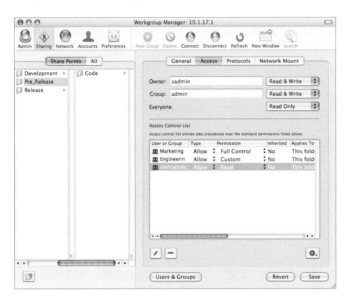

6 Double-click the Contractors group, choose Deny from the Permission Type pop-up menu, and click OK.

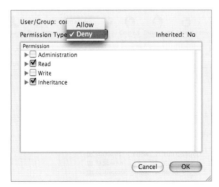

7 Click Save.

Notice that this permission type moves to the top of the list. The Deny access is enforced first. Even though the Contractors group would now have access as part of the Engineering group, it is explicitly denied access.

For this exercise, do not change the ACLs on the Release folder. Take some time to log in as various users and notice how your access changes. The Contractors group was denied access to the Pre_Release folder but picked up Engineering access to the documents in the Release folder.

Clean Up Folders on the Server

You have created the Phantom Project folder and viewed how the workflow can occur when documents are moved from folder to folder. You can now remove the folder from the server.

1   On your client computer, open Workgroup Manager and connect to your server.

2   Click the Sharing button in Workgroup Manager's toolbar, select the Phantom Project share point, deselect the "Share this item and its contents" checkbox, and click Save.

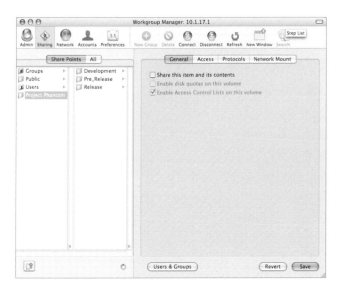

3   Quit Workgroup Manager.

4   In the Finder on the server, delete the folder Phantom Project.

What You've Learned

▶ Authentication gets a user into the server. Authorization determines what the user can do after getting in.

▶ User accounts for Mac OS X Server are created in Workgroup Manager. You can configure two types of accounts with Workgroup Manager: user and administrator. An administrator account is the same as a user account except it has the authority to administer the server.

▶ Group accounts enable administrators to quickly assign a set of permissions to multiple users. You create and manage group accounts in Workgroup Manager. You can add users to groups and group membership to user accounts.

▶ You also use Workgroup Manager to create share points and to assign permissions to the share points.

▶ Mac OS X Server v10.4 added support for access control lists (ACLs), which provide a higher granularity for setting permissions. These ACLs are compatible with ACLs from the Windows world and work in addition to the standard POSIX (UNIX) permissions found on Mac OS X.

References

The following documents provide more information about installing Mac OS X Server. (All of these and more are available at www.apple.com/server/documentation.)

Administration Guides

Mac OS X Server Getting Started (http://images.apple.com/server/pdfs/Getting_Started_v10.4.pdf)

User Management (http://images.apple.com/server/pdfs/User_Management_Admin_v10.4.pdf)

File Services Administration (http://images.apple.com/server/pdfs/File_Services_v10.4.pdf)

Mac OS X Server Command-Line Administration (http://images.apple.com/server/pdfs/Command_Line_v10.4.pdf)

Apple Knowledge Base Documents

You can check for new and updated Knowledge Base documents at www.apple.com/support.

Review Quiz

1. Describe the difference between authentication and authorization, and give an example of each.

2. What is the difference between user and administrator accounts on both Mac OS X and Mac OS X Server?

3. What is the difference between group accounts on Mac OS X and Mac OS X Server?

4. What tool is used to configure user, group, and share point settings on Mac OS X Server? What tool is used to change user and group permissions on Mac OS X?

5. Where do you set file or folder access ACLs?

6. How many characters are allowed in a user short name?

Answers

1. Authentication is the process by which the system requires you to provide information before it allows you to access a specific account. An example is entering a name and password while connecting to an Apple file server. Authorization refers to the process by which permissions are used to regulate a user's access to specific resources, such as files and share points, once the user has been successfully authenticated.

2. User accounts provide basic access to a computer or server, while administrator accounts allow a person to administer the machine. On Mac OS X, the administrator account is typically used for changing settings or adding new software. On Mac OS X Server, the administrator account is typically used for changing settings on the server machine itself, usually through Server Admin or Workgroup Manager.

3. Group accounts on Mac OS X are assigned by default and are difficult to change. Mac OS X Server adds easy-to-use tools for creating, assigning, and changing group accounts.

4. Workgroup Manager is used to configure on Mac OS X Server. Get Info is used to change permissions on Mac OS X.

5. Workgroup Manager

6. 255 Roman characters

6

Lesson Files	Lesson_6/Local_Users
Time	This lesson takes approximately 3 hours to complete.
Goals	Use Open Directory and Directory Access to configure Open Directory search policies
	Use Workgroup Manager to create network user accounts
	Use Open Directory to authenticate a user account
	Configure a local NetInfo directory
	Configure network mounts using Workgroup Manager

Lesson 6
Using Open Directory

This lesson describes how using a directory service can help you manage users and resources on your network. You will learn about the features of Apple's Open Directory and how it can be integrated with other directory services in a mixed environment. You will also learn how to set up and manage directories and user accounts with Server Admin, Workgroup Manager, and Directory Access—the three main tools you'll use with Open Directory. Finally, you will become familiar with common Open Directory issues and learn how to correct them.

Open Directory is extremely versatile when dealing with a variety of other directory services, such as Active Directory, eDirectory, and Network Information Servers (NIS) directory servers. This lesson deals with a Mac OS X Server–to–Mac OS X directory service scenario.

Directory Services Concepts

Giving a user multiple user accounts on different computers can cause problems. For instance, if each computer in a network has its own private authentication database, a user might have to remember a different password for each computer. Even if you assign the user the same password on every computer, if the databases are independent, the information can become inconsistent over time, as the user changes passwords in one location but forgets to do so in another. One strategy to resolve this problem is to create a single authentication database and make it available to all computers.

Directory services provide exactly this kind of central repository for information about the computers, applications, and users in an organization. With directory services, you can consistently maintain information about all the users—such as their names, passwords, and preferences—as well as about printers and other network resources. You can maintain this information in a single location, rather than on individual computers. In both education and enterprise environments, directory services are the best way to manage users and computing resources.

What Is Open Directory?

Apple's extensible directory-services architecture, called Open Directory, is built into Mac OS X and Mac OS X Server and includes authentication services. Because it is an integral part of Mac OS X, several services on Mac OS X and Mac OS X Server use information from Open Directory. For secure login to these services, Open Directory has a built-in authentication authority that uses Simple Authentication and Security Layer (SASL) and Kerberos (for more on Kerberos, see Kerberos_v2.mov on the CD-ROM). Using these authentication authorities, Open Directory can securely store and validate the passwords of users who want to log in to client computers on your network or use other network resources that require authentication. You can also use Open Directory to enforce policies such as password expiration and minimum length and to manage user preferences.

Open Directory can also authenticate Windows users for directory login, file services, print service, and other Windows services that Mac OS X Server provides. Open Directory has been integrated with Samba 3, which allows an Open Directory server to function as a Windows primary domain controller (PDC) or a backup domain controller (BDC).

Another piece to Open Directory is its discovery protocols. Mac OS X and Mac OS X Server can use Open Directory to discover network services, such as file servers, that make themselves known with the Bonjour, AppleTalk, Service Location Protocol (SLP), or Server Message Block (SMB) service discovery protocols.

Overview of Open Directory Components

Open Directory is based on OpenLDAP, an open-source implementation of the Lightweight Directory Access Protocol (LDAP), a standard protocol used for accessing directory-service data. Having a single protocol means that all the Mac OS X and Mac OS X Server computers on your network can work from one set of data. Applications that use directory information need to recognize LDAP only to access the central repository. Because of its open architecture, Open Directory makes it easy to integrate Mac OS X and Mac OS X Server systems into an existing network infrastructure. In addition to LDAP, Open Directory includes plug-ins for several other directory types, including Active Directory, eDirectory, NetInfo, and NIS.

Overview of Open Directory Components

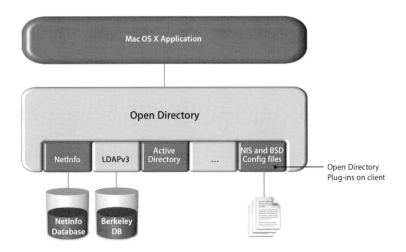

Earlier versions of Mac OS X and Mac OS X Server used the NetInfo protocol for directory services (Mac OS X and Mac OS X Server still use the NetInfo directory format for local directory data). Starting with Mac OS X Server v10.3, this protocol was replaced with LDAP on Mac OS X Server. The Server Admin utility contains features that help administrators migrate from the NetInfo protocol to LDAP. Open Directory accomplishes this because it acts as an intermediary between directories (which store information about users and resources) and the application and system software processes that want to use the information. By default, Open Directory stores directory information in a specialized, open-source database, Berkeley DB, which is optimized to handle many requests and to find and retrieve information quickly. Berkeley DB provides high-performance indexing of hundreds of thousands of user records. Open Directory can store information in one directory or in several related directories, and in several different formats.

Open Directory leverages other open-source technologies, such as Kerberos, and combines them with powerful server administration tools to deliver robust directory and authentication services that are easy to set up and manage. Because there are no per-seat or per-user license fees, Open Directory can scale to the needs of an organization without adding high costs to an IT budget. Administrators can deploy Open Directory configuration information automatically using DHCP or manually using the Directory Access application at the computer.

By default, Mac OS X computers request network configuration information, including LDAP configuration, from a DHCP server. If the DHCP and LDAP servers are set up correctly, the client automatically gets access to network resources, including user authentication services, network home folders, share points, and preferences.

Configuring Open Directory

Using Server Admin, a computer running Mac OS X Server can be set up in four ways:

▶   As a standalone server, the server does not provide directory information to other computers or get directory information from an existing system. The local directory cannot be shared.

▶ As a server connected to a directory system, you can set up the server to provide services that require user accounts and authentication, such as file and mail services, but use accounts that are set up on another server.

▶ As an Open Directory replica, a server hosts a replicated version of a directory. The replica is synchronized periodically with the master. An LDAP server that receives a request from a user takes responsibility for the request, passing it to other LDAP servers as necessary but ensuring a single coordinated response for the user. This helps balance the load by distributing the work between one LDAP master and x number of replicas.

▶ As an Open Directory master, a server can provide directory information and authentication information to other systems as the host of a shared LDAP directory. In addition, the server authenticates users whose accounts are stored in the shared LDAP directory. This is the best use of a Mac OS X server because all users can now be placed in the LDAP directory for remote authentication instead of local authentication.

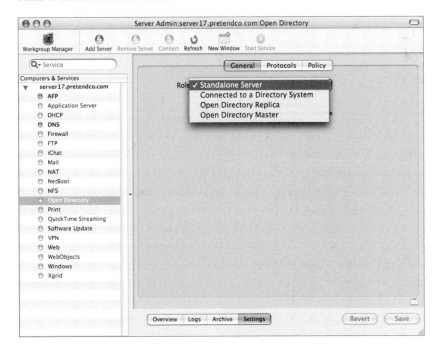

As you plan directory services for your network, consider the need to share user and resource information among multiple Mac OS X computers. If the need is low, then little directory planning is necessary; everything can be accessed from a local server directory. But if you want to share information among computers, you need to set up at least one shared directory.

Connecting to an Existing Directory System

If you are setting up multiple servers, it would be extremely inefficient to populate each server with the same user accounts. Instead, your Mac OS X Server computer can be a node connected to a directory system. In this role, the server gets authentication, user information, and other directory information from a directory system hosted on another server or servers. The Mac OS X server still gets some directory information locally from its own directory and provides authentication based on this information for local users, for example. This puts one server at the pinnacle of your setup and other servers that obtain their directory information from this original server. This server does not have to be an Open Directory server, as discussed earlier.

To configure your server to obtain directory services from an existing LDAP directory:

1   Open Server Admin. Select Open Directory in the Computers & Services ‚ list. Click the Settings button at the bottom of the window, then click the General button near the top of the window. Choose "Connected to a Directory System" from the Role pop-up menu.

2   Use the Directory Access utility (click Open Directory Access in the Settings pane) to enable and configure access to one or more directory systems.

You could also choose to configure Directory Access first, in which case Open Directory will change the server settings from standalone to a node ("Connected to a Directory System") for you.

Configuring an Open Directory Master

Instead of binding to another server for directory services, you can set up Mac OS X Server to host a shared LDAP directory, providing directory information and authentication to other systems. To do so:

1   Choose Open Directory Master from the Role pop-up menu in the Open Directory pane of Server Admin.

2   Enter a user name, a short name, and a password for a new account that will administer the shared LDAP directory. You can use the same user name and password as your initial account.

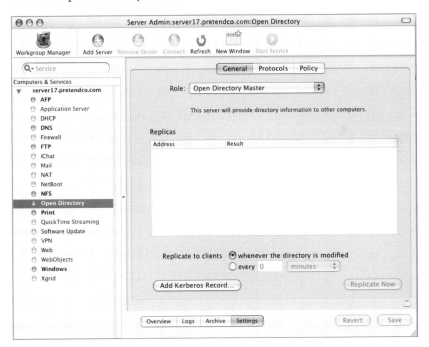

Once you have set up your server to be an Open Directory master, you can configure other computers on your network to access the server's shared LDAP directory.

> **NOTE ▸** Do not configure your server as an Open Directory master during initial setup. Instead, set the role to Standalone Server. Later, when you have verified that domain name system (DNS) and other network services are working the way you want, use Server Admin to configure the server as an Open Directory master. The hostname must match the DNS name.

> **NOTE ▸** Once you have added accounts to the Open Directory directory on your server, do not change the Open Directory role setting. If you do, you will lose all your account information and orphan your users' data.

> **TIP ▸** Determine a schema for your user IDs (UIDs) as you enter user records. Perhaps have your administrators in a separate range for easier searching. Workgroup Manager allows filtering, and UID or GID (group ID) is a powerful way to search for users or groups.

Configure Open Directory

Server Admin is the primary utility for configuring directory services provided by Mac OS X Server.

1   On your Mac OS X computer, open Server Admin, connect to your server as server17.pretendco.com, and authenticate as Server Admin if necessary.

    Make sure your server is resolving DNS correctly. If not, you may need to stop and start DNS.

2   In the Computers & Services list, select Open Directory for your server
and click Settings.

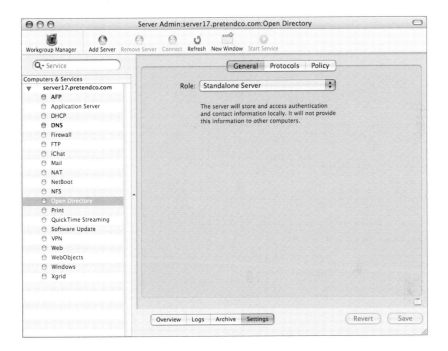

3   From the Role pop-up menu, choose Open Directory Master.

You will be prompted to create an administrator account for the
directory.

4   In the sheet that appears, enter the following values:

▶   Name: *Directory Administrator*

▶   Short Name: *diradmin*

▶   Password: *f00tba11*

▶ Kerberos Realm: *SERVER17.PRETENDCO.COM*

▶ Search Base: *dc=pretendco,dc=com*

5 Click Create and then click Save.

Directory services now create the user and the directory services database. This may take some time.

6 Click Overview and verify the status of the following services:

▶ Lookup Server (lookupd) is: Running

▶ NetInfo Server (netinfod) is: Local only

▶ LDAP Server (slapd) is: Running

▶ Password Server is: Running

▶ Kerberos is: Running

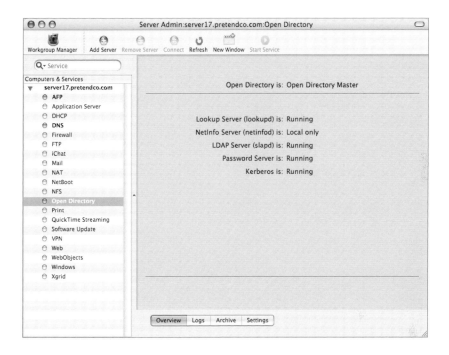

7   Quit Server Admin.

> **NOTE ▶** It is important to always use the fully qualified domain name (FQDN) in the Kerberos Realm field. Kerberos relies upon a valid DNS to function properly. If at any time you see that Kerberos did not start, it is probably due to misconfigured DNS data.

To recap, you began with a NetInfo database for your local users. That database still exists. The administrator of that database is sadmin. You have now created a secondary, shared LDAP database. The administrator of that database is diradmin. Each database is separate and requires different authentication to manage either one (in this case, you have used the same password for both databases). You have also created a Password Server database to store LDAP user passwords and a Kerberos Key Distribution Center. You will learn about those later in this lesson.

Network Users

Once you have created shared LDAP directories, you need to populate them with information. User account information is probably the most important type of information you can store in a directory. User accounts that are stored in a shared directory are accessible to all the computers that search that directory; those accounts are referred to as *network user accounts*.

To create user accounts, use Workgroup Manager. If you click the small globe icon on the upper left of the Accounts pane below the Admin button in the toolbar, you can choose a directory from a pop-up menu. This enables you to create user accounts in different directories. You use the Basic pane to create an account, and then use the other panes to set the account's attributes, such as login shell.

> **NOTE** ▸ If you are creating user accounts that other computers will use, make sure you have chosen a shared directory from the directory pop-up menu before you create the account. Workgroup Manager will display a warning whenever you start to add accounts to the local directory, to help prevent you from accidentally creating an account in the local directory instead of a shared one.

> **NOTE** ▸ New in Mac OS X Server v10.4, you can add users and/or groups from one directory to groups from another directory. This increases the flexibility of your system and servers, but it can be very easy to create an overly complex model across directory servers. Always make sure you know which directory you are editing before making changes.

Setting Up a Basic Network User Account

You can use Workgroup Manager to configure both local and network user accounts. Workgroup Manager is essentially a directory-services editing tool.

Follow the steps on the next page to verify the configuration and verify that Workgroup Manager can see both databases.

1   Open Workgroup Manager on your Mac OS X computer and connect to your server computer using the following settings:

▶   Address: *server17.pretendco.com*

▶   User Name: *sadmin*

▶   Password: *f00tba11*

You should see the LDAP directory but it won't be authenticated.

2   If you do not see the LDAP directory, click the small globe icon at the left, beneath the toolbar, to display the Directory Node pop-up menu, and choose Other.

3   In the "Select a Directory" sheet that opens, select LDAPv3, select 127.0.0.1, and click OK.

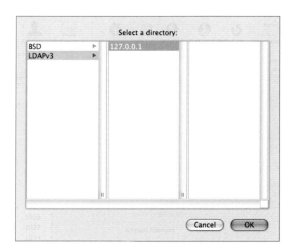

NOTE ▶ Authentication lasts for a set period of time—usually 5 minutes. You may see a locked option if the authentication has timed out.

4 Click the Lock icon on the right under the toolbar and authenticate as diradmin with the password f00tba11.

5 In the left pane of the Workgroup Manager window, click the Users button, then click the New User button in the toolbar.

6 Enter the following values:

▶ Name: *John Jacobs*

▶ Short Names: *john*

▶ Password: *johnjacobs*

7 Click Save.

You have just created a user account in your shared directory domain. John Jacobs is now listed in the left pane. The only user currently in the LDAP directory is diradmin.

The other users you dealt with in Lesson 4 are located in the Local Directory.

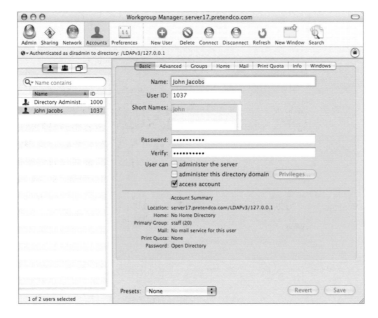

Setting the Account's Password Policy

Once you have created new users, it is useful to establish password policies for their network accounts. (There is more on setting these policies later in this lesson.) Should the users change their passwords next time they log in? Should there be a minimum password length? You can use Workgroup Manager to establish these and other policies for your users.

1   Select the user account John Jacobs and click the Advanced button.

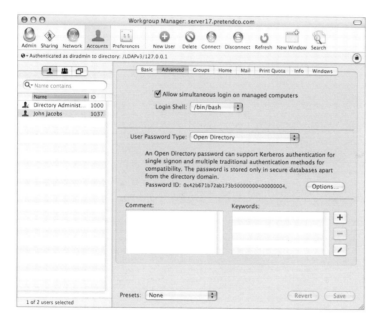

2   Click the Options button.

3   Select the following checkboxes:

▶   Allow the user to change the password

▶   Password must contain at least N characters

▶   Password must be changed at next login

"Allow the user to log in" will already be selected.

4   In the "Password must contain at least *N* characters" textbox, enter *8*.

The next time John logs in, he will need to change his password, and the password will need to be at least eight characters long.

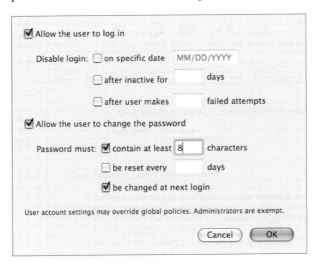

5   Click OK and then click Save.

6   Quit Workgroup Manager.

> **TIP** There are two places to deny access to a specific user account: the Basic pane and the Advanced pane. Changing the settings in the Basic pane will automatically affect the Advanced settings, but changing the data in the Advanced pane does not affect the Basic settings. If you want to deny access to a specific user account, make sure that settings in both the Basic and Advanced panes are configured appropriately. Make sure to save changes so that the new settings will be written to the directory.

Delivery of LDAP Server Information Over DHCP

Once you have an Open Directory master set up, you must configure the client computers to connect, or *bind*, to the server. Using Directory Access on each client computer, you create an LDAP configuration that has the address and search path for your Open Directory master. This method forces you to visit every computer running Mac OS X, which can be quite time consuming if you have a few hundred Mac OS X computers that need to be bound to your server.

An alternative to manually setting the address on each computer is to provide the LDAP binding information through the DHCP service. As explained earlier in Lesson 3, "Using Network Services," you can configure the Mac OS X Server DHCP service to provide connection information for an LDAP server. After the DHCP service has been configured, the client computer requests the address of an LDAP directory server from the DHCP service that also supplies the computer's IP address, router address, and DNS server addresses. That LDAP server's address automatically becomes part of your Mac OS X computer's search path.

Delivery of LDAP Server Over DHCP

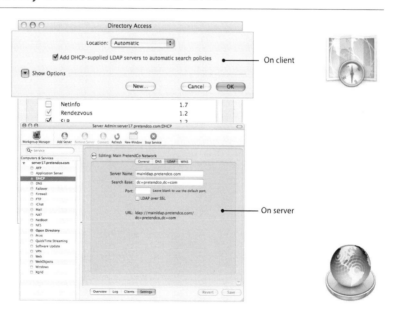

Connecting to the LDAP Shared Directory

You will configure your Mac OS X computer to use authentication services and network user accounts on your Mac OS X server. Once you have configured a parent directory on Mac OS X Server, you need to set the client machines to look for it. You can configure DHCP to provide the information required to locate the parent directory or you can set it up manually. Any client bound to the server can authenticate users using the data in the shared domain. Your Mac OS X computer must be using the static IP address (10.1.17.2) manually assigned in Lesson 3.

Set Static LDAP Binding to Your Server

The Mac OS X computers need to bind to your Open Directory master server to connect. In the following steps, you will set the binding manually and then set the client to use the server for authentication information.

1   On the Mac OS X computer, open Directory Access (located in /Applications/Utilities). If necessary, click the Lock icon and authenticate to make changes.

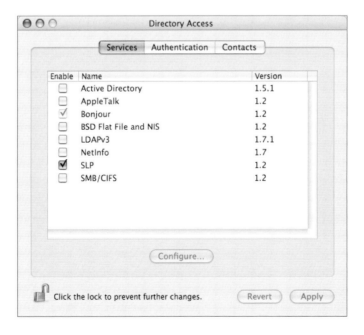

2 Disable NetInfo if it is not already disabled, and enable LDAPv3 if it is not already enabled.

3 Select LDAPv3 and click Configure.

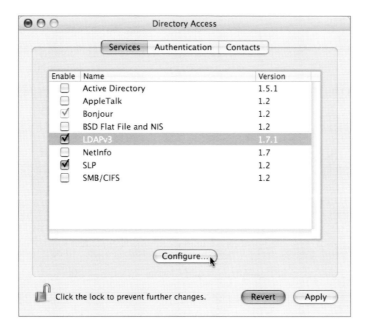

4 Click the Show Options button.

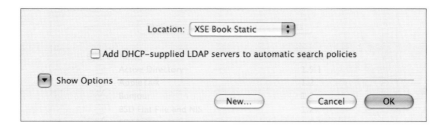

5 Deselect the "Add DHCP-supplied LDAP Servers to automatic search policies" checkbox if it is selected, and then click New.

A new connection dialog appears.

6   Enter *server17.pretendco.com* in the Server Name of IP Address field, and leave the checkboxes set to their default configurations.

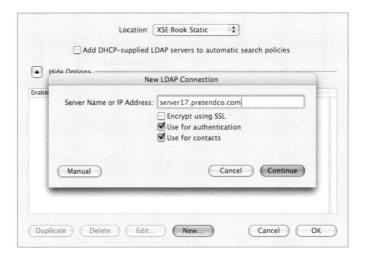

7   Click Continue and then click OK. (Reauthenticate if prompted.)

8   Click OK to close the LDAP configuration window, and then click the Apply button if it's highlighted.

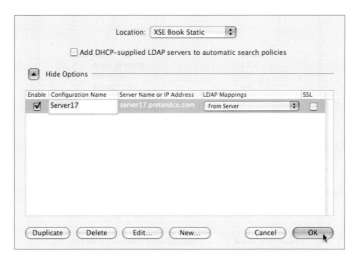

Verify Authentication

Now that binding is complete, you must verify that you are using the server for authentication information.

1   Click the Authentication button in Directory Access and verify that /LDAPv3/server17.pretendco.com is in the list.

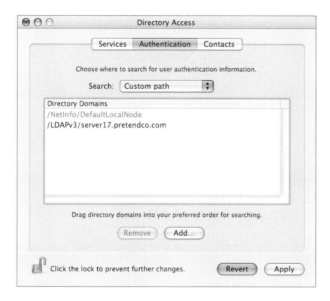

If the server path is not in the list, you will need to add it (you will not need to complete the following steps if the authentication is set for you):

A.   Choose Custom path from the Search menu.

B.   Click Add.

C.   Choose server17.pretendco.com.

D.   Click Add.

E.   Click Apply if necessary.

2   Quit Directory Access.

3   Quit any applications and log out of your Mac OS X computer.

Log In As a Network User

Now that you have set authentication, you can use the user records on the server to log in to the local computer. You will log in as the network user created in the previous exercise.

1 On the client computer at the login window, click Other, then log in as John Jacobs using the password johnjacobs.

Because there is no account record for John Jacobs on the client computer, the client searches the parent directory on the server to find a user account that matches.

2 You are prompted to enter a new password, because you configured directory services to require the password to be changed at the next login.

3 Enter the new password *johnj* into the New Password and Verify Password fields, and then click Log In.

This login fails (and you are told so at the bottom of the login window), because earlier you set the password policy to require at least eight characters.

4   Enter *johnjohn* into the New Password and Verify Password fields, and
    then click Log In.

5   Log out and log back in as your default account on your Mac OS X
    computer.

    This user account is limited, because it has no home folder configured
    yet. This means that John cannot do much of anything in the way of
    saving data or preferences, because he has no place to save them.

Configuring an Open Directory Replica

Open Directory enables you to replicate servers—that is, to create and maintain one or more exact copies of your server's LDAP, password, and Kerberos
databases. Open Directory also provides automatic load balancing between

replicated servers. As a result, you can scale your directory infrastructure and improve search-and-retrieval time on distributed networks. Open Directory replication can also improve client search-and-retrieval time on distributed networks by reducing network traffic between remote sites and ensuring rapid access to directory records, even if the network connection between two locations is lost.

Configuring an Open Directory Replica

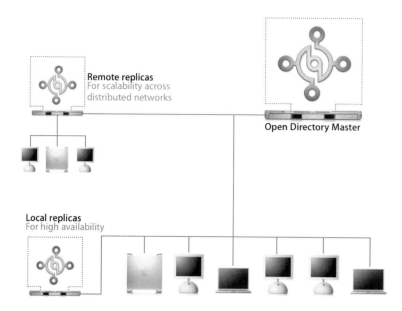

If you already have a master directory server set up, you can configure a second Mac OS X server as a directory replica, to provide the same directory information and authentication information as the master. The replica server hosts a read-only copy of the master's LDAP directory and its Kerberos key distribution center (KDC). The Password Server authentication database is writable on the master and any replicas. When data is transferred from the master to any replica, that data is encrypted as it is copied over. Replicas also need a serial number that is different from that of the master, unless a site license is purchased from Apple Computer.

To configure your server to host a replica of an Open Directory master:

1   Open Server Admin and choose Open Directory Replica from the Role pop-up menu in the Open Directory.

2   Enter the IP address of the LDAP master and a root password on the LDAP master.

3   Enter the name and password of an administrator of the Open Directory master's LDAP directory.

> **WARNING ▶** If this server is already a master, the current LDAP database will be emptied of all its contents.

Once you have set up your server to be an Open Directory replica, other computers can connect to it as needed automatically. The Open Directory master will also update the replica automatically or at specific intervals.

> **TIP ▶** Because replication uses time stamps, it is best to use NTP to synchronize the clocks on all Open Directory masters, replicas, and servers using existing masters. You enable NTP services in Mac OS X Server in Server Admin. You configure a server to use NTP services in the Date & Time pane of System Preferences.

Authentication Methods on Mac OS X Server

Open Directory offers a variety of options for authenticating users whose accounts are stored in directories on Mac OS X Server, including Kerberos and the many authentication methods that network services require. Open Directory can authenticate users by using:

▶   Single sign-on with the Kerberos KDC built in to Mac OS X Server

▶   A password stored securely in the Open Directory Password Server database

▶ A password stored as several hashes—including NT LAN Manager (NTLM), NTLMv2, and LAN Manager—in a file that only the root user can access

▶ A crypt password stored directly in the user's account, for backward compatibility with legacy systems

▶ A non-Apple LDAP server for LDAP bind authentication

In addition, Open Directory lets you set up a password policy that affects all users (except administrators) as well as specific password policies for each user, such as automatic password expiration and minimum password length. (Password policies do not apply to crypt passwords or LDAP bind authentication.) Even though Mac OS X Server supports all of these different authentication methods, you should not use all methods. Crypt password support, for example, is provided for backward compatibility with older computers, but using crypt passwords is not as secure as using the Open Directory Password Server.

Configuring User Authentication

To authenticate a user, Open Directory first must determine which authentication option to use: Kerberos, Open Directory Password Server, shadow password, crypt password, or LDAP bind. The user's account contains information that specifies which authentication option to use. This information is called the *authentication authority attribute*. The authentication authority attribute is not limited to specifying a single authentication option. For example, an authentication authority attribute could specify that a user can be authenticated by Kerberos and Open Directory Password Server.

You can change a user's authentication authority attribute by changing the password type in the Advanced pane of Workgroup Manager. By default, the password type is Open Directory, which means that Mac OS X Server uses either Kerberos or Open Directory Password Server. Open Directory passwords are stored securely in a separate database, not in the user account.

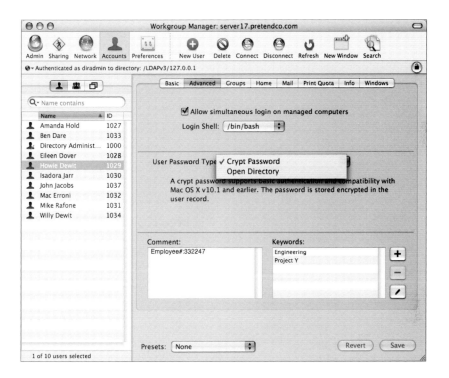

A user's account might not contain an authentication authority attribute. If a user's account contains no authentication authority attribute, Mac OS X Server assumes a crypt password is stored in the user's account. For example, user accounts created using Mac OS X v10.1 and earlier contain a crypt password but not an authentication authority attribute.

> **NOTE** ▶ Crypt passwords are inherently less secure, because they are stored in the directory database and are subject to dictionary attacks. Configure a user account to use a crypt password only if you need to provide compatibility with a computer running Mac OS X v10.1 or earlier.

TIP ▶ If you are using a server that was upgraded from an earlier version of Mac OS X Server, you should examine the password type for all the user records stored on the server. If any records are still using a crypt password, you should upgrade the password type for the account to Open Directory.

Setting Password Policies

Both Kerberos and Open Directory Password Server enforce password policies. For example, a user's password policy can specify a password expiration interval. If the user is logging in and Open Directory discovers that the user's password has expired, the user must replace the expired password. Then Open Directory can authenticate the user.

Password policies can disable a user account on a certain date, after a number of days, after a period of inactivity, or after a number of failed login attempts. Password policies can also require passwords to be a minimum length, contain at least one letter, contain at least one numeral, differ from the account name, differ from recent passwords, or be changed periodically.

Open Directory applies the same password policy rules to Open Directory Password Server and Kerberos. Password policies do not affect administrator accounts. Administrators are exempt from password policies because they can change the policies at will. In addition, enforcing password policies on administrators would subject them to denial-of-service attacks.

Kerberos and Open Directory Password Server maintain password policies separately. Mac OS X Server synchronizes the Kerberos password policy rules with Open Directory Password Server password policy rules.

Setting Open Directory Passwords for LDAP Users

In this section, you will set Open Directory passwords for users in the LDAP (master) database. Before you can do that, however, you must import these users. When you use Workgroup Manager to export and import user records, the passwords are not transferred for security reasons. For example, as part of the upkeep and servicing of a server, it sometimes becomes necessary to move users from one server to another or from one directory node (in this example, Local) to a network-visible node.

Previously you created a list of local users for the server. These users could connect to the file server but are not configured to use the server as a network user. You will now move the users to the network directory node.

Export the Local Users

Follow these steps to export a local user list for import into a network directory:

1   Log in to your Mac OS X computer as your local administrator if you have not already done so, open Workgroup Manager, and authenticate to your server as the local server administrator, sadmin (password f00tba11).

2   Click the small globe icon on the left, beneath the toolbar, to display the Directory Node pop-up menu, and choose Local.

3   If necessary, reauthenticate as sadmin (password f00tba11).

Remember that the local node uses the Server Admin account (sadmin), and the network directory uses the Directory Administrator (diradmin) account (they both have the same passwords for ease of use in this book).

4   Click Accounts, and then click the Users button.

You will now use the filter option in Workgroup Manager to display only the users you want to export.

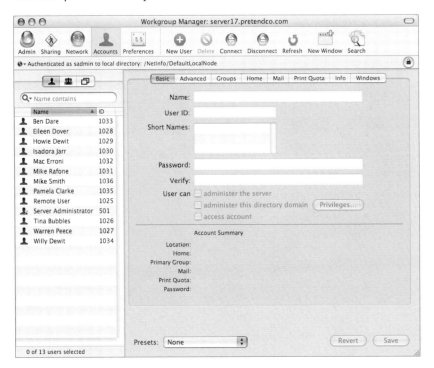

5   Set the filter to display only the user IDs over 1001.

This would display only local users, excluding the sadmin account.

6   Select all the users and choose Export from the Server menu.

You'll get a dialog that warns you that exporting does not preserve user passwords. This is not a problem, since you will be resetting the passwords later.

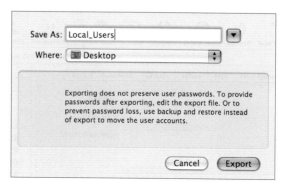

7   Name the file Local_Users and export it to the desktop.

Now that you have an exported list of users, you need to change directory nodes and import the user list into the shared directory node.

8   Clear the filter field to show all users again.

9   Click the small globe icon at the left, beneath the toolbar, to display the Directory Node pop-up menu, and then choose LDAPv3/127.0.0.1.

This is the network-visible node for this server. If you were connected to a larger system, you could use Other to navigate to another network node.

10 Click the Lock on the right under the toolbar and authenticate as diradmin (password f00tba11).

You should notice that the administrative user changes in the displayed user list From Server Administrator to Directory Administrator, noting that you have now changed databases.

11 Choose Import from the Server menu and choose the Local_Users file from your desktop. Click the Import button in the dialog that opens.

You have now copied the users into the network node. Remember, the passwords were not saved when exported, so they were not imported in this step.

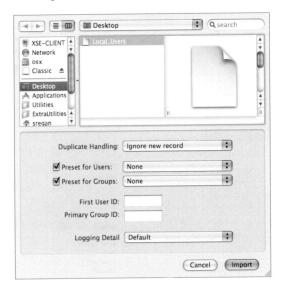

Enable Accounts and Reset User Passwords

To enable the users to log in correctly, you must set the passwords on the accounts you just imported.

1 If necessary, clear the filter on the user list (remove any data that appear in the list and choose Name Contains from the list) to see all the entries.

2   Select all the users, and Command-click John Jacobs and Directory Administrator to deselect those two existing users.

3   Click the Advanced button and choose Open Directory from the User Password Type pop-up menu.

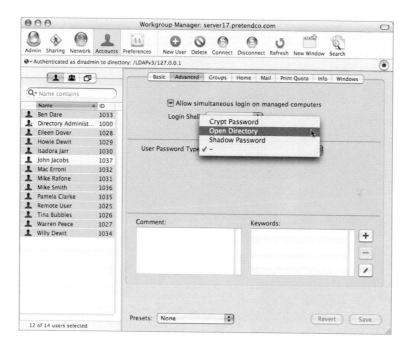

4   In the dialog that appears, enter and verify a new password, *changeme*; click OK to close the dialog; and then click Save.

All the users now have the same password, so you must set them to be changed the next time each user logs in. The Options button now also appears in the Advanced pane when an Open Directory password is being used.

5   Click the Options button and select the following checkboxes:

▶   Allow the user to log in

▶   Allow the user to change the password

▶   Password must be changed at next login

Deselect any other options.

These settings are not realistic because all selected users have the same password. For this book, all passwords are the same (changeme) for ease of use. If you want to have separate passwords for each user, feel free to do so, but write them down so you will not forget them.

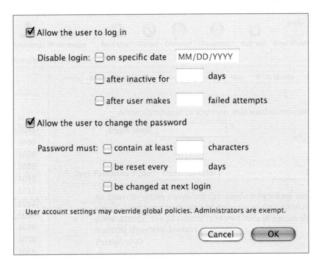

NOTE ▶ If you get an error when attempting to save the password policies, click the Basic tab, reset the selected users' passwords, and save that change. Then go back and set the password policies.

7   Click Save.

You have successfully repopulated the directory node. There are now two sets of user accounts on this server, Local and Network. This situation could cause confusion if users log in without binding to the LDAP directory.

Clean Up the Local Directory Node

Once you have migrated the user list, it's good practice to remove the duplicate entries in the local node. Open Directory uses the first instance of the user name it finds, which may result in users logging in to the wrong account.

1   In Workgroup Manager, click the small globe icon on the left, beneath the toolbar, to display the Directory Node pop-up menu. Choose Local and authenticate as necessary.

2   Select the list of users you exported, taking care not to delete the sadmin or remote user accounts, and click the Delete button.

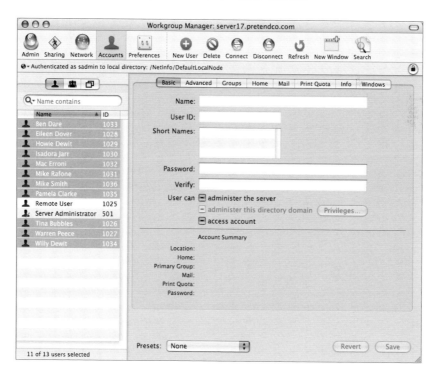

3   Confirm the deletion and quit Workgroup Manager.

4   On your Mac OS X computer, log out as the local Mac OS X administrator and attempt to log in as Mac Erroni with the password changeme. Verify that you need to change the password.

You do not need to complete the login process unless you want to. The fact that you were prompted to change the password is validation of successful operation.

5   Log back in as the Mac OS X administrator.

Single Sign-on and Kerberos

Frequently, a user who is logged in on one computer needs to use resources located on another computer on the network. Users typically browse the network in the Finder and click to connect to the other computer. It would be a nuisance for them to have to enter a password for each connection. If you've deployed Open Directory, you've saved them that trouble. Open Directory provides a feature known as *single sign-on*, which relies on Kerberos. Single sign-on essentially means that when the user logs in, they automatically have access to other services they may need that day, such as email, file servers, VPN connectivity, and others without entering another password.

Kerberos enables you to keep a list of users on a single computer, called the *key distribution center (KDC)*, which is built in to Mac OS X Server once an Open Directory master has been created. When a network user logs in on a Mac OS X v10.2 or later client computer, that computer negotiates with the KDC. If the user provides the correct user name and password, the KDC provides a ticket that enables the user to connect to other servers on the network for the duration of the login session. During that time, the user can access any network service that has been "kerberized" (modified to work with Kerberos) without seeing a password dialog.

Kerberos is one of the components of Open Directory. The reason a user's password is stored in both the Password Server database and the Kerberos principal database is to allow users to authenticate to services that are not kerberized. However, users must enter a password every time they access those services. Open Directory uses Password Server to provide support for those authentication protocols.

Since Kerberos is an open standard, Open Directory on Mac OS X Server can be easily integrated into an existing Kerberos network. You can set up your Mac OS X computers to use an existing KDC for authentication and still use your Mac OS X Server computer as an LDAP server.

One security aspect to using Kerberos is that the tickets are time sensitive. Kerberos requires that the computers on your network be synchronized to within about 5 minutes. Configure your Mac OS X computers and your servers to use the Network Time Protocol (NTP), and synchronize to the same time server so this does not become an issue in preventing you from getting Kerberos tickets.

Backing Up Open Directory Files

You can use the Server Admin application to archive a copy of an Open Directory master directory and authentication data. You can archive a copy of the data while the Open Directory master is in service.

The following files are archived:

▶ LDAP directory database and configuration files

▶ Open Directory Password Server database

▶ Kerberos database and configuration files

▶ Local NetInfo domain and shadow password database

To archive an Open Directory master:

1 Open Server Admin and, in the Computers & Services list, select Open Directory.

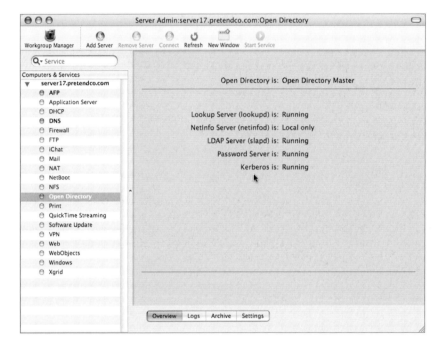

2 Click Archive (at the bottom of the window).

3 Enter the path to the folder where you want the Open Directory data archived, and then click the Archive button.

You can type the folder path or click the Browse button (•••) to select it.

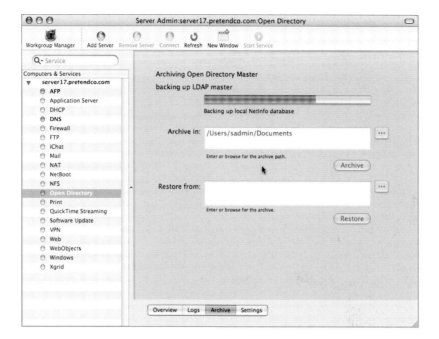

4   Enter a name and password to use in encrypting the archive, and then click OK.

To restore an Open Directory master from an archive:

1   Open Server Admin and, in the Computers & Services list, select Open Directory.

2   Click Archive (at the bottom of the window).

3   Enter the path to the Open Directory archive file, and then click the Restore button.

You can type the path or click the Browse (•••) button to select the archive file.

4   Enter the password to use in decrypting the archive, and then click OK.

> **TIP ▶** Carefully safeguard the backup media that contains a copy of the Open Directory Password database, the Kerberos database, and the Kerberos keytab file. The backup contains passwords of all users who have an Open Directory password, both in the shared LDAP directory and in the local NetInfo directory. Your security precautions for the backup media should be just as stringent as for the Open Directory master server.

> **NOTE ▶** Although you can back up an Open Directory replica, there is no real need to do so. In fact, restoring a replica can be dangerous, because it puts an outdated copy of the master on the network. Since a replica is a copy of the master, the master effectively backs up the replica. If a replica develops a problem, you can just change its role to standalone server. Then set up that server as though it were a brand new server, with a new hostname, and set it up as a replica of the same master as before. Therefore, if you have a reliable backup of the master, you effectively have a backup of all replicas of the master.

Troubleshooting

Because Open Directory includes several services, there are several log files used for tracking status and errors. Fortunately, you can use Server Admin to view status information and logs for Open Directory services. For example, you can use the password-service logs to monitor failed login attempts for suspicious activity, or use the Open Directory logs for all failed authentication attempts, including IP addresses that generate them. Periodically review the logs to determine whether there are numerous failed trials for the same password ID, indicating that somebody might be generating login guesses.

The directory-service error log and the directory-service server log both list which plug-ins loaded successfully and which ones failed. This information is useful when your server is bound to another directory service.

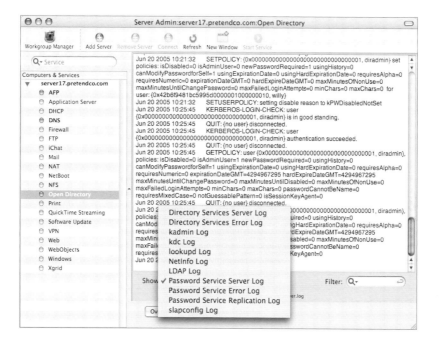

Interpreting log files can be a difficult task, and you may need the help of a more experienced system administrator. In that case, you can email the appropriate log file to the administrator. To find out where in the system the log file is stored, choose the log file from the Show pop-up menu in Server Admin. The path to the log file will be displayed beneath the Show pop-up menu.

Troubleshooting Directory Services

If Mac OS X or Mac OS X Server experiences a startup delay and a message about LDAP or directory services appears above the progress bar, the computer could be trying to access an LDAP directory that is not available on your network.

There are several ways to begin troubleshooting when you are unable to connect to a directory service. These include the following:

▶   Use Directory Access to make sure the LDAP and other configurations are correct.

▶ Use the Network pane of System Preferences to make sure the computer's network location and other network settings are correct.

▶ Inspect the physical network connection for faults.

If you cannot modify the password of a user whose password is authenticated by Open Directory, or if you cannot modify a user account to use Open Directory authentication, one of two things might be wrong:

▶ Check to make sure you are authenticated as that particular directory administrator.

▶ Your administrator user account might not be configured for Open Directory authentication. If you have upgraded from an earlier version of Mac OS X Server, the account might have a crypt password rather than an Open Directory password.

Troubleshooting Kerberos

When a user or service that uses Kerberos experiences authentication failures, try these techniques:

▶ Ensure that DNS is resolving addresses correctly. This is especially important at the time you are promoting a server to Open Directory master. If the DNS does not resolve addresses correctly, the incorrect address will be written to the Kerberos configuration files. Kerberos tickets will not be usable.

▶ Kerberos authentication is based on encrypted timestamps. If there's more than a 5-minute difference between the KDC, client, and service computers, authentication may fail. Make sure that the clocks for all computers are synchronized using the NTP service of Mac OS X Server or another network time server.

▶ Make sure that Kerberos authentication is enabled for the service in question.

▶ If a Kerberos server used for password validation is not available, reset the Open Directory master to use a server that is available.

▶ Make sure that the server providing the kerberized service has access to directories containing accounts for users who are authenticated using Kerberos. One way to do this is to use a shared directory on the KDC server that hosts the user records.

▶ Refer to the password service and password error logs for information that can help you solve problems. You can sometimes detect incorrect setup information, such as wrong configuration filenames, using the logs.

▶ View the user's Kerberos ticket. The Kerberos tickets are visible in the Kerberos application, which is found in /System/Library/CoreServices.

▶ If Kerberos tickets are being granted but the user is still experiencing authentication errors, Kerberos's keytab file on the server may contain duplicate sets of keys.

What You've Learned

▶ Directory services centralize system and network administration, and simplify a user's experience on the network.

▶ Open Directory is Apple's extensible directory-services architecture.

▶ Directories store information in a specialized database that is optimized to handle a great many requests for information and to find and retrieve information quickly. Information may be stored in one directory or in several related directories.

▶ Open Directory uses the LDAP standard to provide a common language for directory access, enabling you to maintain information in a single location on the network rather than on each computer.

▶ The Open Directory pane of Server Admin lets you configure how a Mac OS X server works with directory information.

▶ Workgroup Manager enables you to create both local and network user accounts.

▶ Directory Access is the primary application for setting up a Mac OS X computer's connections with directories and exists on both Mac OS X and Mac OS X Server.

References

The following documents provide more information about installing Mac OS X Server. (All of these and more are available at www.apple.com/server/documentation.)

Administration Guides

Mac OS X Server Getting Started (http://images.apple.com/server/pdfs/Getting_Started_v10.4.pdf)

Upgrading and Migrating to Mac OS X Server v10.4 Tiger (http://images.apple.com/server/pdfs/Migration_v10.4.pdf)

Open Directory Administration (http://images.apple.com/server/pdfs/Open_Directory_v10.4.pdf)

User Management (http://images.apple.com/server/pdfs/User_Management_Admin_v10.4.pdf)

Mac OS X Server Command-Line Administration (http://images.apple.com/server/pdfs/Command_Line_v10.4.pdf)

Apple Knowledge Base Documents

You can check for new and updated Knowledge Base documents at www.apple.com/support.

LDAP

Document 107242, "Mac OS X Server: How to Get More Than 500 Returns From LDAP Server"

Authentication

Document 107543, "Mac OS X Server 10.2, 10.3: Password authentication options for networked environments"

Document 107875, "Mac OS X Server 10.3: Upgrading Password Server users to Kerberos and single sign-on"

Kerberos

Document 107702, "Mac OS X Server 10.3: Kerberos authentication may not work after changing to LDAP master or replica, or Kerberizing a particular service"

Books

Carter, Gerald. *LDAP System Administration* (O'Reilly, 2003).

Bartosh, Michael, and Haas, Jason. *Essential Mac OS X Panther Server Administration* (O'Reilly, 2005).

Garman, Jason. *Kerberos: The Definitive Guide* (O'Reilly, 2003).

URLs

Massachusetts Institute of Technology Kerberos release: http://web.mit.edu/kerberos/www

The Moron's Guide to Kerberos, Version 1.2.2: http://gost.isi.edu/brian/security/kerberos.html

Designing an Authentication System: a Dialogue in Four Scenes: http://web.mit.edu/kerberos/www/dialogue.html

Review Quiz

1. What is the main function of directory services?

2. What standard is used for data storage with Open Directory? What version and level of support is provided for this standard?

3. How can network administrators automatically configure clients with Open Directory configurations?

Answers

1. Directory services provide a central repository for information about the systems, applications, and users in an organization.

2. Open Directory uses the Lightweight Directory Access Protocol (LDAP) standard to provide a common language for directory access. Full read and write support for LDAP is provided with Mac OS X Server.

3. System administrators can use DHCP to dynamically assign IP addresses as well as provide computers with the settings on where to find DNS and LDAP servers on the local network. Armed with these settings, clients can then place requests for directory services to the correct authority.

7

Lesson Files   printme.txt (/Users/Shared/Student_Materials/Lesson7/)

Time   This lesson takes approximately 1 hour to complete.

Goals   Use Server Admin to configure print service on Mac OS X Server

Use Server Admin to share printers over AppleTalk, LPR, IPP, or SMB

Use Server Admin and Workgroup Manager to enable user print quotas on printer queues

Use Server Admin to monitor print jobs for a given queue

Lesson 7
Understanding Print Service

This lesson provides an overview of print service in Mac OS X Server. You will learn how to configure your server to access a printer on the network or on its Universal Serial Bus (USB) port and how to share it as a queue to client computers. You will see how to use the Print pane in Server Admin to manage and monitor printing. Then you'll read about some special features—including printer pools and print quotas—that can make printer management easier. Finally, you will become familiar with print server problems and how to correct them.

Common UNIX Printing System (CUPS) handles print service in Mac OS X Server v10.4, and all print management that you do with the Printer Setup Utility and Server Admin can also be done using the command line.

Print Service Overview

Network environments create many printing challenges for network administrators. In shared printing environments where no one is responsible for managing printers, each user becomes the administrator for each printer he or she uses. Even in cases where a central person is responsible for maintaining printers, there is no guarantee that person will be aware of printer issues as they arise, since different printing protocols provide varying levels of error reporting. Also, printer protocols that support one client may not support other clients on the network. If printers are available to everyone on the network, it may be difficult to prioritize print jobs so that the most important ones print first. Finally, network administrators often want to limit, or at least monitor, the number of pages users are printing so that supplies aren't wasted.

Mac OS X Server provides a server-based print service that enables you to administer printing using Server Admin. Print service offers several features that you and your users don't get with simple network-printer sharing:

▶ You can monitor print jobs and error conditions on the server.

▶ You can hold or delete print jobs before they reach the printer.

▶ You can set page quotas for individual users on specific print queues.

▶ You can administer printers remotely using Server Admin.

▶ Users are less likely to lose their print jobs when they shut down or disconnect their computers.

To use print service, you set up print queues on your server. Users print to these queues instead of directly to printers. When a user prints a document, the print job moves quickly from the queue on the user's computer to the queue on the server. All management of the printing process takes place on the server itself.

Configuring Print Service

Before you set up print queues, consider what kind of client computers your users have and which protocols those computers use to submit print jobs. Server Admin permits the creation of queues with the following protocols:

▶ Line Printer Daemon (LPR): For printing from UNIX computers, Macintosh computers running Mac OS 8.1 or later, and Windows computers running Windows 2000 and Windows NT

▶ Server Message Block (SMB): For printing mainly from Windows computers, although SMB printing is supported under Mac OS X

▶ AppleTalk: For printing from Macintosh computers

▶ Internet Printing Protocol (IPP): For printing from Macintosh, Windows, and UNIX computers

After planning out the supported print environment, use Server Admin to create the individual print queues and set overall printer settings, such as the default queue or logging level. Optionally you can set print quotas on a per-user basis. While Server Admin is used for configuring most Mac OS X Server print service features, Workgroup Manager is used for configuring print quotas for specific user accounts. (Because print quotas are user-based, it is Workgroup Manager, not Server Admin, that is used.) As a final step, use Server Admin to start print service on the server. Once Mac OS X Server is fully configured for print service, you can then configure users' computers for individual printing.

Creating Print Queues

You create a print queue using the Print pane of Server Admin:

1 Click Settings, click Queues, and then click the Add (+) button.

2 Choose the printer's protocol from the pop-up menu in the Configuration sheet.

The protocol you use to access the printer from the server can be different from the protocol you use subsequently to share the queue with client computers. Print service can access a network printer that is using AppleTalk, LPR, or Open Directory. Once you create the queue in the Print pane, you can then share it using any combination of AppleTalk, IPP, LPR, or SMB.

The next few steps depend on the printer's protocol:

▶ For an AppleTalk or Open Directory printer, you select the printer from a list of network printers.

▶ For an LPR printer, you type the printer IP address or DNS name. You can either use the default queue or deselect "Use default queue on server" and type a queue name.

You can also use print service to share a USB printer that is connected directly to the server. In this case, you don't have to create a queue—it appears automatically when the server detects the printer.

> **NOTE ▶** Print service in Mac OS X Server v10.4 supports both PostScript and raster printers.

Sharing a Print Queue

Once you create a queue, you will see the Editing pane for that queue. In the Sharing Name field, type the queue name you want clients to see. For maximum compatibility with all printing protocols, use queue names without spaces, periods, or other nonalphanumeric characters.

Queue names shared via LPR or SMB must use the following characters only: A to Z, a to z, 0 to 9, and _ (underscore). Note that the queue name is encoded according to the language used on the server and might not be readable on client computers using another language. AppleTalk queue names cannot be longer than 32 bytes (which may be fewer than 32 typed characters). Printer Setup Utility won't let you create a queue name longer than that, so this is an issue only if you're creating the queue name from the command-line interface (CLI) or CUPS web interface. And if the client computer is running Windows NT 4.x, make sure the queue name contains only letters and numbers; do not use an IP address as the queue name.

> **NOTE ▶** If you change the print queue name on the server, print jobs that users send to the old queue name will not print. Users must delete the queue and then add it again using the new queue name.

Next, select the protocols to be used for sharing this queue. The protocols available for sharing the print queue are AppleTalk, IPP, LPR, and SMB.

NOTE ▸ If you select SMB, make sure you start Windows services, too.

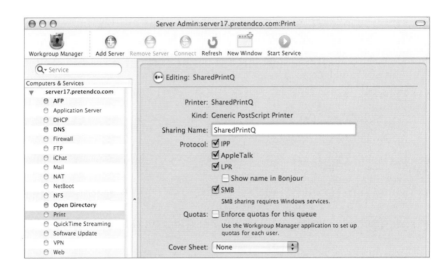

NOTE ▸ Don't confuse the protocols available for *creating* a print queue with the protocols available for *sharing* a print queue. You can create print queues for printers found via AppleTalk, LPR, Open Directory, and USB. Once the print queue is created, you can share it to clients via AppleTalk, IPP, LPR, and SMB.

If you prefer to have a cover sheet printed with each print job for this queue, select the appropriate cover sheet from the Cover Sheet pop-up menu. To complete configuration of this print queue, click Save.

Creating a Printer Pool

Ordinarily each print-service queue you set up is assigned to a single printer. But single-printer queues can cause administrative problems. The printer can become a bottleneck when many users try to print at the same time, and if a printer becomes unavailable, the jobs remain in the queue. The kind of the printer pool is determined by the first printer added.

You can avoid these problems by using a special queue called a *printer pool* (also called a *printer class*), a queue with more than one printer assigned to it. A printer pool offers two main advantages over single-printer queues:

▶ Print jobs are assigned to the next available printer in the pool, so you can have as many jobs printing simultaneously as you have printers assigned to the pool.

▶ If a printer assigned to the pool becomes unavailable, the other printers in the pool continue to print waiting jobs.

To configure a printer pool:

1 Select the printers you want to include in the pool from the main Queue window and click the Create Printer Pool button.

2 When prompted, enter a name for the new printer pool.

3 As with setting up individual printers, select the desired protocols for accessing the printer pool, and whether a cover sheet is desired.

When creating a printer pool, plan ahead. All printers in a pool should be similar enough that the same formatting works on all printers. After you create the printer pool, you can manage the resulting pool queue as you would any other print queue.

> **NOTE ▶** The kind of printer pool is determined by the first printer added. All printers in the pool should be the same model.

Adjusting General Service Settings

You can use print service's General settings in Server Admin to specify a default LPR queue for the server. Setting a default LPR queue makes it easier for LPR clients to print without knowing the names of the queues on the server. A user can choose "Use default queue on server" when adding the printer.

Along with setting a default LPR queue, you should configure the logging options desired for print service. The Logging pane enables you to archive logs on a regular basis, after they've reached a certain maximum log size (which, with CUPS, is twice the maximum log size setting). You can also select the amount of logging detail to be logged. However, the more detailed the logging, the quicker the logs will fill and need rotating.

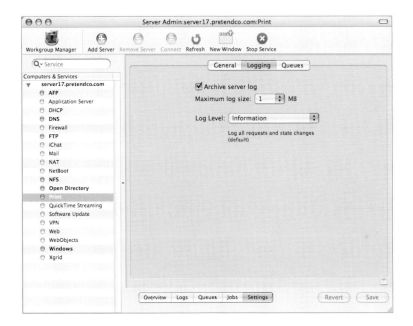

Enabling Quotas for Print Queues

Sometimes users abuse their printing privileges. A user could monopolize a printer so that others cannot use it or could print an unreasonable number of pages, using up supplies and shortening the life of the printer. The print service enables you to control printer usage with a *print quota,* the total number of pages that can be printed during a specified time period. You can establish print quotas per user and per printer. For example, if you set a per-user quota, once a user has printed the specified number of pages, he or she cannot print again until the quota period ends, regardless of the print queue, and the quota is automatically renewed (or until you explicitly renew the quota, which you can do at any time). You can have separate quotas per queue, and not set for all printers. Regardless of the quota version you choose, you set these per user in Workgroup Manager.

Print quotas are most effective when users log in using network user accounts. Network user accounts are covered in Lesson 6, "Using Open Directory."

To configure quotas, you use both Workgroup Manager and Server Admin. Use Server Admin to enable quotas on a queue:

1   In the Print pane, click Settings, and then click Queues.

2   Double-click the queue or click the Edit (pencil) button.

3   From the Editing pane, select "Enforce quotas for this queue."

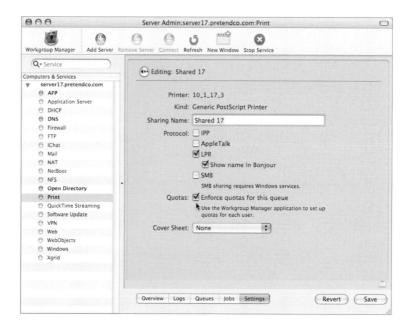

Configuring Print Quotas for User Accounts

Once you set quotas for specific print queues, use Workgroup Manager to configure quotas for individual users:

1   Click the Users button, select a user, and then click Print Quota.

2   In the Print Quota pane, select All Queues or Per Queue to create a single quota that covers all printers or individual quotas, respectively, for each printer.

   If you select All Queues, you must enter the number of pages allowed and the number of days in the quota period. If you select Per Queue, you must also specify the name or IP address of the print server and the name of the queue on that server.

3   If you choose the Per Queue option, after selecting the specific queue, select the specific quota setting for that queue.

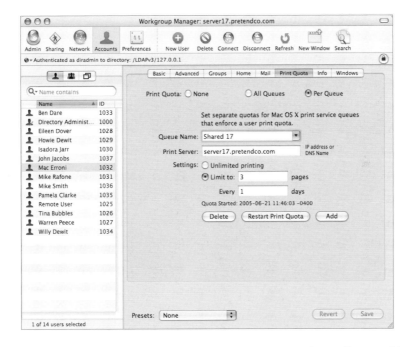

Once the server is fully configured, click Start Service in the toolbar. At this point, you can configure client computers for individual access. Users can browse for a print queue you have shared from Mac OS X Server based on the queue's configuration.

Configuring Client Computers

When you create an LPR print queue, print service announces its presence via Bonjour. If your print queue is shared over AppleTalk, Name Binding Protocol (NBP) allows Mac OS 9 users to see the queue in the Chooser. Queues shared over SMB will show up in the Windows Network Neighborhood using the standard NetBIOS method. Since Samba is responsible for registering your printer, make sure you have configured the correct workgroup name and WINS server in the Windows pane of Server Admin.

IPP is a relatively new printing protocol and is supported on Mac OS X v10.2 and later, Windows ME/2000/XP, and UNIX (Linux, Solaris, HP-UX, IRIX, and AIX).

Configure Client Computers

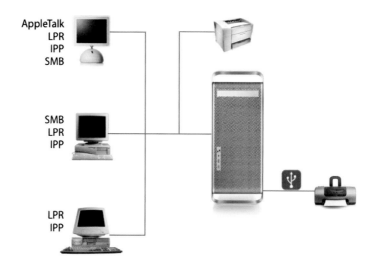

Configuring Printers With Server Admin

In this section, you will configure a bogus print queue (it doesn't actually print to a printer) and use Server Admin to share this print queue. The print queue will be an LPR queue, but you'll see how to make it available through other protocols, such as AppleTalk as well as how easy it is to browse for shared print queues when you use Bonjour.

Create and Configure a Print Queue

Use Server Admin to create and configure a print queue:

1   On your Mac OS X computer, open Server Admin, authenticate if necessary, and connect to your server.

2   In the Computers & Services list, select Print, click the Settings button, and click the Queues button at the top of the window.

The Queues pane appears.

3   Click the Add (+) button to add a new queue.

4   In the dialog that appears, choose LPR from the "Specify a printer to use
    with the new queue" pop-up menu, enter *10.1.17.3* in the "Printer's
    address" field, and click OK.

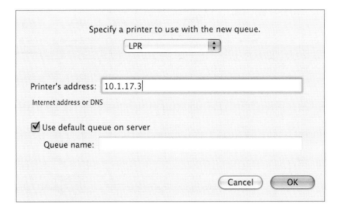

5   In the editing pane, enter *Shared 17* as the sharing name for the new
    queue, select the LPR checkbox to enable sharing the print queue via
    LPR, and select the "Show name in Bonjour" checkbox.

6 Click Save.

7 If necessary, click the back button to return to the Queues pane.

8 Click the Queues button at the bottom of the window to open the Queues list.

Once you create the printer, it may take a short while, but the printer will appear in the Queues list.

9 Click the Start Service button.

You have now created a new print queue and started the print service. It is now time to create a printer on the computer and test the print queue.

Create a Printer on a Mac OS X Computer

Follow these steps to add a new printer and print to it using Printer Setup Utility:

1   On your Mac OS X computer, open Printer Setup Utility, located in
/Applications/Utilities.

2   Click the Add button in the toolbar to add a new printer.

By default, Printer Setup Utility searches for printers using Bonjour. Your print
server will show up in the Printer list with the queue name you gave it earlier.

3   Select the Shared 17 queue and click the Add button at the bottom of the
window.

That print queue is added to the list.

4   Quit Printer Setup Utility.

Test the Print Queue

Now that you've added the print queue to your Mac OS X computer, you'll use TextEdit to test it.

1   On the Mac OS X computer, double-click the printme.txt file located in /Users/Shared/Student_Materials/Lesson7.

The TextEdit application will open the file.

2   Choose File > Print. In the Print dialog, click Print to print the document to the printer you just added in Printer Setup Utility.

3   Switch to the Server Admin tool and click the Jobs button.

The job appears in the list in the Jobs pane of Server Admin. Because there is no actual printer associated with IP address 10.1.17.3, all jobs pause in the queue.

4 Select the print job in the jobs list and click the Delete (–) button to delete it from the queue.

5 Quit TextEdit.

SMB and Authorization

As of Mac OS X Server v10.3, print service automatically enforces authentication on queues shared over SMB. This feature is useful for preventing unauthorized users from using a particular printer and is consistent with the user experience that a Windows server provides.

To add an SMB printer:

1 Select a workgroup from an SMB browse list, then select a server.

An authentication dialog appears.

2 After logging in, select a printer and click Add.

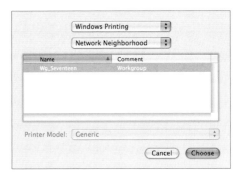

Managing Print Service

Once you have created print queues and shared them, you can use Server Admin to manage them. Sometimes you may need to put a hold on an entire queue, so that you can take a printer offline temporarily but still allow jobs to queue up. Other times, you might need to stop or delete certain print jobs in a queue but allow other jobs to print. You use the Queues pane and the Jobs pane, respectively, for those tasks.

Managing Print Queues

The Queues pane provides a summary of information about each queue, including the number of jobs inside that queue and the status of the queue itself. To see the Queues pane, click the Queues button at the bottom of the Print service window. You can stop the queue by selecting the queue and clicking the Stop button (the square icon). To restart the queue, click the Start button (the triangle icon).

Managing Print Jobs

To see the individual jobs in a queue, click the Jobs button and choose the queue from the "Jobs on the Queue" pop-up menu. For each job, the Queue Status list shows the user who printed it and the name of the document.

> **NOTE ▶** The print server is dependent on the client to send the names of the document and the user. If your print client doesn't embed this information in the print job, the print server can't display it for you.

You can put a job on hold by selecting the job and clicking the Pause button (the two vertical lines) at the bottom of the screen; release the hold by clicking the Start button (the solid triangle). To delete a job, click the Delete (–) button.

Monitoring Print Service

If you're an effective administrator, you probably do more than just watch jobs go through the print queue. The Queues and Jobs panes show a lot of useful information about which users are printing what, but the print log files are the real sources of historical information. To see the logs, select Print from the Computers & Services list, click Logs, and then select Print Service Log or an individual queue's log from the Show pop-up menu.

Log messages for the print service are available through the CUPS logs. Access and error logs are found in /var/log/cups.

Like Mac OS X, Mac OS X Server uses the CUPS daemon, cupsd, to prepare print jobs for a printer. A new feature of Mac OS X Server v10.4 is that you can view the CUPS logs directly in Server Admin instead of having to locate them yourself in the Mac OS X file system.

As stated earlier, you can configure print service to archive the print service logs after they reach a maximum size. This practice ensures that the current logs are a manageable size.

Controlling User Access

Controlling access to your printers does not hide your printers from the clients on the network. The printers are still on the network, as they would be without print service. Some users might bypass print service by adding a network printer directly. This is possible if a client computer has the proper drivers to support the network printer and if the user has network access to the printer. If this happens, the administrator is unable to use Mac OS X Server to monitor printer usage centrally.

Make sure that when users add the queue to the printer list on their client computers using Printer Setup Utility, they access the queue from your server. Tell them which protocol to select (AppleTalk, IPP, LPR, or SMB) and the name of the queue to add. As an additional security measure, the print server can be configured with a second isolated network where the network printer resides. This would ensure the printer is accessible only by using the configured print queue on the server.

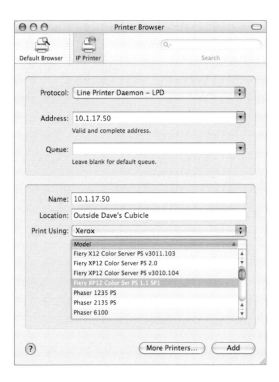

Troubleshooting Print Service

For all print-service troubleshooting, the logs are an invaluable resource. For specific problems, here are some troubleshooting tips:

▶   If print service does not start, check the print-service log for error messages that were generated at the time you tried to start the service.

▶   If users cannot add a queue:

- Verify that the network settings on the client and server computers are correct. Use Network Utility to verify that the computers can communicate.

- Make sure print service is running and verify that the queue is using the correct sharing protocol for that client.

- Make sure the queue name is compatible with any naming restrictions imposed by the client computer. (For details on queue names, see the "Sharing a Print Queue" section, earlier in this lesson.)

▶   If users cannot print to a queue:

- Verify the network settings on the client and server computers.

- Make sure print service is running.

- Make sure the user has added the queue on the client computer.

- If the client computer is running Windows NT 4.x, make sure the queue name contains only letters and numbers, and is not an IP address.

- If you changed the print queue name on the server, tell users to delete the queue and then add it again using the new queue name. Then check the log for the queue.

▶   If jobs in a queue on the server do not print:

- Make sure that neither the queue nor the jobs are on hold. Sometimes large jobs hold up the queue. If you notice a large job that's holding up other jobs, you may want to delete it.

- Confirm that the printer is connected to the network or to the server's USB port.

- Ensure that the printer is turned on, has paper, and is not experiencing a problem such as a paper jam.

- Check the log for that queue.

Monitor Print-Service Activity

Follow these steps to use Server Admin to observe print-server usage as well as usage for individual print queues:

1 On your Mac OS X computer, open Server Admin, authenticate if necessary, and connect to your server.

2 In the Computers & Services list, select Print, then click the Overview button.

The Overview pane displays basic information, such as whether the service is running and how many queues are configured.

3 Click the Logs button.

The Print Service Log shows general print server activity, such as starting and stopping print service, and creating and deleting queues.

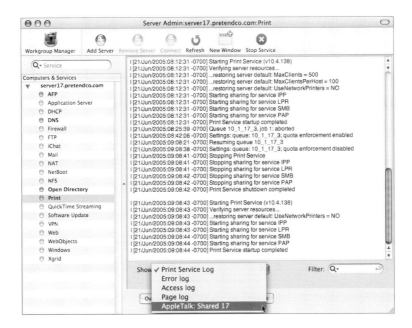

4 At the bottom of the window, choose the log for your queue from the Show pop-up menu.

This log shows activity that is specific to this queue, such as each job's page count and which user submitted it.

5 Click the Jobs button, select any print jobs you currently have, and delete them using the Delete (–) button.

What You've Learned

▶ Print service on Mac OS X Server provides features that simple printer sharing does not provide.

▶ Print service can share print queues using the following printing protocols:

- LPR
- IPP
- SMB
- AppleTalk

▶ You use Workgroup Manager to set specific user print quotas. You use Server Admin to:

- Create and share print queues

- Manage print queues and jobs

- Turn on quotas for a print queue

- View print logs

▶ Windows users must authenticate to the Mac OS X Server print service, as they do with Windows servers.

▶ You can configure printer pools with multiple printers, for availability and volume.

▶ Some users on your network might attempt to bypass the print service features, although you can design your network to prevent this.

References

The following documents provide more information about installing Mac OS X Server. (All of these and more are available at www.apple.com/server/documentation).

Administration Guides

Mac OS X Server Getting Started (http://images.apple.com/server/pdfs/Getting_Started_v10.4.pdf)

Print Service Administration (http://images.apple.com/server/pdfs/Print_Service_v10.4.pdf)

Windows Service Administration (http://images.apple.com/server/pdfs/Windows_Services_v10.4.pdf)

User Management (http://images.apple.com/server/pdfs/User_Management_Admin_v10.4.pdf)

Mac OS X Server Command-Line Administration (http://images.apple.com/server/pdfs/Command_Line_v10.4.pdf)

Apple Knowledge Base Documents

You can check for new and updated Knowledge Base documents at www.apple.com/support.

Books

Bartosh, Michael, and Haas, Jason. *Essential Mac OS X Panther Server Administration* (O'Reilly, 2005).

Regan, Schoun, and White, Kevin. *Mac OS X Server 10.4 Tiger: Visual QuickPro Guide* (Peachpit Press, 2005).

Sweet, Michael. *CUPS Common UNIX Printing System* (SAMS, 2001).

URLs

Common UNIX Printing System: www.cups.org

Apple Developer Documentation: http://developer.apple.com/printing

Review Quiz

1. What types of clients can print via Mac OS X Server, and what are their native printing protocols?

2. Where do you create new print queues?

3. What are the advantages of using print queues compared to having users print directly to printers?

Answers

1. Mac OS (AppleTalk and LPR), Mac OS X (LPR, IPP, and AppleTalk), Windows (SMB, LPR, and IPP), and UNIX (LPR and IPP)

2. The Queues pane of the Print pane of Server Admin. A printer set up with Printer Setup Utility also shows up as a queue available for sharing.

3. You can monitor print jobs and error conditions on the server, hold or delete print jobs before they reach the printer, set page quotas for individual users on specific print queues, and administer printers remotely using Server Admin. Plus, your users are less likely to interrupt their print jobs when they shut down or disconnect their computers.

8

Lesson Files	None
Time	This lesson takes approximately 3 hours to complete.
Goals	Configure Mac OS X Server to control access to files and provide services based on user and group accounts
	Configure Mac OS X Server file services for Macintosh and Windows clients
	Configure Mac OS X Server to share files with Macintosh, Windows, and UNIX clients
	Configure Mac OS X Server to provide file services to FTP clients
	Troubleshoot file services on Mac OS X Server
	Configure Mac OS X Server to provide dynamic automounts

Lesson **8**

Using File Services

This lesson addresses the topic of using Mac OS X Server to share files across a network. It begins by exploring the challenges associated with file sharing and the issues to consider when setting up file sharing. The main focus of the lesson covers setting up share points with appropriate access settings, and configuring the specific sharing protocols that Mac OS X Server will use. This lesson also addresses network mounts and general file-sharing troubleshooting issues to consider when enabling file services on Mac OS X Server.

Mac OS X Server has many different ways to manage share points and permissions. This lesson takes you through using Server Admin and Workgroup Manager to manage file sharing.

Challenges of File Sharing

When setting up file services, there are a number of issues to consider. The obvious issues are what types of clients will be accessing your file server, what protocols they will be using, and what access levels they will need.

At first glance, these questions might seem relatively easy to answer, but the true requirements can get very complex. For example, a network share point might require access by Windows and Mac users, using their native protocols, where both platforms might be reading and writing to the same files at the same time. In other cases, you might need a complex workflow to be supported, such as in a print production environment, where the traditional UNIX permissions model is not sufficient to support the workflow. In other cases, you might have a large number of users and the challenge is managing their appropriate access over a period of time, as user and departmental needs change.

Historically, Mac OS X Server supported multiple platforms, but the experience may not have been optimal. Whereas Mac OS X Server has implemented the UNIX permissions model, Windows NT servers and later have implemented a much different permissions model based on access control lists (ACLs). Accessing a server from a nonnative client, such as a Windows XP client accessing a Mac OS X v10.3 server, might have led to a confusing interpretation of the permissions available to that user, because the Windows client would have been expecting the more granular permissions model. Mac OS X Server v10.4 addresses this issue and others by including support for new features, such as ACLs, both at the file-system and service levels.

The challenge also lies in the setup of the share points themselves. Careless layout of share points results in a more complex permissions matrix than would have been necessary.

Different Protocols for Different Clients

Mac OS X Server includes a number of ways to share files. The method you select depends largely on the clients you expect to serve (although security is another factor to consider). Mac OS X Server provides the following file-sharing services:

▶ Apple File Service (AFS): AFS, which uses the Apple Filing Protocol (AFP), is useful primarily for sharing files with Macintosh clients, whether they are older Mac OS 9 clients or the latest Mac OS X clients.

▶ File Transfer Protocol (FTP): This file-sharing protocol is lightweight in the sense that it is simple and does not have all the features available in the other file-sharing services in Mac OS X. FTP allows you to transfer files back and forth between client and server, but you cannot, for example, open a document over an FTP connection. The primary benefit of FTP is that it is ubiquitous: It is hard to find a TCP-capable computer that does not support FTP.

▶ Network File System (NFS): NFS is the traditional method of file sharing for UNIX-based computers. NFS has its heritage in research facilities and academia in the 1980s. While it can be very convenient and flexible, it suffers from some security holes that do not affect the other protocols. The primary use for NFS is to provide files to UNIX or Linux computers. Although Mac OS X has a core based on UNIX, you should normally use AFS for Macintosh clients.

▶ Windows file service: This service uses the Server Message Block (SMB) protocol. You may also hear this referred to as the Common Internet File System (CIFS). SMB is the native file-sharing protocol for Windows computers but is also used widely in UNIX environments. Mac OS X Server can appear to be a Windows server, even to the extent that it shows up in the Windows Network Neighborhood just as a Windows server would.

▶ NFS resharing: Imagine a big UNIX-based server that speaks only NFS, and a number of legacy Macintosh clients that speak only AFP. How can they communicate? It would seem that Mac OS X, which is both Macintosh and UNIX based, would be a good translator between the two. And, in fact, it is: Mac OS X Server includes the capability to "reshare" an NFS volume with Apple File Service just as it would share a local drive. This lesson does not teach you how to configure NFS resharing.

You can also share a folder over several different protocols simultaneously.

Planning for File Services

When setting up file services on Mac OS X Server, proper initial planning can save you time in the long run.

Setting Up

Follow these guidelines when you first start planning to implement file services.

Plan Your File-Server Requirements

Determine your organizational requirements. How are your users organized? Is there a logical structure to follow for assigning users to groups that best address workflow needs? What types of computers will be used to access your file server? What share points and folder structures will be needed? How will users interact with one another when accessing these share points? These answers will dictate the file services you configure, as well as how you might organize groups and share points.

> **NOTE** ▶ One of your early considerations is whether to use the new access-control features available in Mac OS X Server v10.4. This decision will dictate how you proceed with setting user and group access rights to share points and folders, as well as how files and folders created over time on your will be shared.

Use Workgroup Manager to Configure Users, Groups, Share Points, and File-System Access

The main goal is to end up with a group structure that best matches your organizational needs and allows easy maintenance over time. Setting up users and groups at the beginning is trivial. Setting up users and groups that continue to work as the organization goes through natural changes over time is not as simple as it first appears. But having a logical group structure that can be used to allow and deny access to your server file system will save you from continually having to adjust file-service access later on. Mac OS X Server v10.4 now supports groups within groups, using groups as owners of a folder, and setting access-control lists on folders. Another improvement in Mac OS X Server v10.4 is that users can be members of more than 16 groups.

> **TIP** ▶ For testing of groups, share points, and ACLs, you do not have to have all users entered. You may decide to test with a skeletal set of users and groups that meet the business requirements of your organization. After verifying the groups and share points, you can then enter or import the full set of users.

Use Server Admin to Configure File Services and Access to File Services, and to Start the Services

Server Admin is the main application you use to configure a specific file service—AFP, FTP, NFS, Windows (SMB/CIFS). You first configure the settings for each service, addressing such options as maximum number of clients, guest access, logging levels, and other service-specific settings. Once the services are configured, set and test appropriate access for users to the specific services. For example, you may have one group of users that needs access from both Windows and Mac clients, while another group is using only Linux clients. For security reasons, you might limit the first group's access to the AFP and Windows services, while limiting the Linux users to NFS or FTP services. Once service access has been properly secured, then you can use Server Admin to start each of the services you will be using and let users start accessing their appropriate file service.

> **NOTE** ▶ Service ACLs should not be confused with file-system ACLs, which were covered in Lesson 5, "Authentication and Authorization." Service ACLs will be covered in depth later in this lesson.

Adjust Settings Over Time and Continually Monitor Your File Server for Signs of Problems

There are several ways to monitor your server services and manually adjust user and group settings:

▶ Use Server Admin to monitor logs and queues for specific services, as well as to fine-tune any service-configuration settings as required.

▶   Use Workgroup Manager to adjust users and groups, as well as to modify any file-service ACLs as needed.

▶   Use other appropriate applications as needed, for either monitoring or securing the server.

Once a server is deployed, you'll need to perform regular maintenance. This includes monitoring service usage to determine if it is addressing the needs of the organization, as well as looking for any security issues or unexpected activity. You might use additional software, such as Console, Terminal, or even third-party security software. As organizations change, use Workgroup Manager and Server Admin to adjust groups, users, and access to file systems and services.

Creating Share Points and Setting Access Permissions

After determining server and user requirements and entering at least a sample set of users and groups that represents the organizational structure, the next step in sharing files is to create your share points. A *share point* is any folder, drive, or partition that you mounted on the server. When you create a share point, you make that item and its contents available to network clients via the specified protocols. This includes deciding what items you want to give access to and organizing the items logically. It requires using your initial planning and knowledge of your users and their needs. You might decide that everything belongs in a single share point and use permissions to control access within that share point, or you might set up a more complex workflow. For example, you could have one share point for your copywriters and a separate share point for the copy editors. Perhaps you would have a third share point where they could both access common items or share files among themselves. Setting up effective share points requires as much knowledge of your users and how they work together as it does the technology of share points.

Remember that Mac OS X Server supports different file-sharing protocols for different clients. When you create a share point in Workgroup Manager, you have the option of sharing it via any combination of AFP, FTP, SMB, or NFS. By default, any new share point is shared via AFP, FTP, and SMB. If you want to share it over NFS, you must explicitly enable that service for that share point. For each protocol, you will want to review the Workgroup Manager settings for items such as allowing guest access, creating a custom share point name, and deciding whether service-specific inheritance is to be configured for that service.

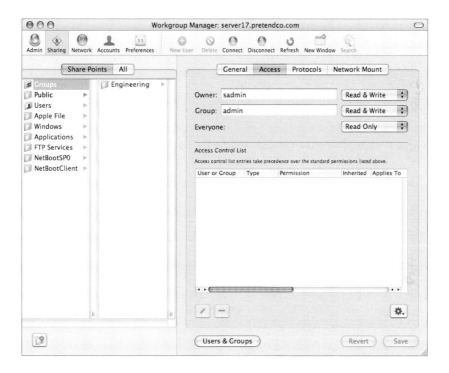

NOTE ▸ If inheritance is applied via file-system ACLs, then the separate inheritance settings, available from Workgroup Manager's Protocols pane for Apple File Service and Windows file service, will not be considered.

Ultimately, how a share point is configured for access, combined with the access settings for each file-sharing service, determine whether users are able to log in via a file-sharing protocol, and if so, what share points they are able to see upon login.

Apple File Service

Apple File Service, which uses the Apple Filing Protocol (AFP), has been the default sharing protocol for Mac OS X and its predecessors for quite some time. As Apple moves forward with an ever widening set of options when dealing with permissions, it is important to understand the basics of POSIX permissions and their role in Mac OS X and Mac OS X Server.

AFP Share Point—POSIX Permissions Versus Inheritance

When determining how to set inheritance with a share point, you will want to first consider whether you will be using ACLs to set access permissions. If so, you should use the inheritance that is associated with ACLs. If you will not be using ACLs to determine access to your share point, you will want to consider the specific options available for either the AFP or SMB sharing protocol.

For example, when configuring a share point with Workgroup Manager, if "Apple File Settings" is chosen in the Protocols pane, you have the ability to use standard POSIX behavior or to inherit permissions from the parent folder for your AFP server. Historically, the inherited model was the only model available in AFP 2.1 and 3.0 (used in AppleShare IP 5.0 through Mac OS X v10.1). In this model, whenever you create a folder on a share point, the new folder inherits the owner, group, and permissions of the parent folder. This is also true if you are copying folders to a mounted server volume or duplicating files on a mounted server volume. However, when you create or copy files on a mounted volume set to use inherited permissions, the group and permissions are inherited from the parent folder, but the owner of the file is the user who created or copied the file.

> **TIP** The inherited permissions model applies only to items when they are created on the mounted volume. If you move an item from one folder to another folder on the same mounted volume, the permissions and ownership of the item do not automatically change.

The other permissions model for new files and folders is the standard POSIX (UNIX) model. This model is available in AFP 3.1, which first appeared in Mac OS X v10.2. In the POSIX model, permissions depend on whether an item is new or a copy of an existing item. When you create a new item on a mounted volume or copy an item to a mounted volume, the new file or folder inherits its group from the enclosing folder, but the owner is always the user who created the file or folder. The difference is that copied files and folders maintain the permissions of the original item. New files and folders have the following predefined permissions:

▶ Owner: read/write

▶ Group: read only

▶ Everyone: read only

This is also known as a umask of 0022. You cannot change these predefined values. Under this model, if you create an item in a folder in which the group has read/write permission, the item will not inherit that permission. If you want to let other group members edit the new item, you must change its permissions manually, using the Finder's Get Info command. Workgroup Manager gives you the option to choose between the POSIX permissions model and the inherited model for each share point shared via AFP.

In the figure below, we are looking at a file with read/write permissions set for the user (owner), group, and others (the first dash indicates a file and then rw- for user, rw- for group, and rw- for others). When this file is placed in an inherited permissions folder with the permissions set as rwx for user, rwx for group, and r-x for others, the file's write access for others is removed because it inherits the permissions of the folder. If that same file is dropped into a folder with POSIX permissions (rwx for user, rwx for group, and r-x for others), that file's final permissions are rw for only the owner, and group and others have read only access. This is due to something called the umask in Mac OS X and Mac OS X Server and has it's roots within UNIX. The default umask is to remove write access to group and others by default, hence the reason here that the file had its write permissions removed regardless of what the folder permissions were.

AFP Share Point—POSIX Permissions Inheritance

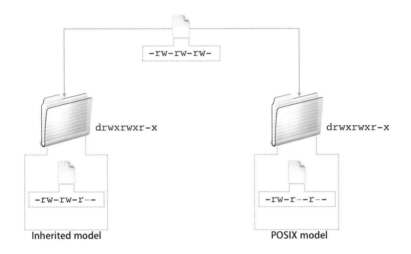

-rw-rw-rw-

drwxrwxr-x   drwxrwxr-x

-rw-rw-r--   -rw-r--r--

Inherited model   POSIX model

NOTE ▶ Setting umask in the Terminal affects only the shell that is currently running. It doesn't have a permanent effect on future shells (unless you change the shell initialization scripts), and it doesn't have any effect on the Finder.

Setting Access to Share Points and Folders

Once you've created a share point and determined the protocols you will use, you can begin to address levels of access within that share point. You need to consider POSIX privileges (ownership and permissions) as well as file-system access permissions (set via ACLs), both of which were discussed in Lesson 5. Previous versions of Mac OS X Server supported POSIX privileges with only a single user and group to define ownership. Mac OS X Server v10.4 adds the ability to have control settings available via ACLs. Using this very flexible system, you can apply access settings to any folder within your share points through inheritance or explicit support.

TIP You do not need to make a folder a share point to set its access level, because Workgroup Manager allows you to browse the file system on your server. Also, you cannot set ACLs via the Finder using the Get Info command, you must use Workgroup Manager.

To configure access settings for share points or folders, use the Access pane when viewing that share point or folder in Workgroup Manager. The standard POSIX settings are listed as Owner, Group, and Everyone in the top half of the pane; access settings using ACLs are set in the bottom half. POSIX privileges are always set for any file or folder in Mac OS X, while access-control settings (via ACLs) can only be set on folders using the Workgroup Manager's interface and not on individual files. To see the result of access-control settings, you can use the Effective Permission Inspector, available from the Action pop-up menu in the lower-right corner of the Access pane.

TIP The best way to validate permissions is by logging in from client computers and testing access from valid user accounts.

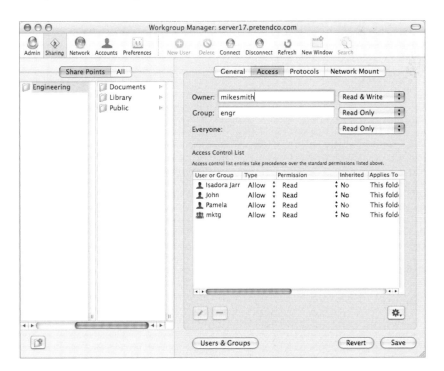

Creating and Enabling Service Access

The General and Access settings you configure in Workgroup Manager are part of the basic configuration steps you need to take regardless of which sharing protocols you decide to use. Although a few additional configuration settings are available from the pop-up menu in the Protocols pane in Workgroup Manager, Server Admin is the main tool for configuring protocol-specific settings.

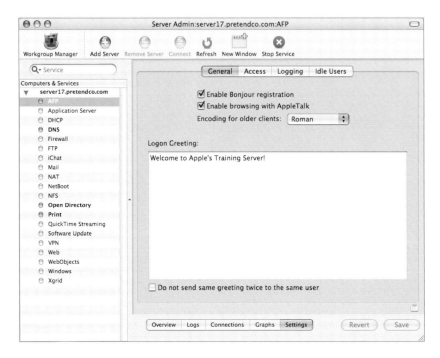

When configuring Apple File Service for Macintosh clients, you must decide how you want clients to find this server. Do you want to require users to type an address when they need to connect, or do you want them to be able to browse and pick the server from a list of servers? Either option may be appropriate, depending on how available you want the server to be.

AFP has two options that enable your clients to browse your server. "Enable browsing with AppleTalk" lets users with Mac OS 9 see your server using the Chooser. On a network that does not support AppleTalk, you can let users browse over IP by selecting "Enable Bonjour registration." This option also enables SLP, if SLP is enabled in the Directory Access application.

The Logon Greeting field lets you specify a message to be displayed when a user connects. The message does not appear when users connect to their home folders.

Controlling Access

AFP gives you the option to use either Kerberos or standard authentication as a method of authenticating users. You can also use SSH (Secure Shell protocol) when the "Enable secure connections" checkbox is selected. If you choose Any Method in the Authentication pop-up menu, AFP will first try to authenticate using Kerberos; if the connection cannot be established using Kerberos or the user cancels the attempted connection with the Kerberos application on his or her computer, it will use standard authentication. This method might cause some confusion for your users if you are not using Kerberos. If this is the case, you should choose Standard from the Authentication pop-up menu.

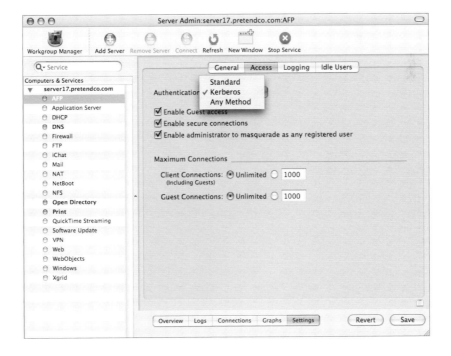

Once the user is authenticated, file permissions control access to the files and folders on your server. One setting deserves to be called out with respect to permissions: the Everyone permissions. When you set Everyone permissions, those permissions apply to everyone who can see the item (either a file or folder) who is not either the owner or part of the default group. You need to understand how Everyone permissions combine with another feature, guest access. As the name implies, guest access lets anyone who can connect to your server use its share points. A user who connects as Guest is given Everyone permissions for file and folder access. If you give read-only access to Everyone on a share point that allows guest access, everyone on your network can see and mount that share point.

If a folder is buried deep within a file hierarchy where guests can't go (because the enclosing folders don't grant access to Everyone), then guests can't use the Finder to browse to that folder. The Everyone permissions apply only to users who have been granted permission to see the enclosing folders but have not been granted permission to see that folder via their user and group settings. If a user knows the full pathname to the enclosed folder, he or she can navigate directly to that folder and view its contents if it has read access, even if the folders enclosing it do not support read access for that user.

Guest access can be very useful, but before you enable it, be sure you understand its implications in your permissions scheme.

Enabling Access

File ACLs control file-system access. Service ACLs control which service a user can access and provide an extra level of control when configuring your server. You can set service ACLs per service or globally for the entire server. It is important to understand the ramifications when enabling ACLs across all services. Therefore, as a cautionary measure, it is best to enable ACLs per service to reduce the amount of confusion for your users.

Logging Activity

Are you concerned that a user is accessing items that he or she should not have access to? Are you getting complaints from your users that their documents are disappearing or that they can't access things they should have access to? For troubleshooting these issues and more, logging is an invaluable resource.

AFP can keep two types of logs: the error log, which is always open by default, and the access log, which you must enable on the server using Server Admin (also used to view the logs). Enable the access log only when needed. Every action taken by a user is logged to this file, so it can become very large very quickly and fill the available space in the file system. Logging all of these events for a busy server with a couple of hundred users can quickly result in a large log file that will be difficult to read through when attempting to diagnose the source of the issue.

Troubleshooting and Monitoring Usage

In addition to the logs, Server Admin gives you graphical information about the current state of your server. You can view the number of connections, which users are currently connected, what protocol they used to connect, and how long they have been connected. In addition, the Graphs pane gives you a historical view of the amount of overall activity that the server has seen recently. You can drag the Graph window out to the Desktop to create a TIFF file of a graph, should you need this for reporting purposes.

Monitoring server usage is a valuable tool to keep track of workflow. You can view graphs and watch for usual traffic patterns, usage spikes, and low usage periods that you could use to plan backups.

Configuring Apple File Service

You use Workgroup Manager to make a folder on your server computer shared via AFP.

Set Up a Folder for Sharing

Before a folder can be shared via any protocol, you must set it up for sharing.

1   If it has not already been done, log in to the server and use the Finder to create a new folder: /Shared Items/*Apple File Services* (where *Apple File Services* is the name of the new folder in the /Shared Items folder).

    You do not have to be physically located near your server to create share points, as you will see later.

2   If Workgroup Manager is not open on your Mac OS X computer, open it and connect to your server as sadmin.

3 Click the Sharing button in the toolbar and then click the Refresh button
on the toolbar to have Workgroup Manager refresh its view of the server.

4 Click the All button on the left side of the window to navigate the entire
contents of the hard drive. Go to the Apple File Services folder you created
in step 1. Then select the Apple File Services folder and make sure it is
highlighted.

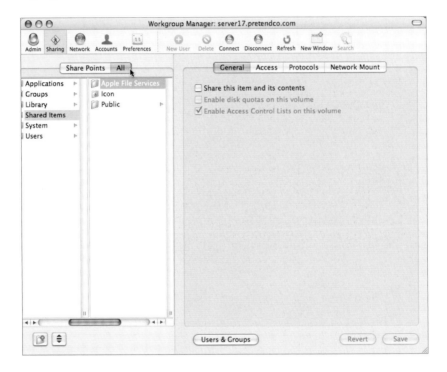

5 In the General pane, select "Share this item and its contents" and
click Save.

This item is now shared. By default, Mac OS X Server v10.4 shares items
over AFP, SMB, and FTP. Since you want this item to be viewable only by
your Macintosh clients, you'll modify the default setting so that the item is
shared only via Apple File Service.

6   Click the Protocols button, and under Apple File Settings make sure that
        "Share this item using AFP" is enabled (it should be enabled by default).

7   From the pop-up menu in the Protocols pane choose Windows File
        Settings, and deselect the "Share this item using SMB" checkbox.

8   From the pop-up menu in the Protocols pane choose FTP Settings, and
        deselect the "Share this item using FTP" checkbox. Click Save.

Now your shared folder named Apple File Services is visible only to Mac clients using AFP.

Configure and Start AFP Service

Since you want to share this folder using AFP, you must configure AFP service with Server Admin and then start the AFP service.

1 On your Mac OS X computer, open Server Admin and authenticate to your server as sadmin. Select the AFP service from the Computers & Services list, and then click the Settings button at the bottom of the window.

2 In the General pane, make sure that "Enable Bonjour registration" and "Enable browsing with AppleTalk" are both selected.

3 Click the Access button, choose Standard from the Authentication pop-up menu, and select the Enable Guest access option. Click Save.

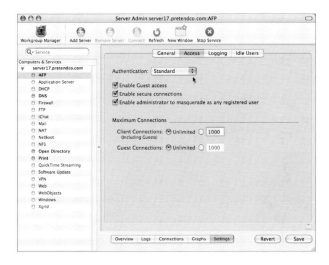

4 AFP should already be running from previous lessons. If it isn't, start it by clicking the Start Service button.

5 On your Mac OS X computer, use Connect to Server to connect to your server at server17.pretendco.com.

6 Connect as a guest user.

7 Select the Apple File Services share point and click OK.

8 Verify that the Apple File Services volume appears on your Mac OS X desktop.

9 Unmount the Apple File Services share point.

Restrict Access to Files

Now that you have shared the Apple File Services folder, modify the permissions to restrict access to the files.

1 On your Mac OS X computer in Workgroup Manager, click the Sharing button in the toolbar and then click the Share Points button on the left side of the window. Navigate to and select the Apple File Services folder.

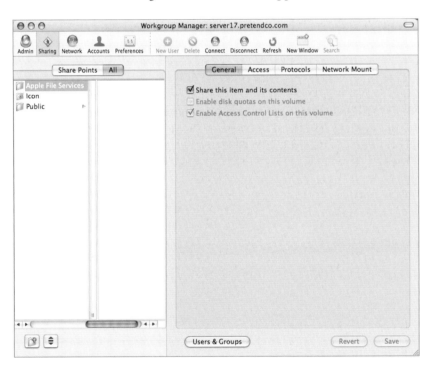

2   Click the New Folder button in the lower-left section of Workgroup Manager to create two folders inside Apple File Services: Press Releases and Tiger Development.

You can create share points using Workgroup Manager without actually going to your server computer.

3   Click the Refresh button on the toolbar to have Workgroup Manager refresh its view of the server.

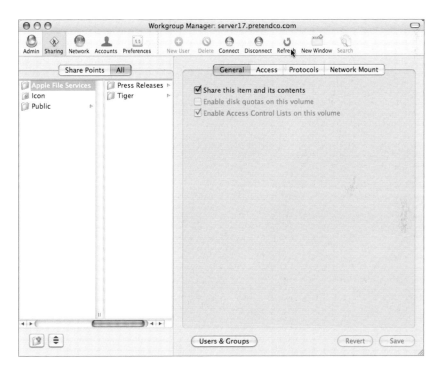

4   Click the Share Points button on the left side of the window, and navigate to the /Apple File Services/Tiger Development folder.

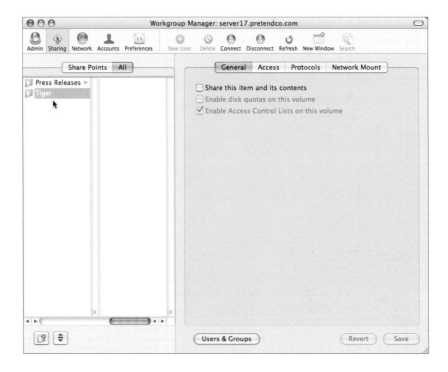

5   In the Access pane, change the permissions as follows:

▶   Owner: ben, Read & Write

▶   Group: admin, Read & Write

▶   Everyone: None

6   Click Save.

Adding Users to the Shared Directory

The Engineering and Marketing groups existed as part of the local network domain. To assign users to groups in a shared network domain, you add them to your server's shared directory.

1   On your Mac O X computer within Workgroup Manager, click the Accounts button and authenticate as needed to the LDAPv3/127.0.0.1 directory.

Before you can create groups in your LDAP directory, you must first delete the groups with the same names from the local directory.

2   Choose Local from the directory pop-up menu.

3   Click the Groups button, and delete the two groups Engineering and Marketing. Click the Refresh button in the toolbar.

You can now add the two groups to the LDAP directory.

4   Choose LDAPv3/127.0.0.1 from the directory pop-up menu.

5   Click the Groups button and add two groups: Engineering (short name: engr) **and** Marketing (short name: mktg).

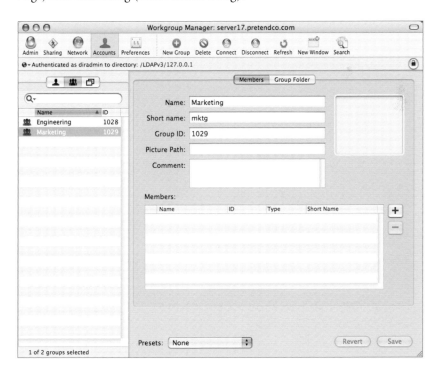

6 Click the Add Group Members (+) button to show the Users & Groups drawer, and add the following users to their respective groups (click Save to save the changes for each group):

▶ To the Engineering group, add Warren Peece.

▶ To the Marketing group, add Warren Peece and Tina Bubbles.

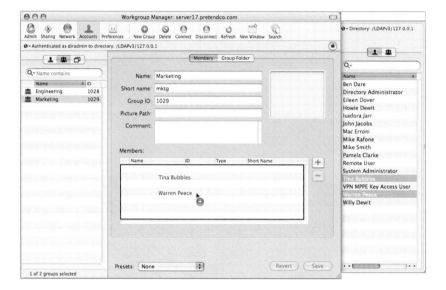

7 Click the Sharing button in the toolbar, and select the Tiger Development folder.

8 Click the Users & Groups button. Then click the Groups button in the drawer and drag the Engineering and Marketing groups to the Access Control List box. Click Save.

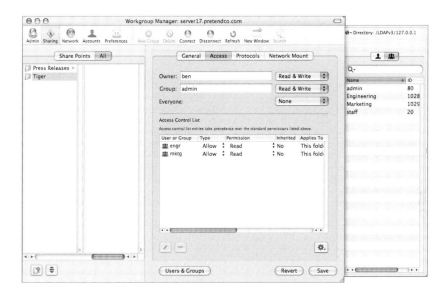

9   In Workgroup Manager, select the Press Releases folder and change the
permissions to the following:

▶   Owner: sadmin, Read & Write

▶   Group: mktg, Read & Write

▶   Everyone: Read Only

10 Click Save.

Restrict Connections to the Server

Now restrict users and groups who can connect through Apple File Protocol to
your server.

1   On your Mac OS X computer, open Server Admin and authenticate if necessary.

2   Select your server (Server17) from the Computers & Services list.

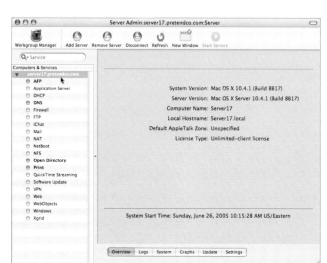

Depending on how you connected to your server with Server Admin, you may see server17.pretendco.com, Server17.local, or 10.1.17.1. Any of these will work.

3   Click Settings, and then click the Access button.

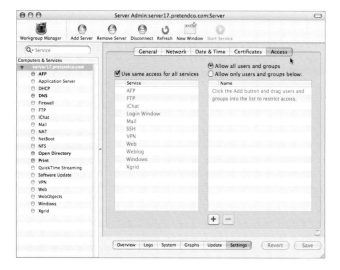

4   Deselect "Use same access for all services" and select AFP from the list.

5   Select "Allow only users and groups below," and click the Add Group Members (+) button.

6   Drag the following users from the Users & Groups drawer:

   ▶ Mike Rafone

   ▶ Tina Bubbles

   ▶ Warren Peece

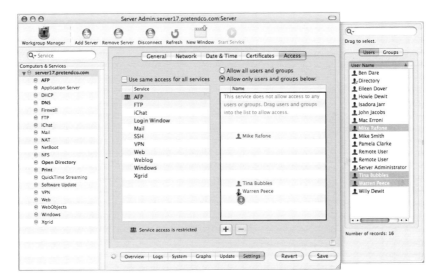

7   Click Save.

8   Using your Mac OS X computer, try to connect to your server as ben, using AFP.

   What happens when you try to connect?

   You cannot connect as ben because ben is not in the approved access list for AFP.

9 Using your Mac OS X computer, connect as Tina (short name: tinabub-bles) and mount the Apple File Services share point.

If you are prompted to set a new password, click OK, then choose Change Password from the Action menu in the Connect to Server dialog. Note which folders you have access to in the mounted share point.

10 Unmount the Apple File Services volume from your Mac OS X computer.

11 Now connect as Warrren (short name: warren) and mount the Apple File Service share point.

Note that Warren has access to the same folders in the mounted share point as Tina.

12 Unmount the Apple File Services volume from your client.

While it can be useful to restrict connections per service/group/user, it will interfere with future exercises in the book.

13 On your Mac OS X computer, open Server Admin and authenticate if necessary.

14 Select your server (Server17) from the Computers & Services list.

Depending on how you connected to your server with Server Admin, you may see server17.pretendco.com, Server17.local, or 10.1.17.1. Any of these will work.

15 Click Settings, and then click the Access button and do the following:

▶ Click the "Allow all users and groups" radio button.

▶ Select the "Use same access for all services" checkbox.

16 Click Save.

17 Choose AFP from the Computers & Services list, and then stop and restart AFP service.

Windows File Service

Mac OS X Server permits you to share files over the SMB protocol. It has some differences with AFP that you must explore. Understanding the fine differences between the two will lead to a better integration when sharing folders.

Windows Share Points

As shown on the next page, when you use Workgroup Manager to configure a share point for use with Windows service (SMB), you have a different set of options as to how new files or folders should behave (these options are ignored if ACLs are configured for the share point):

▶ Inherit permissions from parent: This option means that the new item will have the same permissions as the folder that contains that item.

▶ Assign as follows: This option is the default choice, with the owner receiving read and write access, and Group and Everyone receiving read-only access. The potential issue with the default setting is that users often put a document on the server expecting their coworkers to edit it. With the default settings, this is not possible unless the original author specifically enables read and write access for his or her coworkers. Giving the group read and write access allows this automatically on all new files.

Oplocks are opportunistic locks, a client-side performance enhancement that requires cooperation between the client and server. If a server supports oplocks, the client can cache changes to a file locally and then tell the server that it has written its changes. The server does not let another client write to the file until the first client has finished writing.

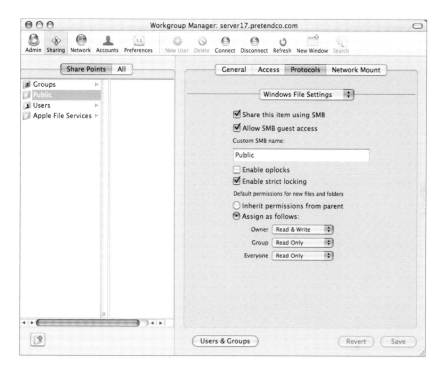

In addition to locking entire files, Windows clients can lock a range of bytes, and Windows servers will honor the lock. Selecting "Enable strict locking" forces the server to treat files with byte-range locks as if the entire file were locked. Choose this option if the volume is being shared over other protocols, such as AFP, so that locked files are not overwritten.

Server Name and Workgroup

The Windows service has a number of configuration options available in Server Admin. Just as Macintosh computers can browse for servers using Bonjour, Windows clients have their own way to find servers on the network, based on a protocol called NetBIOS. The Computer Name field in the

General pane of the Settings pane defines the server's NetBIOS name. It is set automatically, but it is always best to make sure your server's Windows NetBIOS name matches the hostname and the DNS name for your computers. That way, there is no chance for a client computer to get conflicting information if it tries to get the server name using different protocols.

Workgroups are another feature of NetBIOS. The workgroup name is an arbitrary text string used to group servers together. You often see descriptive workgroups, such as MARKETING, RESEARCH, and so on. Your server's Windows service will join whatever workgroup you specify. If you type the name of a workgroup that doesn't exist on your network, your server creates its own workgroup, and Windows computers will see that group.

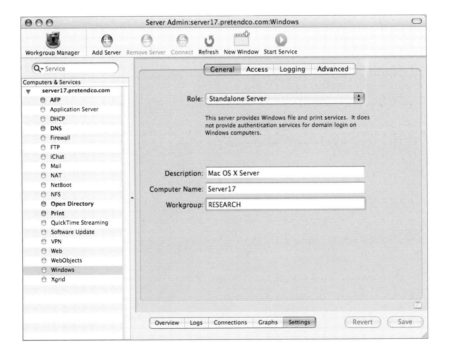

This is also the location where you choose the role of your Windows service on the server. Starting with v10.3, Mac OS X Server can act as a Windows PDC (primary domain controller). Starting with 10.4, Mac OS X Server can act as either a PDC or, now, a BDC (backup domain controller).

Advanced Windows Services

The Advanced pane of the Settings pane lets you set other Windows configuration options:

▶ The Code Page pop-up menu refers to the character set supported by Windows service on this server. The default setting (Latin US) is correct for U.S. English. Other language settings can be chosen from the list.

▶ The Workgroup Master Browser option means your server can become a local master browser. It doesn't mean the server necessarily will be the local master browser, just that it will participate in the election process to determine who will serve as the local master browser.

▶ The Domain Master Browser option is similar to the Workgroup Master Browser, but selecting its checkbox will now result in a possible election between your Domain Master Browser and the Windows Domain Master Browser.

Browsing is a key element of a Windows network. Users can find shared resources on the network by using Network Neighborhood, a Windows utility. A Windows network maintains a list of all the computers connected to it by using central repositories known as *workgroup master browsers* (or simply *master browsers*) and *domain master browsers.*

How do you know whether to select the browser options? You should consult with your Windows administrator. Generally speaking, if you are in a workgroup with a Windows server acting as a domain controller, you should not make Mac OS X Server the domain master browser. In that case, the Windows server is the domain master browser, and adding another domain master browser will result in an election process that the Windows administrator may not want to happen.

▶ Windows Internet Name Service (WINS) is Microsoft's implementation of NetBIOS Name Service (NBNS). WINS resolves NetBIOS names to IP addresses. You can distribute this information using the DHCP service in Mac OS X Server.

How do you know if WINS needs to be configured? Again, you should consult the administrator who is responsible for your Windows computers. Clicking the "Enable WINS server" button makes your Mac OS X Server a WINS server. Selecting "Register with WINS server" allows you to become the client of an existing WINS server by specifying its IP address or name.

▶ Finally, if you want to host home folders for Windows users on your Mac OS X Server, make sure that the "Enable virtual share points" option is selected.

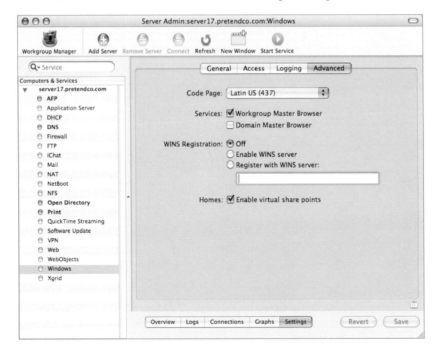

Browsing From a Windows Client

Once you configure your name, your workgroup, and—if necessary—the Advanced settings, Mac OS X Server can be browsed just like any other Windows server on the network. This screen shot shows Mac OS X Server showing up on a small network with no WINS service. A Windows server is creating the Example workgroup, and Mac OS X Server is creating the workgroup named Workgroup.

From a Windows computer, once you have chosen the Mac OS X Server as a share point, the Windows service in Mac OS X Server v10.4 provides support for authentication via the protocols LAN-Manager, NTLM, and NTLMv2 and Kerberos (the last two being one option simultaneously).

Monitoring Activity

Windows service logs are configurable in Server Admin; however, configuration is not quite as flexible as with AFP. Server Admin lets you configure three levels of detail—low, medium, or high—but you can choose a much more verbose level of logging by editing the SMB configuration file directly. Unless you are debugging a particular problem with Windows file sharing, you'll probably want to choose Medium from the Log Detail pop-up menu in the Logging pane. The lower the Log Detail setting, the better you preserve the server's resources.

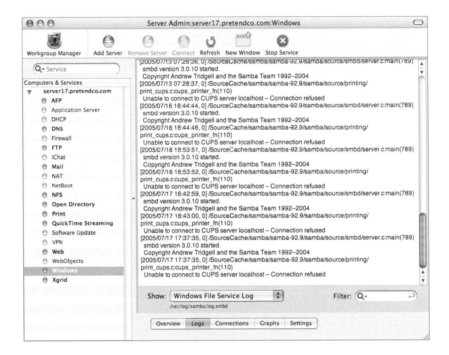

This exercise demonstrates some of the more useful features of Windows file service on Mac OS X Server v10.4. After creating a Windows share point, you will explore the Windows browsing features and browse to your Windows services using the Connect to Server command in Mac OS X.

Configuring Windows File Service

You use Workgroup Manager to share a folder over SMB.

1   On your Mac OS X computer in Workgroup Manager, click the Sharing button in the toolbar, and then click the All button on

the left side of the window. Navigate to and select the Shared Items folder.

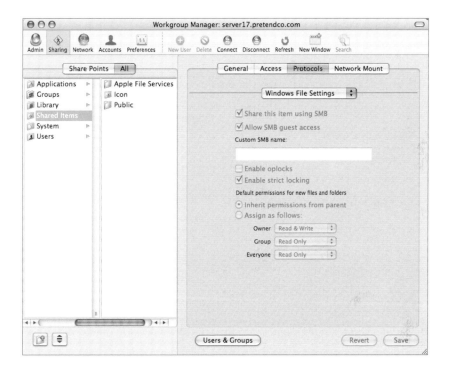

2   Click the New Folder button in the lower-left section of Workgroup Manager to create a folder inside Shared Items called Windows Services.

You can create share points using Workgroup Manager without actually going to your server computer.

3 Click the Refresh button if necessary, and then select the Windows Services folder from the list. Click the General button, select "Share this item and its contents," and click Save.

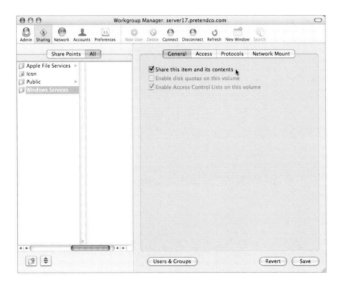

4 Click the Protocols button, and disable AFP and FTP services for this folder.

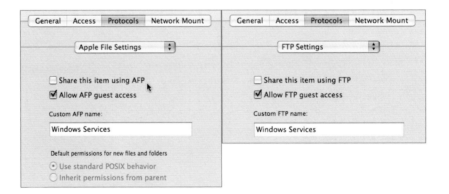

5 From the pop-up menu in the Protocols pane choose Windows File Settings, and in the "Custom SMB name" field type *Windows* and click Save.

All Windows clients will now see a share point called Windows instead of Windows Services.

Configure Access and Start Windows File Service
Now it's time to configure access and start the Windows file service.

1 On your Mac OS X computer, open Server Admin and authenticate if necessary.

2 Select the Windows service in the Computers & Services list, and click the Settings button.

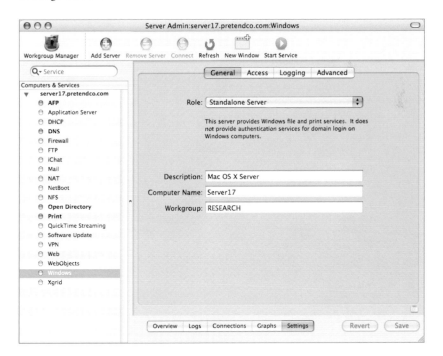

3 In the General pane, enter *server17* in the Computer Name field and *WG_SEVENTEEN* in the Workgroup field.

4 Click the Access button, and select the "Allow Guest access" checkbox.

5 Click the Advanced button. Select "Register with WINS server" from the WINS Registration options, enter *10.1.17.1* in the "Register with WINS server" text box, and click Save.

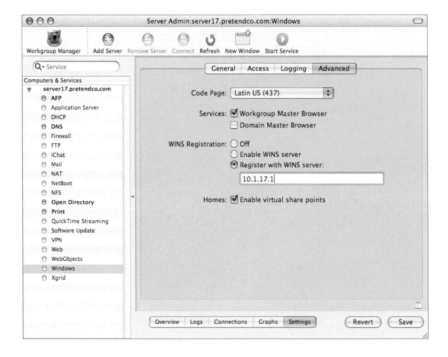

6 Start the Windows service by clicking the Start Service button in the toolbar.

Modify Permissions to Restrict Access

Now that you have shared the Windows Services folder, modify the permissions to restrict access to the files.

1 On your Mac OS X computer in Workgroup Manager, click the Sharing button in the toolbar, and then click the Share Points button on the left side of the window. Navigate to and select the Windows Services folder.

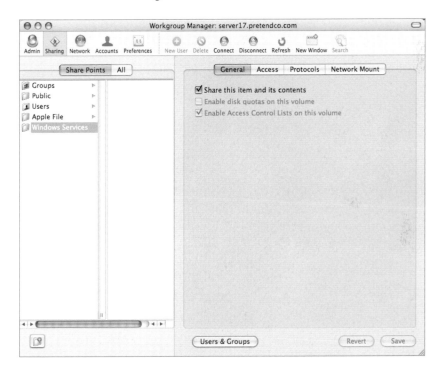

2 Click the New Folder button in the lower-left section of Workgroup Manager to create two folders inside Windows Services: Public and Windows Development.

You can create share points using Workgroup Manager without actually
going to your server computer.

3 Click the Windows Development folder in the Windows Services share
point, click the Access button on the right, and click the Users & Groups
button to open the drawer. Set POSIX permissions as follows.

► Owner: ben, Read & Write

► Group: admin, Read & Write

► Everyone: None

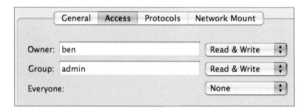

4 Click the Groups button in the drawer, drag the Engineering and
Marketing groups to the Access Control List box, and click Save.

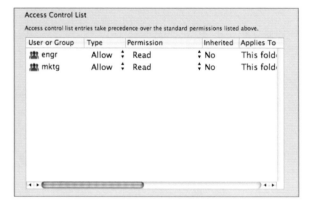

5   In Workgroup Manager, select the Public folder. Change the permissions as follows, and then click Save:

    ▶ Owner: sadmin, Read & Write

    ▶ Group: mktg, Read & Write

    ▶ Everyone: Read & Write

Now you will use the client computer to connect to Windows file service on the server computer over SMB and try to copy some files.

1   On your Mac OS X computer, use the TextEdit application to create a text file. You can enter anything for content.

2   Save the text file on your desktop as mytext.

3   Choose Connect to Server from the Go menu in the Finder, and type the volume address *smb://server17.pretendco.com*.

The SMB/CIFS dialog appears.

4   Choose Windows from the pop-up menu and click OK.

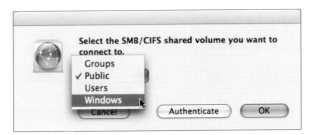

5   Authenticate as needed in this dialog as any valid user and click OK.

6 Copy the mytext file you created from the Mac OS X computer to the mounted network share point Windows Services and into the Public folder.

7 Change the name of the mytext file on your desktop to MyText (notice the case difference).

8 Try to copy this renamed file to the same location on the server as the original file.

> **NOTE ▶** SAMBA (Windows file service) does not currently recognize case sensitivity in files and treats all files the same, regardless of case. Therefore, note that files with the same name but different case structure will get overwritten when using SMB to transfer them.

9 When the server asks you to confirm, click Replace.

10 Unmount your Windows share point from your Mac OS X computer.

NFS Share Point Access

Network File System is considerably different from either AFP or Windows service. The most outstanding difference is that NFS does not support user logins. When you try to connect to Windows or Apple services, the first thing you do is identify yourself with a user name and password. NFS does not give access to users; it gives access to computers. More accurately, it gives access to particular IP addresses. If your computer has one of these IP addresses, NFS lets you connect. It won't prompt you for a name or password.

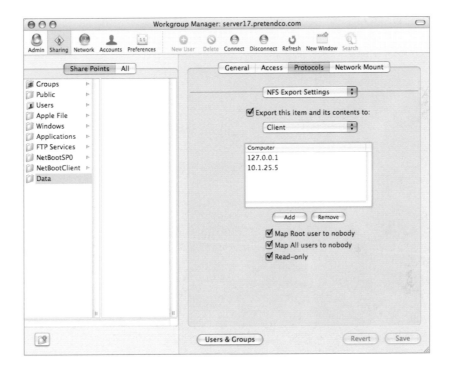

Starting with Mac OS X Server v10.3, NFS file and file-range locks (standard POSIX advisory locks) are enabled by default. This means that two users can safely edit the same file concurrently, as long as they are not editing the same section of the file. If two users attempt to modify the same section of a file, one is locked out in read-only mode until the other is done saving changes.

NFS Trusts the Client for User Authentication

If NFS doesn't prompt you for a name and password, how can it deal with permissions? If you sit down at a client computer and start using an NFS volume, how does it know if you're a member of the group that has access? Who does it assign as the owner for a file you create?

The server simply believes what the client tells it, based upon the user ID provided by the client. The client tells the server that user Jim is creating a folder or deleting a file, and the server believes it. If Jim has access to that file or folder, the operation is allowed. In Mac OS X, the user that the client reports to the server is normally the user who logged in at the login window. Two issues arise with this method of user identification:

▶   User mismatch: Maybe the user really is Jim, and your client is correctly reporting his identity to the server. What if the server doesn't know who Jim is? Or what if there are different Jims—one on the server and one on the client? Remember that each Mac OS X client has a list of users (configured in Accounts preferences), and Mac OS X Server has its own list of users (configured in Workgroup Manager). The two lists may not have any common users, or they may have users who appear to be the same but only coincidentally have the same information. NFS can't keep this straight on its own.

▶   Identity theft: Imagine you are a standard user on the server, but you are the administrator of your own PowerBook running Mac OS X. Since you control that PowerBook, you can create any user you want locally and thus pretend to be whomever you want to be. You can now see why NFS is a security concern.

User Mapping Can Increase Security

One response to the problem of identity theft is to map NFS users. Rather than accept what the client reports, the server can simply pretend that the user is "nobody," and hence the user gets the permissions that are assigned to everyone. You'll almost certainly want to select this mapping for the root user—the all-powerful superuser who can delete any item on a volume. It is just as easy to steal the root user's identity as it is any other user's. Beyond this, you can map all users to nobody and just ignore altogether what the client is reporting for a user. Checking both these options is similar to giving guest access under AFP.

Network Mounted Share Points

You'll often need to make files and folders on a server available to users on client computers. One way to do that is to tell users to connect to the server from the Finder. Connecting from the Finder is easy, but it requires users to remember which server to connect to and where to find the files on that server.

For frequently accessed resources, such as applications, libraries, or fonts, you might want to simplify your users' experience even more. If so, you can make a folder, disk, or partition on a server mount automatically on some or all of the client computers in a domain. You do this by configuring network mount share points.

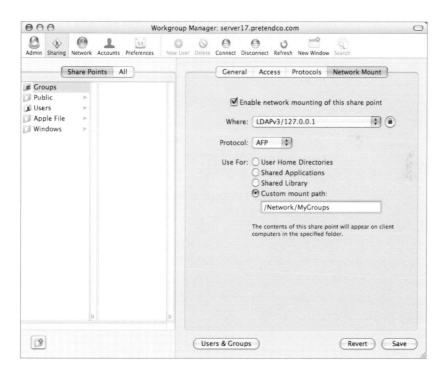

For example, suppose you want to have a specific set of applications available to every user in a given LDAP directory. You could create a share point containing the desired applications and then set the share point to automatically mount into a /Network/Applications folder on client machines that can utilize either the AFP or the NFS protocol. To do this, you configure the share points using Workgroup Manager, and then use the Network Mount button in the Sharing pane to configure those share points to automatically appear in a folder in the Finder windows of supported client computers. Information about these automatically mounted share points is stored in the LDAP directory.

Setting Up a Network Home Folder

You also use Workgroup Manager to set up a network home folder for a network user. The user's home folder can reside in any AFP or NFS share point that the user's computer can access. The share point must be automountable— it must have a network mount record in the directory domain where the user account resides. An automountable share point ensures that the home folder is automatically visible in /Network/Servers when the user logs in to a Mac OS X computer configured to access the shared domain. Apple recommends storing home folders in AFP share points, because AFP provides authentication-level access security, which NFS does not provide. With AFP, a user must log in with a valid name and password to access files.

> **NOTE** ▶ The home folder doesn't need to be stored on the same server as the directory domain containing the user's account. In fact, distributing directory domains and home folders among various servers can help you balance your workload.

When a network user logs in to a Mac OS X computer, the computer retrieves the account information from a shared directory domain on the accounts server. The computer uses the location of the user's home folder, stored in the account, to mount the home folder, which resides physically on a home folder server. Conversely, if you don't set up a home folder for a network user account, any changes the user makes to preferences are lost after logging out.

To set up a home folder for a network user in Workgroup Manager:

1   Click the Accounts button in the toolbar, then select the user in the user list.

2   Click Home to set up the selected user's home folder.

3   In the share points list, select the previously set automounted share point you want to use.

The list displays all the automountable network-visible share points in the search path of the server you are connected to. If the share point you want to select is not listed, try clicking Refresh. If the share point still does not appear, it might not be automountable. In this case, you need to set up the share point to have a network mount record configured for home folders.

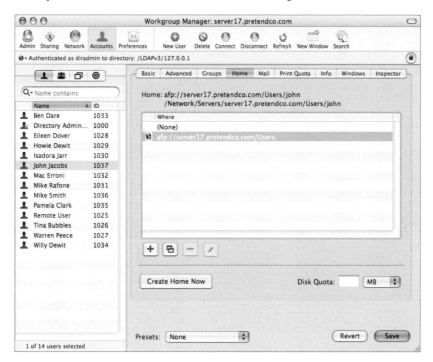

4   Click Create Home Now, and then click Save.

If you do not click Create Home Now before clicking Save, the home folder is created the next time the user restarts the client computer and logs in remotely. The home folder has the same name as the user's first short name. When having Windows users connect, the home folder should be created in advance of the Windows users' initial login.

Optionally, you can use the Disk Quota field in the Home pane to limit the disk space a user can consume to store files in the partition where the user's home folder resides.

For example, when user Sharon places files in user Rafael's folder, the size of the files affects either Sharon's or Rafael's disk quota, depending on the protocol Sharon uses to transfer the files:

▶ If Sharon uses AFP to drop files in Rafael's drop box, Rafael's quota is affected because the owner of the drop box (Rafael) becomes the owner of the files.

▶ If Sharon uses NFS to copy the files to Rafael's folder, Sharon is still owner, and so copying affects Sharon's quota, not Rafael's.

Configuring Network Mounts

Next, you'll configure the /Users folder to be used for network home folders. This is required for your users to log in to local machines using network accounts maintained on the server.

1 If you have turned on Fast User Switching, you may encounter errors, which will prevent them from logging to the Network account if they switch from a local account. Log off all users on your Mac OS X computer except your initial administrator account.

2 On your Mac OS X computer, open and authenticate as sadmin to Workgroup Manager, select the LDAPv3/127.0.0.1 directory, and authenticate again if necessary.

3 Click the Sharing button in the toolbar, and then click the Share Points button on the left side of the window. Navigate to and select the Users folder, and click the Network Mount button on the right.

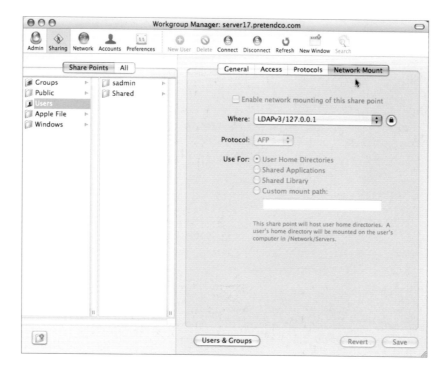

4   Click the lock and authenticate as diradmin.

If you had several other servers that your server was bound to, you would see them in the Where pop-up menu. In this case, all you see is the LDAP directory.

5   Select "Enable network mounting of this share point," confirm that AFP is chosen in the Protocol pop-up menu, and, under Use For, select User Home Directories. Click Save.

6   Click the Accounts button in the toolbar, and make sure you are viewing the LDAP Directory.

This is the shared Open Directory domain you created in a previous lesson. User accounts defined in this domain are accessible from your Mac OS X computer via the network, as you have seen in a previous lesson. While you logged in successfully as another user, that user did not have a home folder.

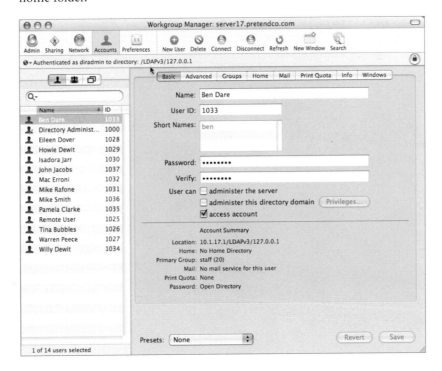

Configuring Users to Utilize the Network Home Folder as Their Home Directory

You have configured the file server to share /Users for network home folders, but you must also point the user account record information to use these home folders.

1 Click the Users button, and select all the users except Directory Administrator. Click the Home button and select the Users share point for your server. Click Save.

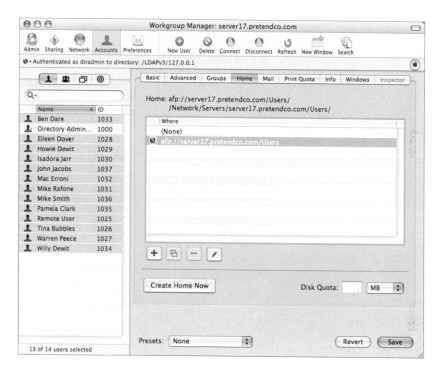

2 On your Mac OS X computer, make sure you have the Location XSE Book Static selected.

3 On your Mac OS X computer, open Directory Access, click the Services button, and select LDAP. Click the Configure button and verify that you are still bound to your server.

Click Cancel once you have verified that the server is still listed in the LDAP list.

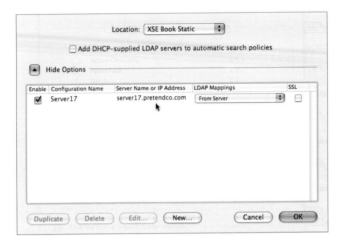

4   In Directory Access, click the Authentication button, and verify that your
     server is still listed in the verification path for your Mac OS X computer.

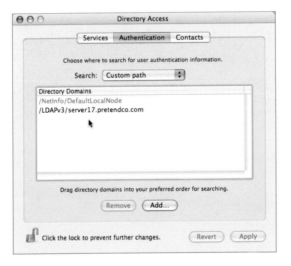

5   Restart your Mac OS X computer.

6   On the Mac OS X computer, log in as Warren Peece.

7   Verify that a new home folder is created in the /Users folder on your server
     computer.

The name of the new home folder matches the short name of the user (in this case, warren).

8 Log out as Warren Peece.

Next, create a new folder, copy some applications into it, and share its contents as a network mount.

1 On the server, create a new folder in /Shared Items. Name the folder Applications.

2 Copy Calculator and Stickies from /Applications to /Shared Items/Applications.

3 On your Mac OS X computer, log in using a local account, then open Server Admin. In the Computers & Services list, select AFP. Click the Settings button, and then click the Access button to verify that "Enable Guest access" is selected; if it isn't, select it and click Save if necessary.

4 On your Mac OS X computer, open and authenticate as sadmin to Workgroup Manager, select the LDAPv3/127.0.0.1 directory, and authenticate again as diradmin if necessary.

5 Click the Sharing button in the toolbar, then click the All button. Navigate to /Shared Items/Applications and click the General button. Select "Share this item and its contents" and click Save.

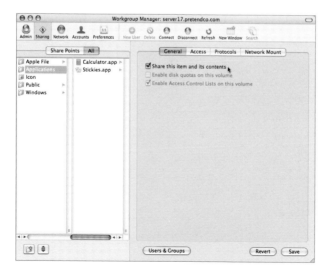

6 Click the Network Mount button. Click the lock and authenticate as diradmin.

If you had several other servers that your server was bound to, you would see them in the Where pop-up menu. In this case, all you see is the LDAP directory.

7 Select "Enable network mounting of this share point," confirm that AFP is chosen in the Protocol pop-up menu, and, under Use For, select Shared Applications. Click Save.

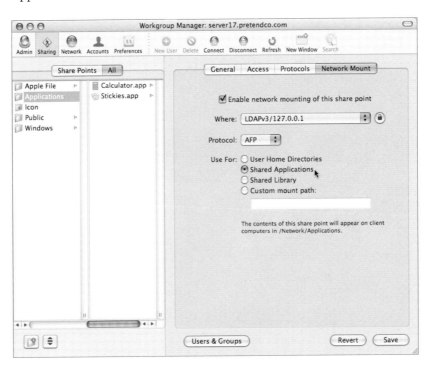

Finally, test your new network mount point.

1   Restart the Mac OS X computer.

Shared volumes mount automatically only at startup. Simply logging in as a network user does not force the volume to mount.

2   Log in as Tina Bubbles.

3   Navigate to /Network/Applications and open Calculator.

When Calculator launches, your client computer has successfully accessed a shared application.

4   Log out from your Mac OS X computer as Tina Bubbles and log back in as your local administrator.

FTP File Service

FTP is a well-known, cross-platform way to transfer files. Mac OS X Server supports this method as a way to transfer files to and from your server.

Enabling FTP

You configure the FTP service in much the same way as you configure the AFP and SMB services—using Workgroup Manager and Server Admin. You use Workgroup Manager to define the share point and folder access, and use Server Admin to configure specific FTP settings. The General pane of the Settings pane of Server Admin lets you control the number of users who can connect to the FTP service, the authentication protocol they use for connecting, and whether to let anonymous users connect. Anonymous FTP users are similar to guest-access users under AFP or SMB.

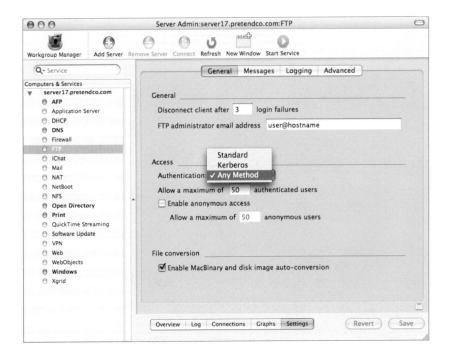

NOTE ▶ Although FTP service uses Kerberos authentication, neither the Finder nor the command-line FTP clients support Kerberos authentication.

By default, all share points you create in Workgroup Manager are shared via AFP, SMB, and FTP. Simply turning on the FTP service gives access to these share points. The Advanced pane of the FTP service lets you modify this behavior. By enabling Home Directory with Share Points from the "Authorized users see" pop-up menu, you can force users to see only their home folders. FTP share points appear as a subfolder inside users' home folders. This is a good way to prevent users from having access to other users' home folders. The most restrictive option is "Home Directory Only." This selection gives users access only to their own home folders. If you have FTP share points set up, anonymous users have access to those share points.

When providing access via FTP, *passive FTP* can be a useful option. Passive FTP is commonly used to access an FTP server behind a firewall. If your network administrator doesn't allow any FTP access through your firewall, this option will not help you, but a common firewall configuration is to allow passive FTP but not full FTP. This is a client-side option. There is nothing you need to configure on the server, but you may need to explain to your users that they must use passive FTP to connect to your server.

FTP File Conversions

One hidden, but very useful, feature of the Mac OS X Server FTP service is its ability to perform automatic file conversions. The FTP server can automatically compress, archive, and encode files on the fly at the time they are requested. There are a few situations where this comes in particularly handy:

▶ MacBinary: Many files created with Classic applications, as well as many applications created for Mac OS 9, use a special type of file called a *forked* file. This type of file can cause difficulties with FTP, so the server encodes the file in MacBinary format before sending it. To request this type of encoding, simply add the extension .bin to the file you are requesting. For example, if the FTP server has a copy of SimpleText, you can ask for SimpleText.bin, and the server will encode and send the SimpleText file in MacBinary format. MacBinary can be combined with both .tar and .gz compressions.

▶ Automatic archiving: If you need an entire folder of documents, just ask for the folder with .tar added at the end before the transfer. The server creates a single archive file of the folder, and you can expand it after you have downloaded it. Be aware that this feature doesn't perform compression.

▶ Disk-image creation: When you include the .dmg extension in the URL, the FTP server converts the download into a disk-image file. This also works when downloading an application that has .app in the filename. In this case, the server automatically creates a .dmg file for the downloaded application.

▶ Automatic compression: If you are copying a large document, you can compress it by adding .gz to the end. This uses a UNIX-style gzip program. It does not preserve resource forks. A useful shortcut is to chain archiving and compression. If you want a folder called bigfolder, you can ask for bigfolder.tar.gz, and the folder will be archived and compressed before it is sent.

Monitoring FTP Activity

The FTP server has a log that you configure in the Logging pane of the Settings pane. You can have the log keep track of uploads or downloads. You can view the activity in the FTP Log pane by clicking the Log button at the bottom of the Server Admin window.

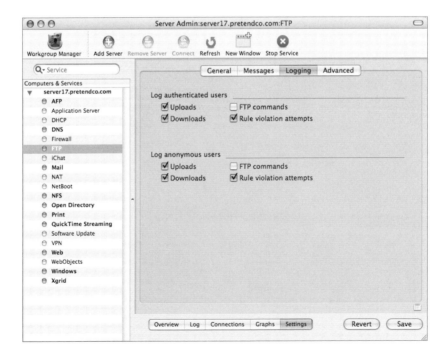

Selecting the "FTP commands" checkbox in the Logging pane logs the actual
FTP protocol commands that the client sends to the server. The "Rule violation
attempts" selection logs permission errors, such as when a user is denied access
to an item. Both of these log items show up in the System log instead of the FTP
activity log.

Configuring FTP Service

You use Workgroup Manager to share a folder over FTP.

1   On the server, use the Finder to create a new folder inside /Shared Items
called FTP Services.

2   Use TextEdit to create a file, and save it as ftp_file in the FTP Services
folder you just created.

3   If Workgroup Manager is not open on your Mac OS X computer, open it
and connect to your server as sadmin.

4   Click the Sharing button in the toolbar, then click the All tab on the left
side of the window. Navigate to and select the FTP Services folder you
created in step 1 (click the Refresh button if necessary).

5   In the General pane, select "Share this item and its contents" and click Save.

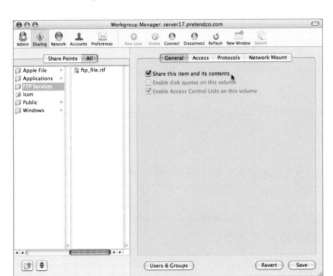

6   Click the Protocols button and do the following:

   ▶   Select Apple File Settings from the pop-up menu and disable "Share this item using AFP."

   ▶   Select Windows File Settings from the pop-up men and disable "Share this item using SMB."

   ▶   Select FTP Settings from the pop-up menu and enable "Share this item using FTP."

7   Click Save.

   Now your shared folder is visible only to FTP clients.

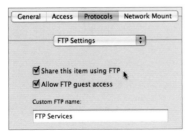

Now that you have shared the FTP folder, modify the permissions to control users' access to files.

1   On your server, use the Finder to create two new folders, Public and Development, in your FTP Services folder.

2   In Workgroup Manager on your Mac OS X computer, click the Refresh button and select the Development folder.

3   Click the Development folder in the FTP Services share point, click the Access button on the right, and click the Users & Groups button to open the drawer. Set POSIX permissions as follows:

   ▶   Owner: ben, Read & Write

   ▶   Group: admin, Read & Write

   ▶   Everyone: None

4   Click the Groups button in the drawer, and drag the Engineering group to the Access Control List box. Click Save.

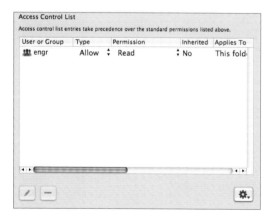

5   In Workgroup Manager, select the Public folder and change the permissions as follows:

▶   Owner: sadmin, Read & Write

▶   Group: mktg, Read & Write

▶   Everyone: Read & Write

6   Click Save.

Next, you'll start the FTP service and allow access to FTP for certain users and groups.

1   On your Mac OS X computer, Open Server Admin and authenticate if necessary.

2   Select the FTP service from the Computers & Services list, and click the Settings button.

3   Choose Standard from the Authentication pop-up menu, and click Save. Click the Start Service button.

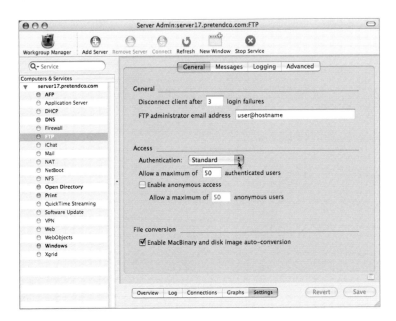

4 Select your server (Server17) in the Computers & Services list.

Depending on how you connected to your server with Server Admin, you may see server17.pretendco.com, Server17.local, or 10.1.17.1. Any of these will work.

5 Click Settings and then click the Access button.

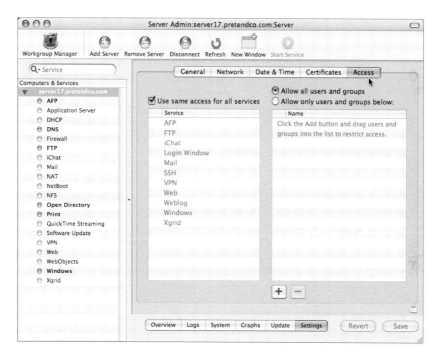

6 Disable any older AFP Access settings.

7 Deselect "Use same access for all services" and select FTP from the list.

8 Select "Allow only users and groups below" and click the Add Group Members (+) button.

9   Drag users Mike Rafone and Tina Bubbles from the Users & Groups drawer.

10 Click Save.

Finally, you'll use the client computer to connect via FTP on the server.

1   Using your client computer from the Finder, try Connect to Server as warren, using ftp://server17.pretendco.com.

You cannot connect as Warren because access has not been permitted; only Mike and Tina have access.

2   Using your client computer, connect as tinabubbles and note which folders you have access to in the mounted share point.

3   Unmount the FTP volume from your client computer.

4   Using your client computer, connect as Mike and note which folders you have access to in the mounted share point.

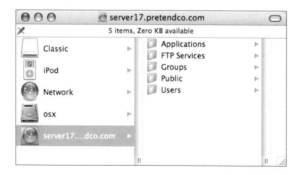

5   Unmount the FTP volume from your client computer.

Although it can be useful to restrict connections per service group user, it will interfere with future exercises in this course.

6   On your Mac OS X computer, open Server Admin and authenticate if necessary.

7 Select your server (Server17) from the Computers & Services list.

Depending on how you connected to your server with Server Admin, you may see server17.pretendco.com, Server17.local, or 10.1.17.1. Any of these will work.

8 Click Settings, then click the Access button, and do the following:

▶ Choose the "Allow all users and groups" button.

▶ Select the "Use same access for all services" checkbox.

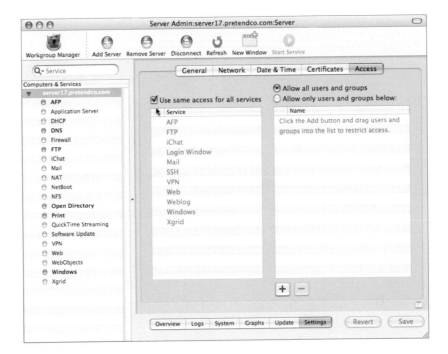

9 Click Save.

10 Choose FTP from the Computers & Services list, and stop and restart FTP service.

Troubleshooting File Services

Whether AFS, SMB, NFS, or FTP, troubleshooting file services on Mac OS X Server typically involves the following considerations:

▶ User access: What users or groups should have access to the specific files and folders on the server, and are their appropriate permissions set correctly?

▶ Platform and protocol access: From what clients are users trying to access the server, such as Mac OS X, Mac OS 9, Windows, or Linux systems? What protocols are they using when accessing the server?

▶ Special needs: Are there any special circumstances, such as users' needing concurrent access to files or access to files in a nonnative format to the system they are using?

For troubleshooting access settings, you will want to first address whether or not you are using ACLs, and test access by using the Effective Permissions Inspector and by logging in from remote clients. Here the biggest issue will be starting with an appropriate logical group structure and maintaining it over time.

While multiple platforms are supported through the different sharing protocols (AFP, SMB, FTP, NFS), this can become tricky either when trying to provide concurrent access to the same files or when platform specific issues come into play. Concurrent access means that multiple users are trying to access or modify the same files at the same time. Many times this is dependent on the specific cross-platform applications' knowing how to allow multiple users to access the same file. Now that Mac OS X Server v10.4 includes support for ACLs and these ACLs are compatible with ACLs from the Windows platform, permissions mapping between Windows clients will be in line with what Windows users expect to see. Previous to Mac OS X Server v10.4, this was not necessarily the case.

Another consideration is if the clients will be storing forked files on the share point. If you use Mac OS Extended for an SMB share point or an NFS export, files created or copied onto the server from the client side will have shadow files instead of resource forks. These files will not look right when viewed from the server. Conversely, files created from the server side will look wrong from the client, which cannot see the resource forks. If you use a UFS volume, files will look correct from both computers because both expect shadow files.

Case-Sensitivity Issues in File Sharing

Case sensitivity becomes an issue if you are copying files between two computers and only one of them has a case-sensitive file system. Beginning with Mac OS X Server v10.3, drives can be formatted as HFS+ case-sensitive volumes. Suppose you have two files, Makefile and makefile, in the same folder on a case-sensitive Mac OS X server. If you were to copy those files to a Mac OS X client computer, which is by default not case sensitive, you would run into problems. The operating system would attempt to overwrite one file with the other. When you copy files from a non-case-sensitive file system to a case-sensitive file system, you might have a problem with executable files. For example, suppose you had an executable script called Runscript on your case-insensitive file system. If you were to copy that file, without altering its name, to a case-sensitive file system, users would be able to run it from the command line only by typing *Runscript*. This could be problematic if the documentation called for typing *runscript* (all lowercase).

You need to be aware of the issues associated with case sensitivity now that Mac OS X Server can easily be configured to be case sensitive, while the Mac OS X client cannot. Not much can be done to synchronize case-sensitive and case-insensitive systems. You need to work around the incompatibility. Given that NFS, FTP, and AFP are case-sensitive protocols, mounting a share point using any of these protocols enables you to see the different case-sensitive files and download whichever one you'd like.

More specifically, SMB does not seem to be a case-sensitive protocol, but it has a distinct preference for uppercase filenames. For example, if your share point contains the files Runscript and runscript, and you use SMB to download either of these files to the client, only Runscript is downloaded, whether you asked for Runscript or runscript. Similarly, if you try to move runscript to a different folder in the share point, Runscript is moved, not runscript. Also, if you upload a local file named runscript to an SMB share point that already contains Runscript and runscript, you are prompted to replace the existing file, but then the operation fails and Runscript is deleted.

Here's what happens: When you attempt to copy runscript to the server, SMB detects the existence of a file with the same name and asks if you want to replace it. Once you click OK, SMB deletes the file Runscript and then attempts to copy runscript to the server. However, that operation fails because runscript still exists on the server. If you try the upload again, however, it succeeds, since now there is only one runscript on the server. When you tell the server to replace the file, it does so without confusion.

A Comparison of File-Sharing Protocols

This chart gives a short comparison of the file-sharing protocols you have seen thus far. There really isn't one best protocol. Instead, think of the protocols as different tools at your disposal to give different types of access.

File-Sharing Protocols Comparison

	AFP	SMB	NFS	FTP
Native platform	Mac OS	Windows	UNIX	Multi-platform
Security	Authentication is normally encrypted	Authentication is normally encrypted	No user authentication	Uses cleartext passwords
Browsable	Bonjour, SLP	NetBIOS	Bonjour, SLP	Bonjour
Example URL	afp:// server17.example.com/ SharePoint	smb:// server17.example.com/ Share	nfs:// server17.example.com/ Volumes/Data/ nfs_share	ftp:// server17.example.com/

AFP and SMB are both full-featured file-sharing protocols with reasonably good security.

NFS is not as secure as the other protocols, but it is very convenient for UNIX clients. Be careful before you "export" (share) a volume over NFS. With a Mac OS X server and a Mac OS X client, NFS volumes are browsable in Connect to

Server; that is, a user can find them by browsing through a list of servers in the Connect to Server window.

FTP is useful because it offers maximum compatibility. However, FTP also offers a minimum feature set, and its passwords are sent over the network as cleartext unless you are using the Kerberos option and a supported Kerberos FTP client—something the Mac OS X Finder lacks.

Mac OS X supports SFTP, a secure alternative for FTP that uses SSH to encrypt the entire FTP connection. Of the four file-sharing protocols, only AFP has built-in support for encrypting connections.

What You've Learned

▶ The first step when implementing file-sharing services is to plan out the shared services needed.

▶ A share point is any folder, drive, or partition that you make available to network clients. Share points are created and configured in Workgroup Manager. A share point can be shared over AFP, SMB, NFS, or FTP. Access control lists can be used to set very flexible restrictions on share points and folders.

▶ AFS allows Macintosh clients to access share points over AFP and is configured in Workgroup Manager and Server Admin.

▶ Windows service allows share points to be accessed by Windows clients over SMB.

▶ NFS provides UNIX systems with access to share points. Unlike AFP and SMB, NFS relies upon the IP address of the computer for authentication. You can use Mac OS X to reshare NFS volumes, to allow other Macintosh clients to access NFS volumes on other servers.

▶ Mac OS X Server provides FTP access for share points as well. Mac OS X Server's FTP service provides the additional feature of automatically encoding, archiving, or compressing a file on the fly, based upon the extension that the client adds to the filename.

▶ Network mount share points and network home folders also can be configured on Mac OS X Server.

References

The following documents provide more information about installing Mac OS X Server. (All of these and more are available at www.apple.com/server/documentation.)

Administration Guides

Mac OS X Server Getting Started (http://images.apple.com/server/pdfs/Getting_Started_v10.4.pdf)

Mac OS X Server Upgrading and Migrating for Version 10.4 or Later (http://images.apple.com/server/pdfs/Migration_v10.4.pdf)

Mac OS X Server File Services Administration for Version 10.4 or Later (http://images.apple.com/server/pdfs/File_Services_v10.4.pdf)

Mac OS X Server Windows Services Administration for Version 10.4 or Later (http://images.apple.com/server/pdfs/Windows_Services_v10.4.pdf)

Mac OS X Server User Management for Version 10.4 or Later (http://images.apple.com/server/pdfs/User_Management_Admin_v10.4.pdf)

Mac OS X Server Command-Line Administration for Version 10.4 or Later (http://images.apple.com/server/pdfs/Command_Line_v10.4.pdf)

Apple Knowledge Base Documents

You can check for new and updated Knowledge Base documents at www.apple.com/support.

Document 301272, "Mac OS X Server 10.4: Limit SMB connections to improve server reliability"

Document 107697, "Mac OS X Server 10.3 or later: SMB print queue names must not exceed 15 characters"

Document 107077, "Mac OS X Server: How to Reshare NFS Exports via AFP"

Document 152363, "Mac OS X 10.3 Help: Managing network and Internet services using Mac OS X Server"

Document 301183, "Mac OS X 10.4 Tiger: "Connection failed" error when connecting to an AFP server"

Document 301601, "Mac OS X Server 10.4: Inherit permissions does not work for AFP service"

Document 301310, "Mac OS X Server 10.4: Windows users cannot modify ACL permissions on the server"

Document 301069, "Mac OS X Server 10.3, 10.4: How to make a hidden directory a share point"

Books

Regan, Schoun, and White, Kevin. *Mac OS X Server 10.4 Tiger: Visual QuickPro Guide* (Peachpit Press, 2005).

Bartosh, Michael, and Haas, Jason. *Essential Mac OS X Panther Server Administration* (O'Reilly, 2005).

URLs

Mac OS X Server File Sharing Issues: www.afp548.com

Apple Developer Documentation: http://developer.apple.com/qa/qa2001/qa1312.html

Review Quiz

1. Name four file-sharing protocols supported by Mac OS X Server and their principal target clients.

2. How does Mac OS X Server support browsing for Windows clients?

3. What is the primary security concern with NFS?

4. What does FTP file conversion do?

Answers

1. AFP for Macintosh clients; SMB for Windows clients; NFS for UNIX clients; and FTP for multiple, cross-platform client access

2. On smaller networks, Mac OS X Server uses NetBIOS to advertise its presence. On larger networks, Mac OS X can be a WINS server, or it can use an existing WINS server. If there are no other servers on the network, Mac OS X Server can be a workgroup master browser or a domain master browser.

3. NFS has no user-authentication process: NFS trusts that the client is who it claims to be. Beyond a security concern, this can also be a management issue if the client and server aren't working with a unified user list.

4. FTP file conversion is a feature of the FTP server that automatically encodes a file or folder requested by an FTP client. The client appends .tar, .bin, or .gz to the end of the filename, and the server does the appropriate encoding.

9

Lesson Files   None

Time   This lesson takes approximately 4 hours to complete.

Goals   Create and configure home folders for network user accounts

Create and manage access to shared group folders

Manage user, workgroup, and computer preferences

Create and configure network browsing and the /Network experience

Create mobile accounts and configure Mac OS X Server for mobile home folders

View and edit an application's preferences

Lesson **9**
Managing Accounts

If you run an organization with several hundred users, how can you make sure they all have the same items in their Dock? What about their experience browsing the network? Printers? The Finder interface? In previous lessons you learned management techniques involving the user name, password, and home folder. There are many other aspects to user account management and it is important to understand how these various aspects interact with each other. When applying other types of management to your user and group accounts, consider that there is also a third type of management—computer list accounts—to add to your options. Careful planning will reveal the best way to implement your management, whether it be based on user accounts, group accounts, computer list accounts, or a combination of all three.

This lesson covers the following areas of account management:

▶ Concepts and tools—Describes account management and its main tool, Workgroup Manager.

▶ User, group, and computer list accounts—Describes how to use Workgroup Manager to manage users, groups, and computers.

▶ Preference management—Describes how to use Workgroup Manager to customize and control the Mac OS X user experience.

▶ Managing the view of /Network—Describes network browsing.

▶ Mobile accounts and mobile users

▶ Troubleshooting preferences

Concepts and Tools

Account management encompasses everything from setting up accounts for network access and creating home folders to fine-tuning the user experience by managing preferences and settings for users, groups, and computers. The term "managed client" refers to a user, group, or computer whose access permissions and preferences are under administrative control.

With effective account management, you can:

▶ Provide users with a consistent, controlled interface while allowing them to access their documents from any computer

▶ Control permissions on mobile computers

▶ Reserve certain resources for specific groups or individuals

▶ Secure computer use in key areas such as administrative offices, classrooms, or open labs

▶ Customize the user experience using group folders

▶ Customize Dock settings

Workgroup Manager

Workgroup Manager is an account-management tool that, among other capabilities, provides centralized, directory-based management of users, groups, and computers from anywhere on your network. You can create standardized desktop configurations, set system preferences, establish and enforce password policies, and control access to hardware, software, and network resources. Your settings are automatically cached so the preferences and user permissions you've defined remain in effect even when computers are offline.

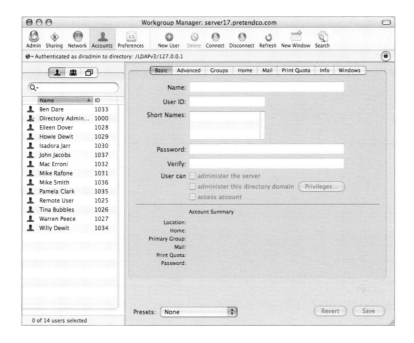

You can also configure systems to open predefined applications, mount resources on the desktop when users log in to specific groups, and provide users with network-based home folders, allowing them to access their own personalized desktop, applications, and files from any computer on the network. You can also configure the way users can view the network topology. When users open the /Network folder on their systems they will see the resources determined by the server administrator. The hierarchy of the resources can also be set using the Network Views settings.

Workgroup Manager stores preferences and policies for users, groups, and computers in an LDAPv3 directory server using Apple's Open Directory architecture. Naturally, you can use the existing hardware and directory domains you already have (such as another server on your network providing user directory information). Based on open standards, Open Directory works with any LDAPv3 server, thereby protecting your investment in standards-based network resources. Also, Open Directory works with Apple's legacy NetInfo and with proprietary directory technologies such as Microsoft's Active Directory.

Workgroup Manager Inspector

Workgroup Manager is a directory-services editor and the user interface is customized for entering data specific to managing user, group, computer, and preference records. The Workgroup Manager application enters the data into the directory in a known format, and other applications and utilities may also save data in the directory. Applications may also store preference-type XML data, which could be added to the attributes of user records, for example. When you need to dig deeper into the attributes and associated values of those attributes, Workgroup Manager provides the Inspector for viewing and editing this raw data. The Inspector is enabled as a Workgroup Manager preference so once it's enabled, click any specific record and select the Inspector to bring up the XML data stored for that entry.

Basic type casting is handled for you in the editor and there is minimal error checking at this level. Manual editing using the Inspector is a power-user option. As a read-only tool, the Inspector is a powerful debug tool.

Managing User, Group, and Computer List Accounts

When you log in to a Mac OS X system using a local user account, both the user account information and the home folder are stored on that computer. This arrangement is difficult for an administrator to manage, as the user configuration on each computer has to be managed individually and locally. Mac OS X Server provides two additional types of user account—created and managed by Workgroup Manager—that can be used in Mac OS X:

▶ Network: A Mac OS X Server user account with the following characteristics:

The account information can reside in any Open Directory domain accessible from the Mac OS X Server that needs to use the account. A directory domain can reside on a Mac OS X computer (for example, the LDAP directory of an Open Directory master) or it can reside on a non-Apple server (for example, an LDAP or Active Directory server). The user's home folder can be stored on the same server as the directory domain that contains the user's account, or it can be stored on another file server.

▶ Mobile: A Mac OS X Server user account with the following characteristics:

Two synchronized accounts. The main account resides in a shared directory domain. The second account is a copy of the main account and resides in the local domain of the user's computer. The user's home folder resides locally, in the user's computer.

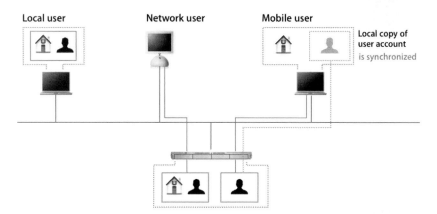

Setting Up a Network Home Folder Review

As discussed in Lesson 8, you also use Workgroup Manager to set up a network home folder for a network user. The user's home folder can reside in any Apple Filing Protocol (AFP) or Network File System (NFS) share point that the user's computer can access. The share point must be automountable—it must have a network mount record in the directory domain where the user account resides. An automountable share point ensures that the home folder is visible in /Network/Servers automatically when the user logs in to a Mac OS X computer configured to access the shared domain. Apple recommends storing home folders in AFP share points, because AFP provides authentication-level access security, which NFS does not provide. With AFP, a user must log in with a valid name and password to access files.

> **NOTE ▸** The home folder doesn't need to be stored on the same server as the directory domain containing the user's account. In fact, distributing directory domains and home folders among various servers can help balance the workload among servers.

When a network user logs in to a Mac OS X computer, the computer retrieves the account information from a shared directory domain on the accounts server. The computer uses the location of the user's home folder, stored in the account, to mount the home folder, which resides physically on a home folder server. Conversely, if you don't set up a home folder for a network user account, any changes the user makes to preferences are lost after logging out.

To set up a home folder for a network user in Workgroup Manager:

1   Select the user in the user list.

2   Click Home to set up the selected user's home folder.

3   In the share points list, select the previously set automounted share point you want to use.

   The list displays all the automountable network-visible share points in the search path of the server you are connected to. If the share point you want to select is not listed, try clicking Refresh. If the share point still does not appear, it might not be automountable. In this case, you need to set up the share point to have a network mount record configured for home folders.

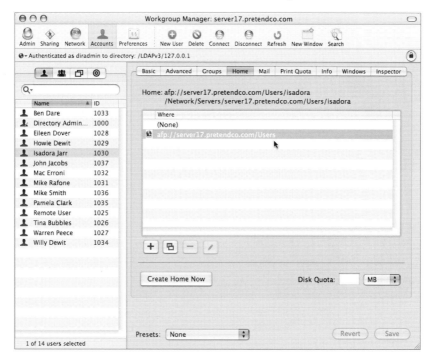

4 Click Create Home Now, and then click Save.

If you do not click Create Home Now before clicking Save, the home folder is created the next time the user restarts the client computer and logs in remotely. The name of the home folder has the same name as the user's first short name. When having Windows users connect, the home folder should be created in advance of the Windows user's initial log in.

Optionally, you can use the Disk Quota field in the Home pane to limit the disk space a user can consume to store files in the partition where the user's home folder resides.

Setting Home Folders for All Users

You will set and create home folders for all users who do not yet have home folders.

1 On your Mac OS X computer, open Workgroup Manager and authenticate as necessary.

2 Click the Accounts button in the toolbar and then click the globe icon below the toolbar. Choose /LDAPv3/127.0.0.1 from the pop-up menu.

3 Select all the users and deselect the Directory Administrator account.

4 Click the home button. Select the path of afp://server17.pretendco.com/ Users, click the Create Home Now button, and then click Save.

Even if you already have home folders for some of the users, this will not change those settings.

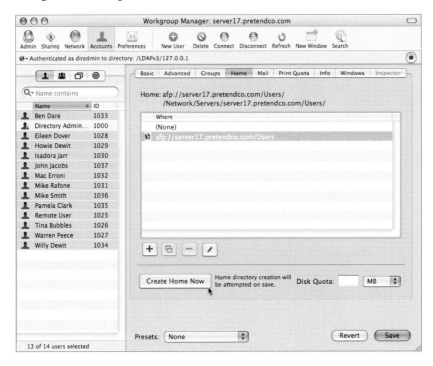

5 On your server, navigate to the /Users folder and verify that all the home folders were created.

6 Verify you have a home folder for Pamela by logging in as Pamela from your Mac OS X computer, then log back out and back in as your local administrator.

Managing Preferences for Users in a Workgroup

Although you can set up preferences individually for users with network accounts, it's more efficient to manage preferences for the workgroups to which they belong. Using workgroups allows you to manage users regardless of which computers they use. Using Workgroup Manager, you can provide all users in a workgroup with the same access permissions for media, printers, and volumes.

> **NOTE ▶** It is important to note the difference between a workgroup and a group. A group is a file system designation. It is used to handle access to the file system (as in owner, group, everyone). It is specific to the file system, server, or computer. A workgroup is a directory-service record separate from any specific file system or server. It is used as a method of associating similar preferences for sets of user records.

A user can be assigned to one or more workgroups and during login, the user selects a workgroup under which to log in. The user then has all the permissions and access privileges assigned to that workgroup.

> **TIP** Administrative users are given an option to disable management. Once selected, this option is hidden but is visible again if the Option key is pressed during login.

Setting Up a Group Folder

You can use Workgroup Manager to set up a group folder for use by members of a particular workgroup. A group folder offers a way to organize documents and applications of special interest to group members and gives group members a way to pass information back and forth among themselves.

To set up a group folder in Workgroup Manager (you will do this in a later exercise):

1   Select the group and click the Group Folder button.

2   Select a listed share point to set up a group folder in it.

If the predefined Groups share point or any other existing share point is not listed in the Group Folder pane, create a mount record for it in the Network Mount pane of the Sharing window in Workgroup Manager.

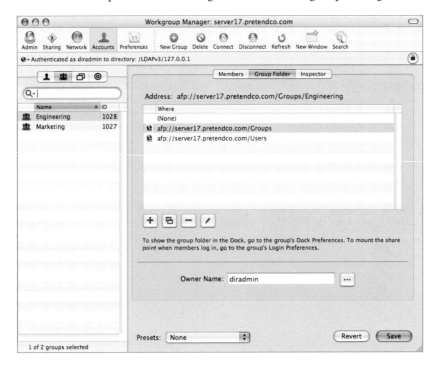

3   In the Owner Name field, click the Browse (…) button to choose an owner (Directory Administrator) from a list of users in the current directory domain.

A common mistake is to not assign an owner to the folder. This will result in errors. The group folder owner is given read/write access to the group folder.

4   Click Save.

5   Create the group folder using the sudo CreateGroupFolder command in Terminal on the server.

> **NOTE** ▶ You need to run CreateGroupFolder manually on the server containing the groups, because it is not automatically executed.

> **TIP** ▶ There are at least two ways in which you can facilitate a group member's access to the group folder when the user logs in: You can set up Dock preferences to make the group folder visible in the Dock, or you can set up login preferences so that the share point in which the group folder resides appears on the desktop.

Managing Computer List Accounts

A *computer list account* is a list of computers that have the same preference settings and are available to the same set of users and groups. You create and modify these computer lists in Workgroup Manager. Computer lists that you set up appear in the searchable list on the left side of the window. Computer list settings appear in the List, Access, and Cache panes on the right side of the window.

When you set up a computer list, make sure you have already determined how computers are identified. Use descriptions that are logical and easy to remember (for instance, the description might be the computer name). You must use the built-in Ethernet address for a computer's address information. This information is unique to each computer. The client computer uses this data to find preference information when a user logs in. An easy way to add computers to a list is to use the Browse (...) button. When you select a computer from the browse list, Workgroup Manager automatically enters the computer's Ethernet address and name for you. It is best to use a computer list for resources in a specific area as well as computers of a specific type, such as portables. For example, all kiosk computers might have the same login preferences or all computers in a lab might have the same default printer preferences. Where preferences are associated with users, workgroups are more efficient.

When a computer starts up, it checks directory services for a computer list record that contains its Ethernet address. If it finds one, it uses settings for that computer list. If no record is found, the computer uses settings for the default Guest Computers computer list. You can add up to 2000 computers to a computer list but a computer cannot be a member of more than one computer list.

> **NOTE ▶** Computers are *not* part of any access control lists (ACLs). They should not be confused with groups.

Macintosh computers are not the only computers that you can add to a computer list. If you want users to log in to a Mac OS X Server primary domain controller (PDC) from Windows workstations, add these workstations to the Windows Computers computer list, which Workgroup Manager creates by default.

> **TIP▶** Although you can add different types of computers to a computer list (for example, iMac and PowerBook computers), in some cases it is more effective to create homogeneous computer lists (for example, create one list for iMac computers and another for PowerBook computers). In this way, you can avoid hardware incompatibilities when you configure computer lists.

Creating a Computer List

To set up a computer list account in Workgroup Manager:

1   Click Accounts.

2   Click the globe icon below the toolbar and open the directory domain where you want to store the new account.

3   If necessary, click the lock and enter your user name and password.

4   Click the Computers button.

5   Choose Server > New Computer List or click New Computer List in the toolbar.

6   Type a list name in the List Name field.

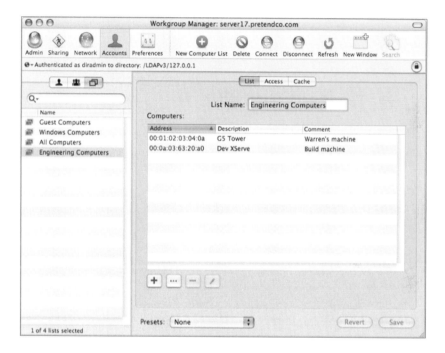

7   Click Add Computer (+) to add a computer to the list, and then type the computer's name and Ethernet address in the Address field. Alternatively, you can click Browse (…), and Workgroup Manager enters the computer's Ethernet address and name for you.

8   Type a description, such as the computer name, and type a comment.

Comments are useful for providing additional information about a computer's location, configuration (for example, a computer set up for individuals with special needs), or attached peripherals. You could also use the comment field for additional identification information, such as the computer's model or serial number.

9   Continue adding computers until your computer list is complete.

10   Click Access. To restrict computer access to certain workgroups, select "Restrict to groups below" and add workgroups to the list.

11   Save the account.

> **NOTE ▶** Computers added to the computer lists at this stage are available in the Managed Network View section of Workgroup Manager. Resources may reside at specific computers (for example, web or file servers).

> **TIP ▶** When there are only a few computers to manage, it is useful to enter them into a computer list or lists. In this way they are accessible via group accounts, user accounts, and computer list accounts. This list is also less likely to change frequently.

Creating a Guest Computers List

If an unknown computer (one that isn't already in a computer list) connects to your network and attempts to access services, that computer is treated as a guest. Settings chosen for the Guest Computers list apply to these unknown or guest computers. Using the Guest Computers list (or just a single computer list) is not recommended for large numbers of computers. Most of your computers should belong to regular computer lists. This makes managing them easier.

During server software installation, a guest computer record is automatically created only in the original directory domain. Afterward, you can create additional Guest Computers accounts in other directory domains. After the account is created, "Guest Computers" appears in the list of computer lists. Each directory domain can have only one Guest Computers list. Depending on network organization and setup, you may not be able to create a Guest Computers list in certain directory domains.

Select the "Define Guest Computer preferences here" option in the List pane if you want to set up managed preferences. Then, click Cache and set an interval for clearing the preferences. Select the "Inherit preferences for Guest Computers" option in the List pane if you want guest computers to have the same managed preference settings as the parent server. Finally, to restrict access to the Guest Computers account to certain groups, use the Access pane.

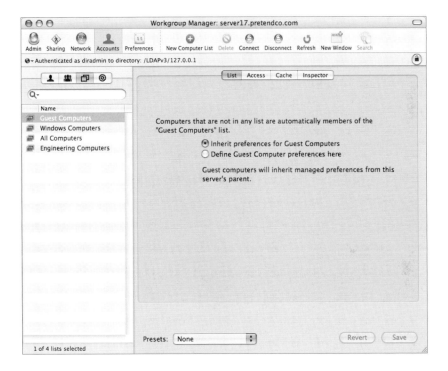

NOTE ▶ You cannot add or move computers to the Guest Computers list, and you cannot change the list name.

Managing Workgroups and Computer Accounts
Once you have computers assigned to your computer lists, you can assign workgroups to the lists. Different sets of users may access the same sets of

computers (for example, different shifts in a workplace or different classes in a computer lab, or any time you have multiple-use computers).

In the figure below, only members of the Marketing and WidgetMaster 3000 groups can access computers in the Marketing Computers list, which have sensitive information and special applications that no one else should have access to.

Similarly, only members of the WidgetMaster 3000 and Engineering groups can access computers in the Engineering Computers list.

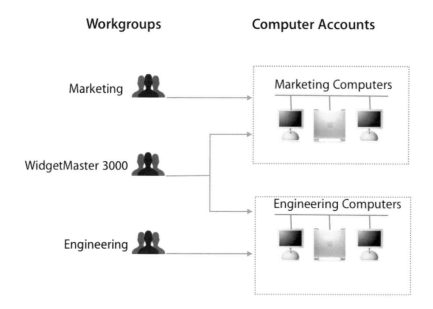

Managing Preferences

When you manage preferences, you centrally control the configuration of specific system settings. You also control users' ability to change those settings, as well as their ability to access applications, printers, removable media, or even certain computers. Information about preferences and their settings in user, group, or computer records is stored in a directory domain accessible to Workgroup Manager, such as the LDAP directory of an Open Directory master. In addition, a copy of group preferences is stored on the workgroup's folder and a copy of user preferences is stored in the user's home folder (the Home folder on Mac OS X computers).

After user, group, and computer list accounts are created, you can start managing preferences for them using the Preferences pane in Workgroup Manager. To manage preferences for Mac OS X clients, you should make sure that each user you want to manage has either a network or local home folder.

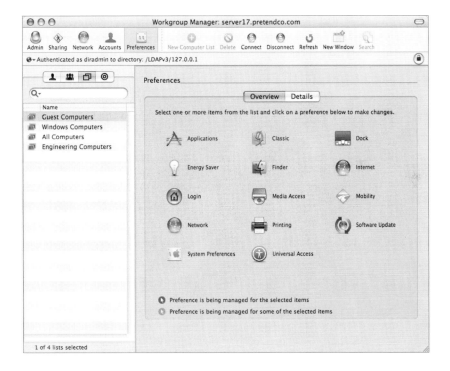

Which Preferences Can Be Managed?

In addition to various other settings for user, group, and computer list accounts, Workgroup Manager provides control over these preferences:

Preference	What You Can Manage
Applications	Applications available to users
Classic	Classic startup settings, sleep settings, and the availability of Classic items such as control panels
Dock	Dock location, behavior, and items
Energy Saver	Available only for computer lists; sleep configuration for the computer
Finder	Finder behavior, desktop appearance and items, and availability of Finder menu commands
Internet	Email account preferences and web browser preferences
Login	Login window appearance, mounted volumes, auto logout, and items that open automatically when a user logs in
Media Access	Settings for CDs, DVDs, and recordable discs, plus settings for internal and external disks such as hard drives
Mobility	Creation and management of mobile accounts and synchronization
Network	Configure Proxy Settings for Internet services
Printing	Available printers and printer access
Software Update	Software Update server to connect for Software Update service
System Preferences	System preferences available to users
Universal Access	Settings to control mouse and keyboard behavior, enhance display settings, and adjust sound or speech for users with special needs

When you manage preferences for a user, group, or computer, an arrow icon appears next to the managed preference in the Preferences pane to indicate that you're managing that preference. If the arrow is dimmed, it means that you have selected two or more accounts in the list at the left of the window, and that for some of the selected accounts this item is managed, while for others it is not.

When Do You Want to Manage Preferences?

With Workgroup Manager, you have three options for managing a preference:

▶ If you don't want to manage settings for a particular preference, select *Never* in the management bar. If you provide users with access to an unmanaged preference, they can change settings as they want. Never is the default management setting for all preferences.

> **TIP** ▶ If you do not manage a particular preference, the user and system preferences are set to default values until changed by the end user. For example, if you do not set any managed preferences for Dock placement, the Dock uses the default location at the bottom of the screen.

▶ If you want to manage a preference initially for accounts but allow the user to make changes if they have that privilege, select *Once* in the management bar. When a user logs in, preference files in their home folder are updated and time-stamped with any preferences that are managed once. If you update settings for a preference that is managed once, Workgroup Manager applies the most recent version to the user's preference files the next time the user logs in. For some preferences, such as Classic preferences or Media Access preferences, Once is not available. You must select Never or Always.

▶ You can force preference settings for an account by selecting *Always* in the management bar. The next time the user logs in, the preference settings are those selected by the administrator. A user cannot change a preference that is Always managed, even if the user is allowed access to that prefer-ence (for example, by using settings in the System Preferences pane of Workgroup Manager's application preferences to make the preference visible to the user).

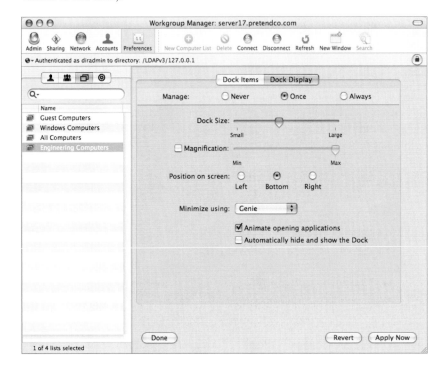

Not all settings make sense in all cases (for example, application access does not make sense in the Once setting, as Once is essentially the same as Always). Mac OS X v10.4 also introduces the notion of "Often." This persistent setting allows the user to change the preferences but resets them the next time the computer boots or a user logs in.

NOTE ▶ The Often option is only available via the Preference Manifest screen. This is available by selecting Details on the main preference screen.

Managing User, Group, and Computer Preferences

Follow these steps to manage user, group, and computer list account preferences:

1   Click Preferences.

2   Click the globe icon below the toolbar and open the directory domain where you want to store the new account.

3   If necessary, click the lock and enter your user name and password.

4   Select the user, group, or computer lists you want to manage.

5   Click the icon for the preference you want to manage.

6   In each pane for that preference, select a management setting (Never, Once, or Always). Then select preference settings or fill in the information you want to use.

7   Click Apply Now.

You might want to manage preferences at the user level only for specific individuals, such as directory domain administrators, teachers, or technical staff. You should also consider which preferences you want to leave under user control. For example, if you aren't concerned about where a user places the Dock, you might want to set Dock Display management to Never.

A more efficient way to manage user preferences is to do it at the workgroup level. Workgroup preferences are shared among all users in the group. Setting some preferences only for groups instead of for individual users can save time, especially when you have large numbers of managed users. In some cases, it may be more efficient to manage preferences for computers instead of for users or groups. These options are all part of proper planning when preparing to manage accounts.

Managed Preference Precedence—Inherit

If you manage the same preference for user, group, and computer list accounts, which preference setting takes precedence? This can be a complicated question, because in some cases the preferences override each other while in others they are combined.

To simplify preference management, you might decide to manage certain preferences at only one level. For example, you could set Login preferences only for workgroups, set Dock preferences only for computers, and set Finder preferences only for users. In such a case, if a user logs in at a managed computer with a managed user account that is a member of a workgroup, the user will inherit each of the managed preferences from each of the managed accounts.

	Login	Dock	Finder
Workgroup	Address Book	"Not Managed"	"Not Managed"
Computer	"Not Managed"	Right	"Not Managed"
User	"Not Managed"	"Not Managed"	☑ Snap to grid
Result:	Address Book	Right	☑ Snap to grid

Managed Preference Precedence—Override

In cases where you have set managed preferences at more than one level, and the preference setting can only have one value, the override rule applies: Managed user preferences override managed computer preferences, which in turn override workgroup preferences. For example, if you are managing Internet preferences and decide to set the Home Page field to www.mac.com for a workgroup and to www.apple.com for a computer list that the workgroup is allowed to access, what does the user get when using one of the managed computers? Since computer preferences override workgroup preferences, the user will see www.apple.com after launching Safari.

	Internet
Workgroup	Home Page: **www.mac.com**
Computer	Home Page: **www.apple.com**
User	"Not Managed"
Result:	Home Page: **www.apple.com**

TIP In general, it's most efficient to manage preferences at the workgroup level. Then you can use the override rule to grant additional privileges to specific users, or to set specific preferences on certain computers.

Managed Preference Precedence—Combine

If a preference can have more than one value, and you set different values for it at the user, computer, and workgroup levels, Workgroup Manager combines these values. For example, if you configure managed Login preferences for a workgroup to launch the Address Book application and Login preferences for a particular user in that workgroup to launch the Chess application, both applications launch when that particular user logs in under that workgroup.

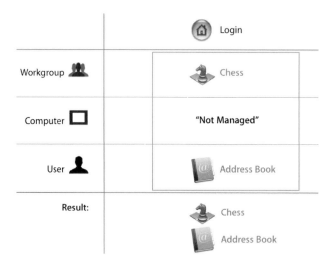

Preference Manifests

Applications store their preference data in specific formats, which are known only to the application developers. Therefore, Workgroup Manager has no way of determining or decoding these formats. With Mac OS X v10.4, Workgroup Manager introduces the notion of *preference manifests.*

Applications that adhere to the manifest format can have their preference data imported and stored with user, group, and computer list accounts. When the manifest settings are saved, the application preferences will also be managed.

Workgroup Manager will do simple checking for the manifest format when you click Add in the Details pane.

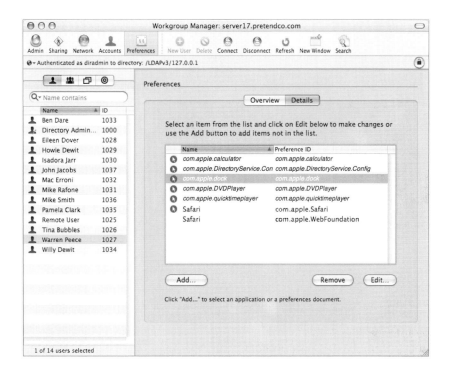

Edit Preference Manifests

All Workgroup Manager preferences (such as Dock, Finder, System Preferences, etc.) are editable using the preference manifest edit function once they have been initially managed. Select the preference you want to view or edit and an XML editor is displayed. You can edit entries here and set them to be managed always, often, or once. This is the only place where the Often setting is available. Workgroup Manager will make a best effort to display record types in known formats. Not all the options configurable may be displayed. Only those settings with values are displayed and no error check-ing is applied to the fields (for example, it would be possible to set a font size to 240 instead of 24).

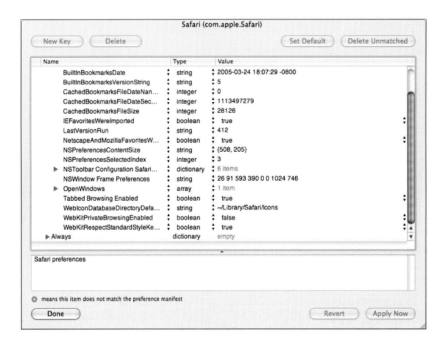

Restrict Access to Applications

You will use the Applications pane in the Preferences pane to specify which applications Pamela Clark can open.

1 Open Workgroup Manager on your Mac OS X computer and authenticate if necessary.

2   Select Pamela Clark in the Accounts list and click the Preferences button in the toolbar.

3   Click the Applications button in the Preferences pane and select Always as the management choice.

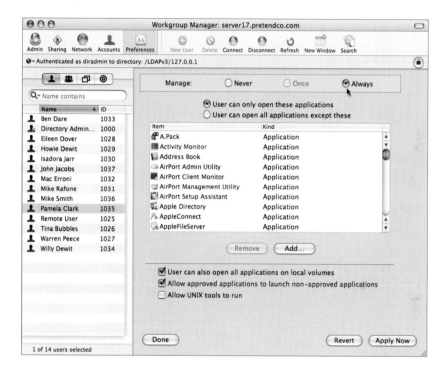

4   Deselect the "User can also open all applications on local volumes" option and select "User can only open these applications."

5   Select Directory Access, NetInfo Manager, and System Preferences, click Remove, and then click Apply Now.

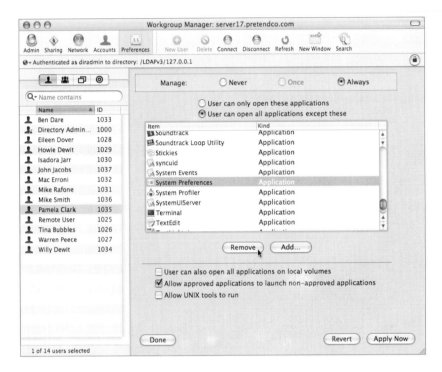

6   Log out of your Mac OS X computer and log back in as Pamela. (You can use Fast User Switching for this if you want.)

7   Click System Preferences in the Dock. What happens?

Go to the Applications folder and double-click System Preferences. What happens?

In both instances you cannot launch System Preferences.

8   Attempt to open NetInfo Manager located in the Utilities folder within the Applications folder.

You cannot launch NetInfo Manager.

NOTE ▶ System Preferences is an application. By not allowing access to this application, you have prevented Pamela from viewing or changing any system preferences.

Restrict Access to Selected System Preferences

In the following steps, you allow Pamela to access a selected number of system preferences.

1   Log in as your local administrator and select Pamela Clark in Workgroup Manager. Click the Preferences button in the toolbar.

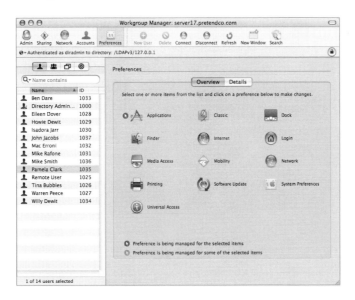

2 Click the Applications button, click Add, choose System Preferences from the list of applications, click Add again, and click Apply Now.

You must add the System Preferences application back to the list of applications that the user can manage. If you do not do this, then attempting to manage various system preferences is a moot point.

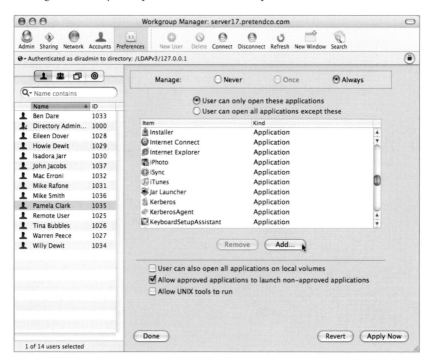

3 Click the Preferences button in the toolbar and click the System Preferences button in the Preferences pane.

4   Select Always as the management choice and deselect the Accounts and Energy Saver preferences. Click Apply Now.

5   Log out or use Fast User Switching and log back in as Pamela.

This will reset the preferences for the user Pamela. Preferences are configured when the user logs in to the system.

6   Open System Preferences.

In the System Preferences window, the Accounts and Energy Saver preferences are dimmed and cannot be changed by Pamela.

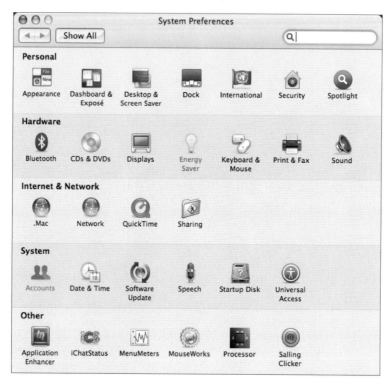

7 Log out as Pamela and log back in as your local administrator.

Managing Preferences on a Network

You will use Workgroup Manager to manage Login, Dock, Finder, and Printer preferences for given accounts. You will then set print quotas.

Configure Login Preferences

These steps show you how to use the Login pane under Preferences in Workgroup Manager to make the Mail application open the first time a user logs into a Mac OS X computer.

1   Open Workgroup Manager and connect to your server as sadmin. Click the globe icon under the toolbar and select the LDAPv3/127.0.0.1 domain from the pop-up menu.

2   Select the Accounts button in the toolbar, select the user Mike Smith, and then click the Preferences button in the toolbar.

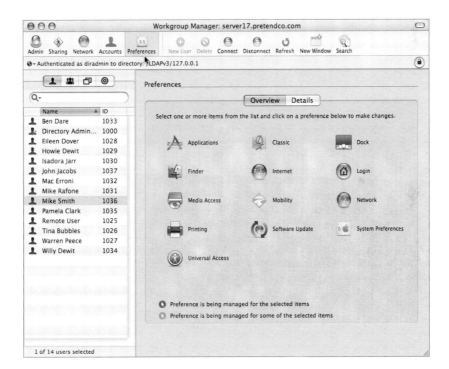

3   Click the Login button in the Preferences pane and select Once as the management choice in the Login Items pane. Click the Add button to add the Mail application (located in /Applications) and click Apply Now.

The Mail application will always open automatically when Mike logs in, unless he changes his login options and removes Mail from the list of applications that open automatically at login.

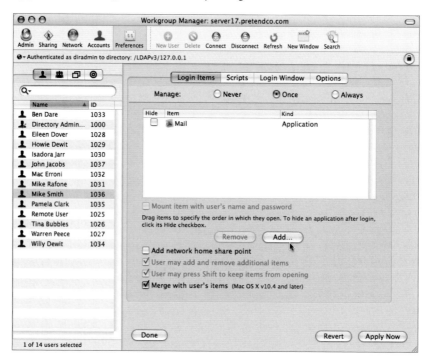

4   Open System Preferences on your Mac OS X computer, click the Accounts preferences pane, click Login Options, and select the "Enable fast user switching" checkbox.

5   Use Fast User Switching to switch to the login window and log in as Mike Smith.

Notice that Mail starts automatically.

6   Quit Mail by clicking the Cancel button.

7   Open the Accounts pane in System Preferences, select the Mike Smith account, and click Login Items.

Notice that Mail has been added to the list of items that open automatically when Mike logs in.

8   Select Mail from the Login Items list and click the Delete (–) button.

Mail will not start the next time Mike logs in because the preferences were set to Once. Therefore Mike has the freedom to choose whether to keep Mail as a login item or not.

9   Log out as Mike Smith and log back in as the local administrator.

You *must* log out as Mike Smith so the next preference changes will take effect. Just doing Fast User Switching from Mike to your local administrator will not show the newer preferences.

Since you are using Fast User Switching, Workgroup Manager is still running.

Configure Dock Preferences

Use the Dock preferences pane to add three applications (Grab, Stickies, and TextEdit) and the Applications folder to Mike Smith's Dock and to set the size of the Dock.

1   In Workgroup Manager, select the Mike Smith account and click the Preferences button in the toolbar.

Notice that because you previously managed Login preferences, it has an arrow next to the icon.

2   Click the Dock button in the Preferences pane, select Always as the management choice, click the Add button next to the Applications list, and add the following applications:

▶ TextEdit

▶ Calculator

▶ Stickies

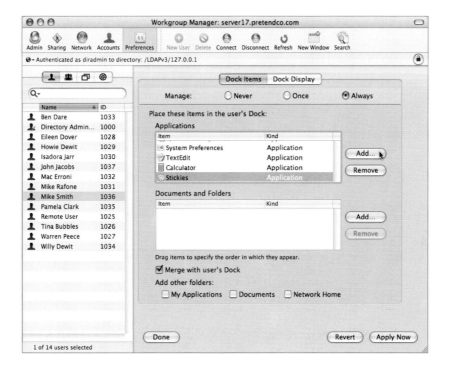

3   Click the Add button next to the Documents and Folders list, navigate to
    the Applications folder, click Add, make sure "Merge with user's Dock" is
    selected, and click Apply Now.

4   Click the Dock Display button, select Always as the management choice,
    set the Dock Size to Large, select "Automatically hide and show the Dock,"
    and click Apply Now.

When Mike logs in, the Dock will contain Calculator, Stickies, and TextEdit; it will be large; and it will be hidden until the pointer is moved to the bottom of the screen.

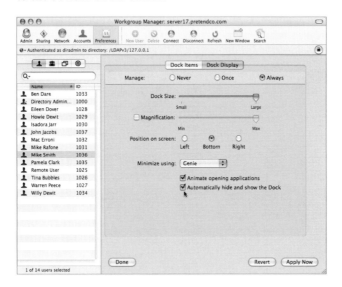

5   Use Fast User Switching and log back in as Mike Smith.

Verify that the Dock settings you just defined in Workgroup Manager have taken effect. Verify that the change is persistent and that Mike can't remove the contents of the Dock.

6   Log out as Mike Smith and log back in as the local administrator.

Since you are using Fast User Switching, Workgroup Manager is still running.

Configure Finder Preferences

Next, you will use Workshop Manager to configure Finder preferences to restrict the views and remove some menu item commands.

1   In Workgroup Manager, select the Mike Smith account and click the Preferences button in the toolbar.

Notice that because you previously managed Login preferences and Dock preferences, they have arrows next to the icons.

2 Click the Finder button in the Preferences pane, select Always as the management choice, click the Views button, and select Always as the management choice. Next set the Icon Size to Large.

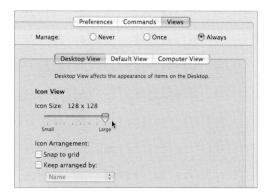

3 Click the Commands button, select Always as the management choice, and deselect the following checkboxes:

▶ Go to iDisk

▶ Burn Disk

▶ Go to Folder

▶ Restart

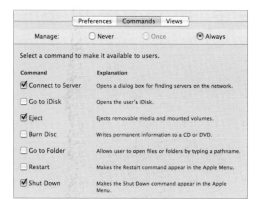

4 Click Apply Now.

5 Use Fast User Switching to log back in as Mike Smith and verify the following:

▶ The hard disk icon is extremely large.

▶ The Restart option is missing from the Apple Menu.

▶ Go to My iDisk and Go to Folder are missing from the Go menu.

▶ The Burn Disk option is missing from the File menu.

6 Log out as Mike Smith and log back in as the local administrator.

Since you are using Fast User Switching, Workgroup Manager is still running.

Configure Printer Preferences

Next, you will configure Mike Smith's printer preferences so that he always has access to a specific printer.

1 In Workgroup Manager, select the Mike Smith account and click the Preferences button in the toolbar.

Notice that because you previously managed Login, Dock, and Finder preferences, they have arrows next to the icons.

2 Click the Printing button in the Preferences pane, select Always as the management choice, and click the Printer List button.

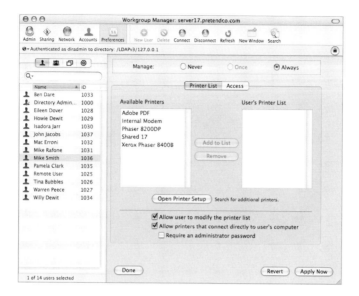

3   In the Printer List pane in the list of available printers, select Shared 17 (this was a printer created in Lesson 7) and click the Add to List button.

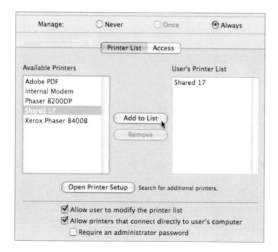

4   Deselect the checkboxes at the bottom of the Printer List pane to prevent Mike from using any other printers.

5 Click the Access button. In the User's Printer List, select Shared 17, click the Make Default button, and click Apply Now.

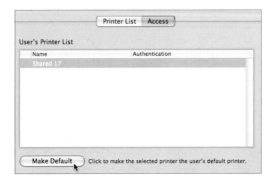

6 Use Fast User Switching to log back in as Mike Smith and open Printer Setup Utility (located in /Applications/Utilities). Verify that Shared 17 is the default printer.

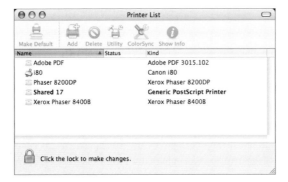

7 Log out as Mike Smith and log back in as the local administrator.

Since you are using Fast User Switching, Workgroup Manager is still running.

Impose Quotas on a Print Queue

Next, you'll use Workgroup Manager to specify how many pages Mike can print per day.

1   In Workgroup Manager select the Mike Smith account, click the Accounts button in the toolbar, and click the Print Quota button.

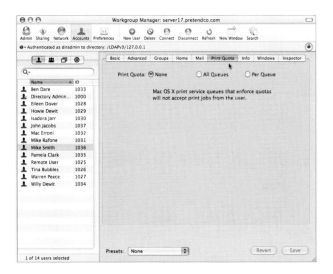

2   For Print Quota, select All Queues, enter the following values, and then click Save:

▶   Limit to: *20*

▶   Every: *1*

Managing Workgroup Accounts

You will use Workgroup Manager to configure Application preferences, Dock preferences, and Finder preferences for a group. You will then log in to the Mac OS X computer and observe how group preferences work with user preferences.

Create Groups With Workgroup Manager

First, you will create a group to share preferences.

1   In Workgroup Manager on your Mac OS X computer select the
LDAPv3/127.0.0.1 domain from the Directory drop-down menu.

2   Click the Accounts button in the toolbar and then click the Group button
to verify the two groups you previously created.

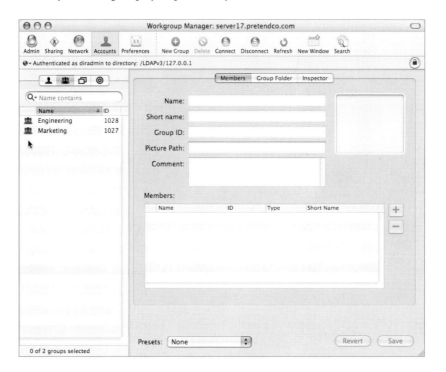

3   Add Mike Smith and Pamela Clark to the Engineering group and
click Save.

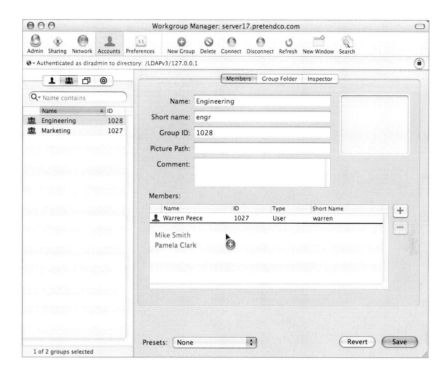

Specify Preferences for Groups

Configure preferences for the Engineering group.

1   Select the Engineering group in Workgroup Manager, click the Preferences button in the toolbar, and click the Applications button in the Preferences pane.

2   Select Always from the Manage options and set the following:

   ▶   Select "User can open all applications except these."

   ▶   Select all the applications in the list and click the Remove button.

   ▶   Deselect "User can also open all applications on local volumes."

▶ Deselect "Allow UNIX tools to run."

▶ Select "Allow approved applications to launch non-approved applications."

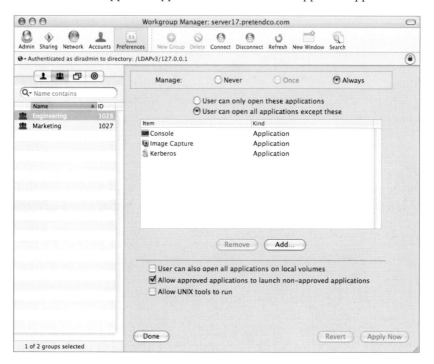

3 Click the Add button and add the following applications to the approved list:

▶ Image Capture (located in /Applications)

▶ Console (located in /Applications/Utilities)

▶ Kerberos (located in /System/Library/CoreServices)

4 Click Apply Now.

5 In Workgroup Manager, click the Preferences button in the toolbar and select the Dock preferences. Click the Dock Items button.

6   Select Always from the Manage options and click the Add button to add the following applications to the Dock:

▶   Image Capture (located in /Applications)

▶   Console (located in /Applications/Utilities)

▶   Kerberos (located in /System/Library/CoreServices)

7   Click Apply Now.

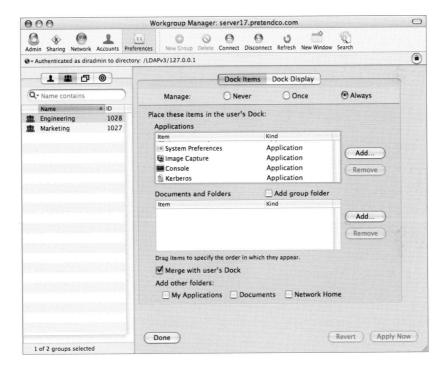

8   Click the Preferences button in the toolbar in Workgroup Manager and select the Finder preferences. Click the Preferences button that is in the

Finder Preferences pane, select Always from the Manage options, and select the "Always open windows in column view" checkbox.

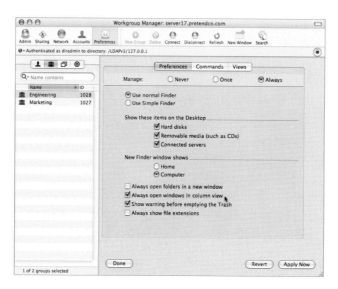

9   Click the Views button, select Always from the Manage options, click Desktop View, and set Icon Size to Small.

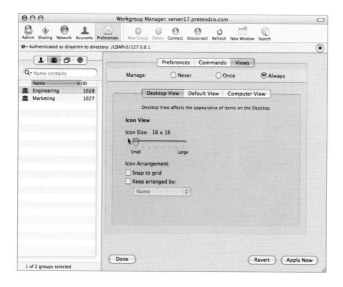

10 Click Apply Now.

Check Group Preferences Against User Preferences

You will now learn how group preferences work with user preferences.

1 Use Fast User Switching to log back in as Mike Smith.

Recall that Mike is a newer member of the Engineering group.

Notice how Mike's Finder preferences, which specify large icon size, took precedence over the group's preferences. Also notice that Mike's Dock has both Mike's applications and the Engineering group's applications. Verify that Mike also still does not have access to the Restart option under the Apple menu and his Go menu is still altered.

2 Log out as Mike and log in as Warren Peece (another member of the Engineering group).

Notice that Warren's hard drive icon is small and the Image Capture application has been added to the Dock in addition to the other applications that were specified by the Engineering group. Verify that Warren does, however, have access to the Restart option under the Apple menu as well as access to the other Go menu options.

3 Log out as Warren and log back in as the local administrator.

Since you are using Fast User Switching, Workgroup Manager is still running.

Create Group Folders

You will now use the CreateGroupFolder command to manually create group folders.

1 In Workgroup Manager on your Mac OS X computer, select the LDAPv3/127.0.0.1 domain from the Directory pop-up menu.

2 Click the Sharing button, click the Share Points button, and select the Groups folder from the list. Then click the Network Mount button on the right.

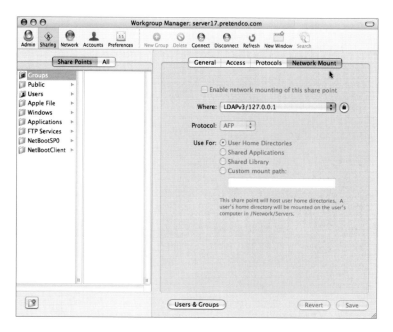

3 Click the Lock icon and authenticate as diradmin. Select "Enable network mounting of this share point," ensure that AFP is the protocol used for User Home Directories, and click Save.

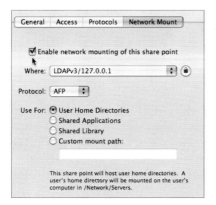

4   Click the Accounts button in the toolbar, click the Group button, and select the Engineering group.

5   Click the Group Folder button and select afp://server17.pretendco.com/ Groups from the list of share points shown. Click the Browse (…) button to choose mikesmith in the Owner Name field, and then click Save.

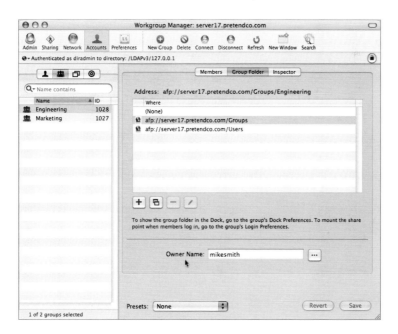

6 On your Mac OS X computer, open the Terminal application (located in /Applications/Utilities) and type *ssh root@10.1.17.1* and press Return.

If this is the first time you have connected to your server via the terminal (exactly what you are doing here), type *yes* at the prompt about the RSA Fingerprint and press Return.

7 Enter the password for sadmin (root's password on Mac OS X Server is initially the same as the administrator's account during the setup process).

8 Type *CreateGroupFolder* and press Return.

In the Finder on your server, notice that a new group folder is created in /Groups called Engineering.

9 Type *exit* in the Terminal and press Return to exit the ssh connection and then quit the Terminal application.

Configure the Group Folder to Be Available to Members

You can make the group folder automatically available to members of the group when they log in to their computers by changing the Login and Dock preferences.

1 In Workgroup Manager on your Mac OS X computer, select the LDAPv3/127.0.0.1 domain from the Directory pop-up menu.

2 Select the Engineering group in Workgroup Manager, click the Preferences button in the toolbar, and click the Dock button in the Preferences pane. Then click the Dock Items button, select the "Add group folder" checkbox, and click Apply Now.

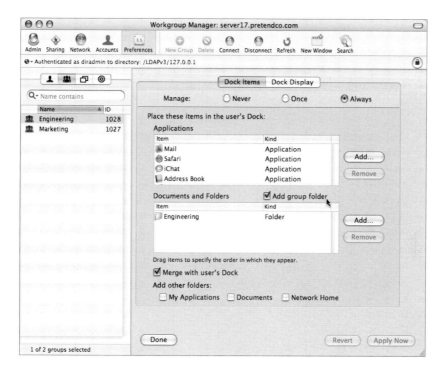

3 Click the Preferences button in the toolbar and click the Login button to reveal the Login preference options.

4 Select Always from the Manage options and select "Add group share point." Then select the share point "Groups" from the Login Items window and place a checkmark in the "Mount item with the user's name and password" checkbox. Click Apply Now.

5 Use Fast User Switching to log back in as Mike Smith, and verify that the Engineering folder is in the Dock and the Groups share point is mounted on the Desktop and that you have access to the Engineering group folder.

6 Log out as Mike Smith and log back in as the local administrator.

Since you are using Fast User Switching, Workgroup Manager is still running.

Managing Computer Access

Now you will create a computer list, add a group to it, and configure its Application, Dock, and Finder preferences. You will then log in to the client and observe how computer list preferences work with group and user preferences. Finally, you will enable Auto Log-Out for the computer list.

> **WARNING** ▶ While this lesson is non-destructive, if you do not follow the steps exactly, you will not be permitted access to your applications again. If you have not already backed up, do so now.

1 In Workgroup Manager on your Mac OS X computer, select the LDAPv3/127.0.0.1 domain from the Directory pop-up menu.

2 Click the Accounts button in the toolbar and click the Computer List button.

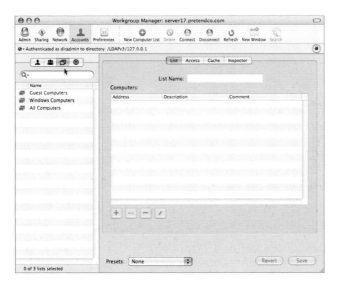

3   Select the Engineering Computers list and click the Delete button in the toolbar.

Computers can be members of only one list; we will assign the Mac OS X computer to a new list.

4   Click New Computer List in the toolbar and in the List Name field, type *XSE Course*.

5   Click the Browse (…) button at the bottom of the pane, choose your Mac OS X computer from the list, and click Connect.

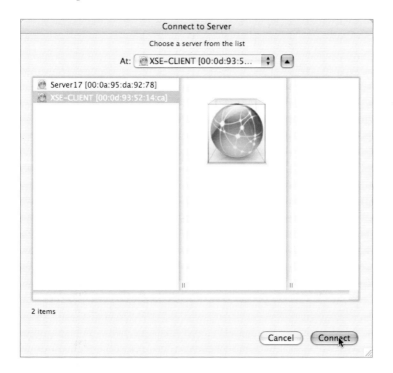

Your Mac OS X computer will be listed by XSE-CLIENT because you have a static IP address and that is the computer and Bonjour name of your Mac OS X computer.

6   Click Save.

7 Click the Preferences button in the toolbar and select the Finder preferences. Click the Preferences button located in the Finder Preferences pane, select Always from the Manage options, and then select the "Always open folders in a new window" checkbox.

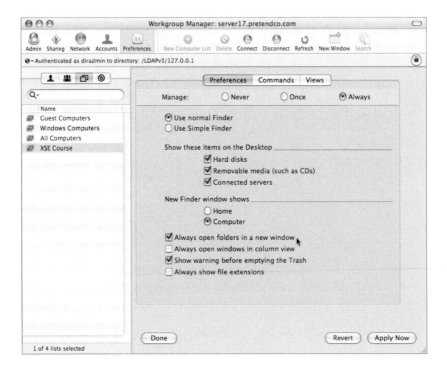

8 Click Apply Now.

9 Click the Accounts button in the toolbar, select the XSE Course from the computer list, click the Access button and select "Restrict to groups below." Add Engineering to the list of groups using the Add Group (+) button and click Save.

Only members of the Engineering group have access to the Mac OS X computer.

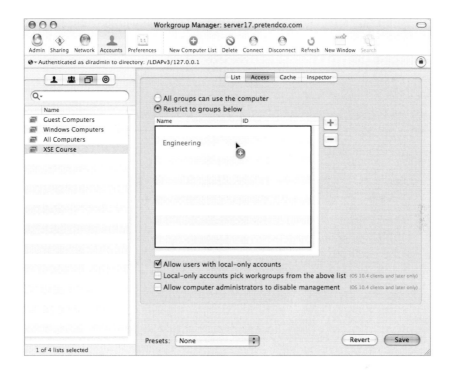

10 Use Fast User Switching and attempt to log in as Tina Bubbles.

    You cannot log in because Tina is not part of the Engineering group.

11 Attempt to log in as Mike Smith and verify that restricted access allows
    Mike to log in because he is part of the Engineering group.

12 Log out as Mike and log back in as the local administrator.

    Since you are using Fast User Switching, Workgroup Manager is still running.

Configuring Computer List Preferences

Configure the Application preferences for the XSE Course computer list to
allow users to open the Chess application.

1   In Workgroup Manager on your Mac OS X computer, select the
    LDAPv3/127.0.0.1 domain from the Directory pop-up menu.

2   Select XSE Course from the Computer List and click the Preferences button in the toolbar.

3   Click the Applications button in the Preferences pane, select Always from the Manage options, and allow users to only open the Chess (located in the Applications folder) and Workgroup Manager (located in the Server folder inside the Applications folder) Applications. Do not allow users to open applications on local volumes.

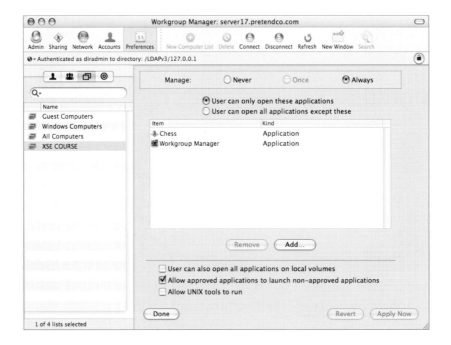

4   Click Apply Now and then click Done.

Clicking the Done button is another way to get back to the main Preferences pane of Workgroup Manager. It is not a requirement that you use this button, rather an optional step.

5   Click the Dock button in the Preferences pane and then click the Dock Items button. Select Always from the Manage options, and click the Add button to add Chess to the Dock.

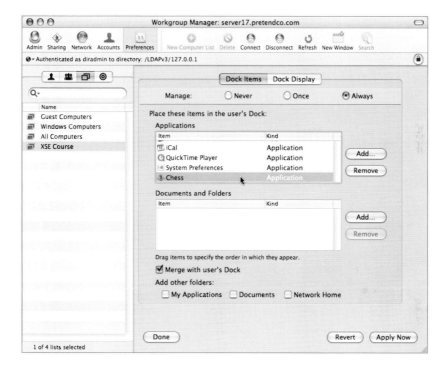

6   Click Apply Now and then click Done.

7   Click the Finder button in the Preferences pane and then click the Preferences button located in the Finder Preferences pane. Select Always from the Manage options and select the following:

▶ "Always open folders in a new window"

▶ "Always open windows in column view"

▶ "Always show warning before emptying the Trash"

▶ "Always show file extensions"

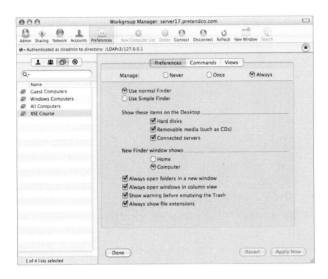

8   Click Apply Now and then click Done.

9   Click the Login button in the Preferences pane and then click the Options
    button. Select Always from the Manage options and select the "Log out
    users after x minutes of inactivity" checkbox (where x is 5 minutes).

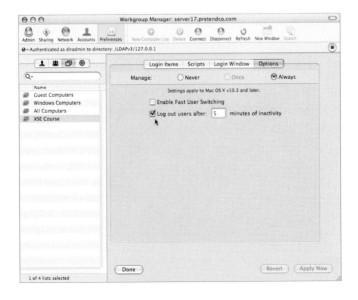

10 Click Apply Now and then click Done.

11 Use Fast User Switching to log back in as Mike Smith and observe how computer list preferences interact with group and user preferences.

Notice that Mike's Finder preferences, which specify that the desktop icons be set to large, take precedence over the Group preferences, which are set to small. Also notice that Mike can open only the Chess application, which now shows up in his Dock, and the Workgroup Manager application (although Mike cannot actually use Workgroup Manager, he can launch it). Along with Chess, the three applications we specified for the Engineering group account preferences, Image Capture, Kerberos, and Console, also show up in the Dock. The restriction to only launch Chess and Workgroup Manager is a computer list account preference.

12 Log out as Mike and log in as Warren Peece (another member of the Engineering group).

Notice how Warren's Finder preferences, which specify that the desktop icons never be managed, has the icon size for the desktop set to small by his group association. Also notice that Warren can open only the Chess application, which now shows up in his Dock, and the Workgroup Manager application (although Mike cannot actually use Workgroup Manager, he can launch it). Along with Chess, the three applications we specified for the Engineering Group account preferences, Image Capture, Kerberos, and Console, also show up in the Dock. The restriction to only launch Chess and Workgroup Manager is a computer list account preference.

13 Log out as Warren and log in as Pamela (another member of the Engineering group).

Notice how Pamela's Finder preferences, which specify that the desktop icons never be managed, has the icon size for the desktop set to small by her group association. Also notice that not only can Pamela launch Chess and Workgroup Manager, she can also launch System Preferences, which was specified by her user account application preferences. However, she cannot access the Accounts and Energy Saver preference panes, as specified by her System Preferences preference management.

14 Log out as Pamela and log back in as the local administrator, then launch Workgroup Manager. Select the Engineering Computers account list, click the Preferences button in the toolbar, click the Applications icon, and click the option to Never manage applications again for this computer list. Click Apply Now. If any other management arrows exist next to preference management icons, click on those icons and set the manage option to Never and click Apply Now.

15 Restart the Mac OS X computer, login as the local administrator, and confirm you can access all applications.

Managing Network Browsing

In the Finder, a user can open the /Network folder to browse for network servers. Typically all network services that announce or publish themselves do so using Bonjour, SLP, or AppleTalk. In Mac OS X Server v10.4 you can configure and customize this user experience to show the user exactly what you want him or her to see.

The Network Option in Workgroup Manager creates entries in the server's directory that will be displayed to clients of the directory when they attempt to access the /Network folder or browse the network. This managed network-browsing feature allows you to customize the user's view of what is on the network.

Create the View

There are three ways to configure a Network view for clients on the same physical network as the Mac OS X Server computer:

▶ Named view is for those specific computers listed in Workgroup Manager. When bound to the directory they will see the specified view.

▶ Default view is what is seen by users who are bound to the directory (for example, many DHCP clients), but do not have specific managed preferences.

▶ Public view is seen by clients who connect to the network but are not bound in any way to the directory service.

Customize the View

Once you have set up the view to be managed, you use Workgroup Manager to customize what is displayed in each zone or neighborhood. Neighborhoods are groupings of services. They are similar to AppleTalk zones, for those familiar with that implementation.

Using Workgroup Manager you can populate the neighborhood with individual services, including all published services, such as Bonjour servers. User-friendly names can be given to each of the layouts to facilitate client browsing. Once the layout is created, settings for each service can be determined. This is handled on a computer-record level. Services such as afp:// or http:// are aligned with specific computer records.

> **NOTE ▶** Computer records created elsewhere in Workgroup Manager are usable in the Managed Network interface as well.

Configure Managed Network Browsing

You will create managed /Network views in the three types of views: Named, Default, and Public. You will create a customized view for server clients. In each case you will need to restart the client machines for the changes to be registered. The /Network information is read in when the client starts.

1 In Workgroup Manager on your Mac OS X computer, select the LDAPv3/127.0.0.1 domain from the Directory pop-up menu.

You are about to create a Default view for users bound to this Directory Master. "Default" is a reserved word, unique to this implementation.

NOTE ▶ The term "Default" has meaning only in the context of managed network views. If you name a network view with the name Default, it will behave as described here.

2 Click the Network button in the toolbar.

If prompted with a Create Managed View configuration sheet, leave the Default view settings.

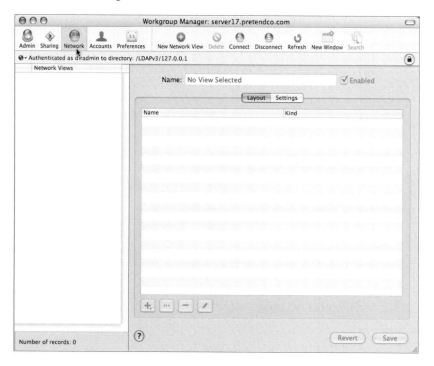

3   Click New Network View in the toolbar. Verify that only the Default view
is selected and click Create.

4   On the lower-left side of the layout pane, click the Add Item (+) button.
Choose New Neighborhood from the pop-up menu and enter *Server17
Zone* in the Name column. Click Save.

5   Select the Server17 Zone, click the Add Item (+) button, and choose
Dynamic List from the Add pop-up menu.

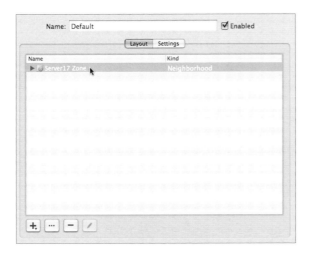

6   Choose /Bonjour/local and click Add.

You will see a list of the services that broadcast availability using the Bonjour protocol, and you have set the Default user view. The /Bonjour/local option now shows up under the Server17 Zone neighborhood (which itself appears as a folder in the Layout pane).

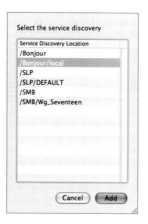

7 Click Save. Click the Settings button and verify the "Client Finder will add to Network view" option is selected. Click Save if necessary.

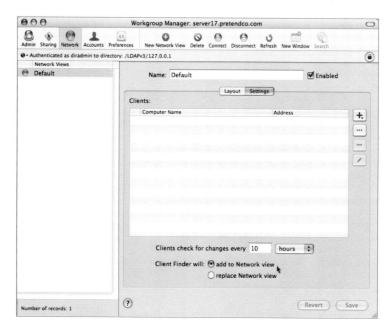

Create the Public View

You will create the Public view for users who are not bound to this Directory master. "Public" is a reserved word, unique to this implementation.

> **NOTE ▶** The term "Public" has meaning only in the context of managed network views. If you name a network view with the name Public, it will behave as described here.

1   Click the Layout button and click New Network View in the toolbar. Select "a named view" and click Create.

2   Name the new view Public. Create a new neighborhood named Public Servers by clicking the Add Item (+) button and choosing New Neighborhood from the pop-up menu. Click Save.

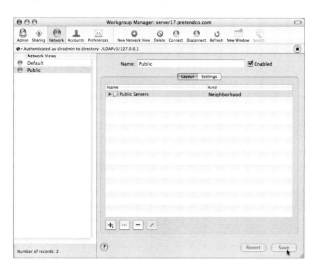

3   Create a dynamic listing by clicking the Add Items (+) button and choosing Dynamic List from the pop-up menu. From the dialog that subsequently appears, choose /SMB/Wg_Seventeen. Click Add and then click Save.

4   Click Settings and verify the "Client Finder will add to Network view" option is selected. Click Save.

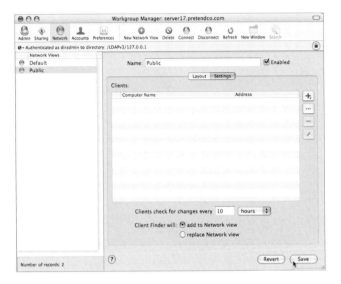

5   Click the Layout button and click New Network View in the toolbar. Select "a named view" and click Create.

6   Name the new view Development and create a new neighborhood named Private Zone. Click Save.

7   Select Private Zone, choose Show Computers from the Add Items pop-up menu, and drag XSE-CLIENT to the Layout pane.

You must add a URL for this computer.

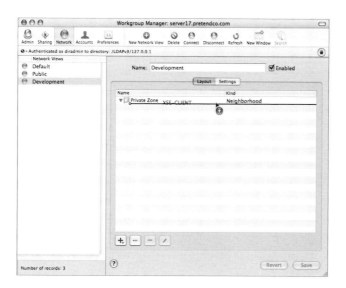

8   Click the Edit button.

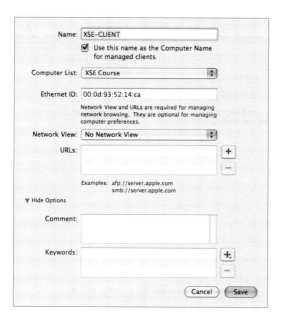

9   Click the Add URL (+) button and enter *afp://xse-client.local.*

10   Click the Add URL (+) button again and enter *http://xse-client.local.*

11   Click Save to close the dialog, and click Save again.

There are now two URLs associated with XSE-CLIENT.

12   Click the Settings button and verify the "Client Finder will add to Network View" option is selected, and click Save.

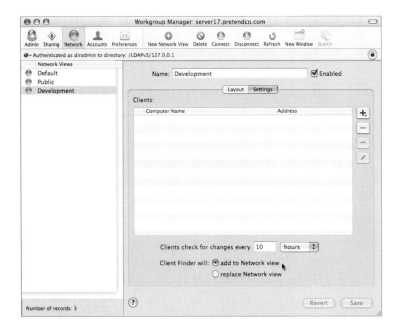

Test the Network Views on the Mac OS X Computer

Test your configuration with a client that is bound to directory services and one that is not.

1   On your Mac OS X computer, open Directory Access located in /Applications/Utilities and authenticate as the local administrator. Deselect LDAP and click Apply.

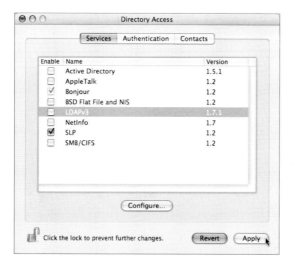

2   Restart the Mac OS X computer.

3   Log in as your local administrator, open a Finder window, and click the Network folder.

Notice the view of the Network has the Default view that you created.

4   Open Directory Access located in /Applications/Utilities and authenticate as the local administrator, recheck LDAP, and click Apply.

5   Restart the Mac OS X computer.

6   Log in as your local administrator, open a Finder window, and click the Network folder.

Since the directory service knows about the computer account, it sees the Named view. Without a known client, the Default view would be visible.

7 In Workgroup Manager on your Mac OS X Server, select the LDAPv3/127.0.0.1 domain from the Directory pop-up menu.

8 Click the Accounts button in the toolbar and then click the Computer List accounts button. Select the XSE Course computer list and click the Delete button in the toolbar to delete the XSE Course computer list.

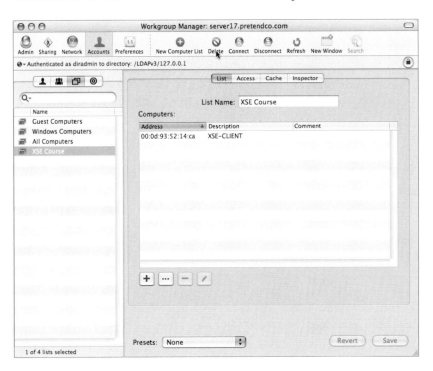

9 Confirm your deletion in the confirmation dialog.

10 Restart your Mac OS X computer and log in as your local administrator account.

Managing Mobile User Accounts

Network user accounts provide a great deal of administrative control, but they are useful only for computers that are constantly connected to the network. If a computer is disconnected from the network, it no longer has access to network user accounts or home folders. To help manage accounts on computers that are not always connected to the network, such as portables, Mac OS X Server v10.3 and later provides the Mobile Accounts managed preference, which allows you to create mobile user accounts.

A mobile user account is a Mac OS X Server user account that resides in a shared domain but is copied to the local computer. This allows a user to log in to a portable computer using the network account even when the computer is not connected to a network. New in Mac OS X Server v10.4 is file synchronization with the server account. Files can be set to be automatically copied from the user's network home folder.

When a computer is connected to the network and the mobile user logs in, the operating system authenticates the user using the account information stored in the shared domain to which the computer is bound. The mobile account on the computer is updated automatically, including any managed preferences. When the computer is disconnected, the user logs in using the local account, which provides the same level of administrative control as that of the network account. In either case, whether the computer is connected to the network or not, the home folder is stored locally on the computer.

Creating and Deleting Mobile User Accounts

To create a mobile user account:

1 Open Workgroup Manager, select a network user account, and then click Preferences in the toolbar.

2   Click Mobility and set the management setting to Always.

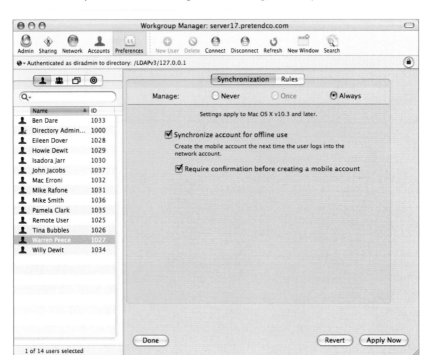

3   Select "Synchronize account for offline use."

4   Select "Require confirmation before creating a mobile account" if you want to allow the user to decide whether to create a mobile account at login.

If this option is selected, the user sees a confirmation dialog when logging in. The user can click Create to create the mobile account immediately, or can click Continue to log in as a network user without creating the mobile account.

5   Click Apply Now.

TIP ▶ If you manage only the creation of a mobile account for a network user, the user's local home folder becomes the default home folder. Any files that were stored in the network home folder are not copied to the local home folder. There is no file synchronization unless you set up rules.

You can also create mobile user accounts by managing the Mobility preference for a workgroup or computer list. For example, if you manage the Mobility preference for a workgroup, all members of the workgroup become mobile users. This can serve to be very useful in a large setting of portables, such as a school full of iBook computers. Similarly, if you manage this preference for a computer list, all users of the computer become mobile users.

If a user no longer requires a mobile account, you should select "Not ever" as the Mobility preference in Workgroup Manager. In addition, you might want to delete the local copy of the account. Both the mobile account and its local home folder are deleted. You must have a local administrator account and password to delete a mobile account. To delete a mobile account:

1   Open System Preferences on the client computer.

2   Click Accounts.

3   Select the account you want to delete.

    The mobile account should have the word "Mobile" beneath it.

4   Click the Delete User (–) button, and then click OK.

Account Synchronization

Creating a mobile account is useful because a user can authenticate with the network information, and the owner of the files on the local and network folders is the same. You can set up rules for automatically copying files. For each preference set you can establish which files can be synchronized at login and logout. These files are currently only copied from the home folder path.

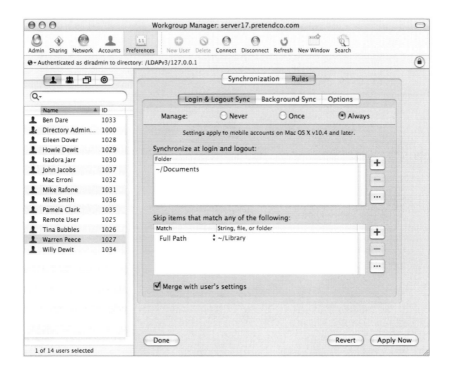

NOTE ▶ While you can set up mobile accounts for your Mac OS X v10.3 users, only users of Mac OS X v10.4 can take advantage of the synchronization rules.

Account Synchronization of Home Folders

The Rules pane lets you designate which files you want synchronized. These files will be synchronized with the corresponding folder on the server. Because the mobile account is a duplicate of the Network account, all the permissions and ownership are identical. You can set up folders to copy and decide whether the copy takes place in the background. You can also determine which files should not be copied.

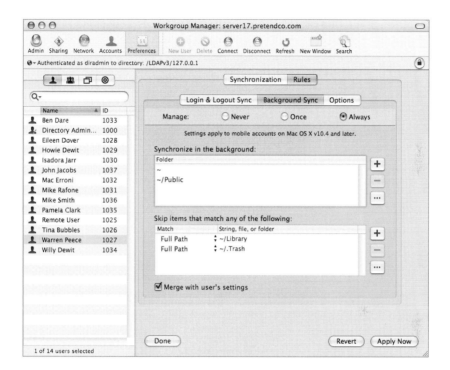

TIP ▶ Cache files, temporary files, and settings specific to the mobile account such as printer settings can be set to never be cached. Limit what is synchronized to essential files and important data. Network administrators may want to preclude music and photos as a rule.

Account Synchronization Options

The Options tab lets you set the timing for the synchronization of files. This can be done on a set time interval or manually. This option is only for the file synchronization and does not affect preferences if they have been selected.

Preference synchronization is currently not supported in Mac OS X Server v10.4.

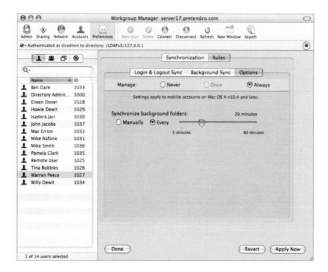

Configure Mobile Computing

You will use one of the accounts you set up previously and set up a synchronized mobile user account for that person.

1   In Workgroup Manager on your Mac OS X computer, select the LDAPv3/127.0.0.1 domain from the Directory pop-up menu.

2   Select Ben Dare from the Accounts list and click the Preferences button in the toolbar.

3   Click the Mobility button, select Always from the Manage options, and select the following checkboxes:

▶   "Synchronize account for offline use"

▶   "Require confirmation before creating a mobile account"

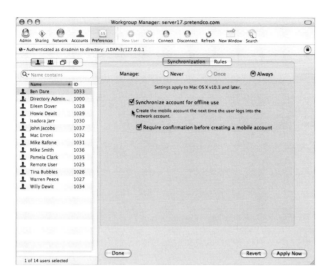

4 Click the Rules button, click the Background Sync button, and select Always from the Manage options. Delete the tilde (~) from the "Synchronize in background" list by selecting it and clicking the Delete (-) button.

The default is to copy the entire Home Directory path except those folders listed in the Skip pane. Configure it to synchronize only the Documents folder.

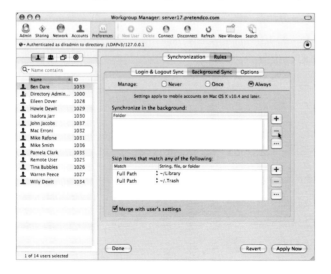

5 Click the Add (+) button and enter ~/*Documents* so you are synching just the Documents folder.

6 With the Documents folder configured, set the synchronization schedule. For this lesson, the schedule should be minimal.

7 Click the Options button, select Always from the Manage options, and verify the timing slider is set to 5 minutes. Click Apply Now.

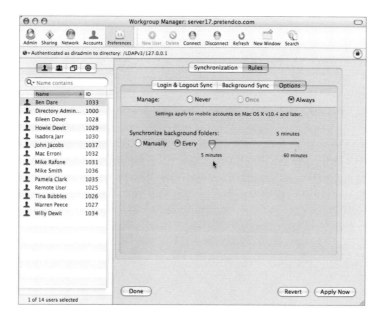

8 Quit Workgroup Manager and restart your Mac OS X computer.

Verify Mobility Account From the Client

The Ben Dare account is now configured to exist locally on each system he successfully logs in to, and files stored in ~/Documents will be synchronized with the Network account.

1 On the Mac OS X computer, log in as Ben.

2 Click the Yes button when the confirmation dialog asks if you want to create a portable home directory.

3 Open TextEdit, create a text file, and save it to the ~/Documents folder.

4 Wait 5 minutes.

5 On the server, view Ben's Document folder type with the Terminal by typing *sudo ls -al /Users/ben/Documents/*.

6 Enter the sadmin password when asked.

This will show all of Ben's documents without actually logging in as Ben on the server.

The file should appear after about 5 minutes.

7 On your Mac OS X computer, log out as Ben and log back in as the local administrator.

Troubleshooting

The majority of problems encountered initiate from users not being able to connect. This happens primarily at login. Check the following issues when troubleshooting account management:

▶ Check the Directory Service binding. Is the client bound to the correct directory?

▶ Is the Directory Server exported correctly?

▶ Check the user, group, and computer list settings. Are the settings too restrictive? For example, is guest access denied and a new computer online?

▶ Check the preferences by logging in as a similar user. This works best if most preferences are shared by the group.

▶ Use the Inspector to view the raw preferences. It is especially useful if settings are set manually and copied into the user records. The Details functionality can also serve as a quick check for a set of preferences.

What You've Learned

▶ Account management encompasses everything from setting up accounts for network access and creating home folders to fine-tuning the user experience by managing preferences and settings for users, groups, and computers.

▶ Workgroup Manager is an account-management tool. It provides centralized directory-based management of users, groups, and computers—from anywhere on your network.

▶ The account information for a network user resides in a shared domain, and the user's home folder resides on a home folder server. Network users can log in from any client on the network and have access to their home folders.

▶ A mobile user has two synchronized accounts. The main account resides in a shared domain, and a copy of the main account resides locally on the user's computer. The mobile user's home folder is stored locally. You can configure the user's files to be synchronized.

▶ A group folder offers a way to organize documents and applications of special interest to group members, and gives group members a folder where they can pass information back and forth.

▶ You can use the Export and Import commands in Workgroup Manager to back up and restore user and group accounts.

▶ A computer list is a list of computers that have the same preference settings and are available to the same users and groups. You can create and modify lists in Workgroup Manager.

▶ You can manage the user's experience of /Network by configuring network browsing. This also allows you to display services that may not advertise themselves automatically, such as a web server.

References

The following documents provide more information about installing Mac OS X Server. (All of these and more are available at www.apple.com/server/documentation.)

Administration Guides

Mac OS X Server Getting Started (http://images.apple.com/server/pdfs/Getting_Started_v10.4.pdf)

System Imaging and Software Update Administration (http://images.apple.com/server/pdfs/System_Image_and_SW_Update_v10.4.pdf)

Apple Remote Desktop 2 Administration Guide (http://images.apple.com/server/pdfs/Apple_Remote_Desktop_Admin_Guide.pdf)

Deploying Mac OS X Computers for k-12 Education (http://images.apple.com/server/pdfs/Deploying_Mac_OS_X_for_K12_Education.pdf)

Apple Knowledge Base Documents

You can check for new and updated Knowledge Base documents at www.apple.com/support.

URLs

MacEnterprise: www.macenterprise.org

Review Quiz

1. What is the difference between a local user account and a network user account?

2. How is a mobile user different from a network user?

3. Can a user be a member of more than one workgroup?

4. Can a computer be a member of more than one computer list?

5. How many user records can you import at one time using the Import command in Workgroup Manager?

6. How many computers can you add to a computer list in Workgroup Manager?

7. What is the difference between a group and a workgroup?

8. In Workgroup Manager, how can you configure preferences for user, group, and computer list accounts to avoid overrides?

9. Name two ways to review raw preference data in Workgroup Manager.

10. What folders are synchronized for mobile account users running v10.3?

11. What is the term used for a managed network grouping?

12. What folders are synchronized with mobile accounts?

Answers

1. In the case of a local user account, the home folder and account information are stored locally. But in the case of a network user account, the home folder is stored on a remote home folder server, and the account information resides in a shared domain.

2. A mobile user is a network user whose Mobility preference is managed. When you manage this preference, the next time the user logs in, Mac OS X Server creates two things: a copy of the user's account in the local domain of the user's computer, and a local home folder, which becomes the user's default home folder. Important: Any documents that were stored in the network home folder are not copied to the local home folder.

3. Yes

4. No

5. Each file you import can contain up to 10,000 records.

6. Up to 2000 computers

7. A workgroup is a group that has managed preferences.

8. By setting each preference for only one type of account. For example, you could set printer preferences only for computers, set application preferences only for workgroups, and set Dock preferences only for users. In such a case, no override occurs for these preferences because the user inherits them without competition.

9. Inspector and Details

10. Trick question—None; it only works for v10.4.

11. Neighborhood

12. Only those in the Home folder hierarchy

10

Lesson Files
/Users/Shared/Student_Materials/Lesson_10/
PretendCo_Biz_Plan.rtf

/Users/Shared/Student_Materials/Lesson_10/Fonts/*

Time
This lesson takes approximately 1 hour to complete.

Goals
Create NetBoot and Network Install images, and configure the server to allow NetBoot and Network Install

Learn how to install custom packages and configure startup disks with Apple Remote Desktop Admin

Use PackageMaker to create a custom installation package

Lesson 10
Implementing Deployment Solutions

Knowing how to use time efficiently is a very important aspect of an administrator's job. When managing several hundred Mac OS X computers, an administrator needs a solution that is both speedy and flexible for performing day-to-day management of the computers. When computers need to be set up for the very first time, what software should be installed? Should they have the latest software updates? Should they have a full complement of non-Apple software, such as Adobe Creative Suite or Microsoft Office? What about shareware programs and the necessary work-related files? Safety videos? Mandatory PDFs?

Before you can push out data to a computer, you must decide *how* to push out that data and in what state. Apple has several applications to assist you with this process, and there are several third-party tools that also complete the tasks of image creation and deployment. Apple has several applications—including System Image Utility, asr, Apple Remote Desktop (ARD), and NetBoot Service—to help you with this process.

There are also some third-party tools that perform image-creation and deployment tasks. These include:

► NetRestore (Mike Bombich Softtware)

► Radmind (University of Michigan)

► Iceberg (WhiteBox)

With the advantage of these and other deployment software tools, you can build an automated system that needs very little user interaction to function.

Deployment Issues

One significant challenge for Mac OS X administrators today is the deployment of software to multiple computers. Whether it is operating system (OS) releases and updates or commercial applications, installing the software manually is labor-intensive. Mac OS X Server provides services and technologies to aid in this deployment. NetBoot and Network Install simplify OS rollout and upgrades. When used with ARD, PackageMaker enables you to create and deploy custom packages from one location to multiple targets.

Deployment Solutions

Mac OS X Server includes two solutions that address deployment needs: NetBoot and custom packages. The other is custom installation via Apple Remote Desktop Admin's Install Packages feature.

Deployment Solutions

	Netboot NetInstall	Custom Packages/ARD
Operating System	✓	–
Applications	✓	✓
Files	–	✓
Suite of Apps	✓	✓

There are two basic mechanisms for deploying software over the network—client-driven and administrator-driven. The NetBoot service is an example of client-driven technology. Users can choose to start up their computers from a NetBoot server by selecting the network image in the Startup Disk pane of System Preferences. While in lab situations administrators may do the actual choosing, in real life each individual client can choose when or if to access the NetBoot server as long as they have administrative privileges on that particular computer. This is sometimes referred to as *pull technology*. When a client system boots up, it pulls data from the server. In this case, the disk image on the server is the operating system itself or an installation package.

In administrator-driven technology, an administrator selects multiple computers from a common console and installs software on those computers. This one-to-many interface is often referred to as *push technology*. ARD is an example of this technology. Using the Install Packages feature, identical software can be installed upon multiple targets at once.

There are pros and cons to each approach. Client-driven technology requires a server, while administrator-driven requires little, if any, client interaction. ARD—which is not part of Mac OS X Server and must be purchased separately—requires less network bandwidth than NetBoot.

> **TIP** Choosing the best method for you depends on your unique setup. NetBoot is perhaps best suited to lab and LAN environments. ARD is more useful with smaller installation efforts across a network. It also has other features, which are covered in Appendix A, "Introduction to Apple Remote Desktop."

Managing Computers With NetBoot

Think about the ways you boot your computer. Most often, your computer starts up from system software located on the local hard drive. This local startup provides you with a typical computer experience of running applications, accessing information, and accomplishing tasks. Sometimes when you perform OS installations or system upgrades, you need to boot from a CD-ROM or DVD-ROM.

Managing a single standalone computer isn't much of an inconvenience. However, imagine managing a lab of computers. Every time you need to upgrade the operating system or install a clean version of Mac OS X, you would need to boot each computer in the lab from the installation CD or DVD. Even with a set of installation discs for each computer, it would still be time-consuming to update or refresh the entire lab.

Mac OS X Server provides a service called NetBoot, which simplifies the management of operating systems on multiple computers. With NetBoot, client computers start up using system software that they access from a server instead of from the client's local hard drive. With NetBoot, the client obtains information from a remote location. With other startup methods, the client is booting off a local source, such as the internal hard drive, CD, or other device.

NetBoot

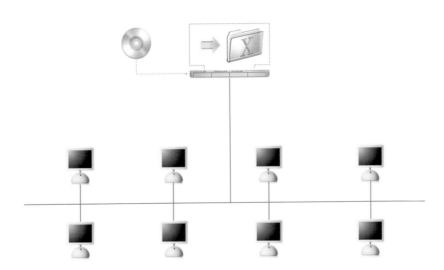

NetBoot is most effective in situations where there is a high frequency of user turnover and where a large number of computers are being deployed with a common configuration. The ability to deploy standard configurations across multiple computers makes NetBoot ideal for computing environments such as:

▶ Classrooms and computer labs: NetBoot makes it easy to configure multiple, identical desktop systems and repurpose them quickly. With NetBoot, you can reconfigure systems for a different class simply by restarting from a different image.

▶ Kiosks and libraries: With NetBoot, you can set up protected computing environments for customers or visitors. For example, you can configure an information station with an Internet browser that connects only to your company's website, or set up a visitor kiosk that runs only a database for collecting feedback. If a system is altered, a simple restart restores it to its original condition.

▶ Computational clusters: NetBoot is a powerful solution for data centers and computational clusters with identically configured web or application servers. Similarly purposed systems can boot from a single NetBoot image maintained on a network-based storage device.

The requirements for NetBoot to function vary slightly. To boot Mac OS X using NetBoot or to use Network Install, the client computer must have a minimum of 128 MB of RAM and 100Base-T Ethernet or faster network connections. (NetBoot using Mac OS 9 also requires only 64 MB of RAM.) For NetBoot deployments of 10 to 50 clients, a 100Base-T switched network is required. Gigabit Ethernet is required for booting more than 50 clients (although Apple has no official test results for configurations beyond 50 clients). Apple does not support the use of AirPort wireless technology with NetBoot clients.

NetBoot Startup

There are two types of NetBoot startup:

▶ A standard NetBoot startup (using a NetBoot boot image) provides a fairly typical computing experience, since clients start up using software that they access from a server.

▶   A Network Install startup sequence (using a NetBoot Install image) enables you to perform fresh installations of your operating system (much like installing from a CD-ROM), install applications or updates, or install configured disk images.

Keep these two types of NetBoot startup in mind while you work through the remainder of this lesson.

With NetBoot, you create disk images on the server that contain Mac OS X or Mac OS X Server system software. Multiple network clients can use each disk image at once. Because you are setting up a centralized source of system software, you need to configure, test, and deploy only once. This dramatically reduces the maintenance required for network computers.

When you start up from a NetBoot image, the startup volume is read-only. When a client needs to write anything back to its startup volume, NetBoot automatically redirects the written data to the client's shadow files (which are discussed later in this lesson, in the section "Understanding Shadow Files"). Data in shadow files is kept for the duration of a NetBoot session. Because the startup volume is read-only, you always start from a clean image. This is ideal in lab and kiosk situations where you want to ensure that users never alter the startup volume.

NetBoot Client Startup Process

When a client computer boots from a NetBoot image, it performs a number of steps to start up successfully:

1   The client places a request for an IP address.

    When a NetBoot client is turned on or restarted, it requests an IP address from a Dynamic Host Configuration Protocol (DHCP) server. While the server providing the address can be the same server providing the NetBoot service, the two services do not have to be provided by the same computer.

2   After receiving an IP address, the NetBoot client sends out a request for startup software. The NetBoot server then delivers the boot ROM file ("booter") to the client using Trivial File Transfer Protocol (TFTP) via its default port, 69.

3   Once the client has the ROM file, it initiates a mount and loads the images for the NetBoot network disk image.

The images can be served using HTTP or network file system (NFS).

NOTE ▶ Mac OS 9 clients used Apple Filing Protocol (AFP) for mounting during NetBoot.

4   After booting from the NetBoot image, the NetBoot client requests an IP address from the DHCP server.

Depending on the type of DHCP server used, the NetBoot client might receive an IP address different from the one received in step 1.

NetBoot Client Startup

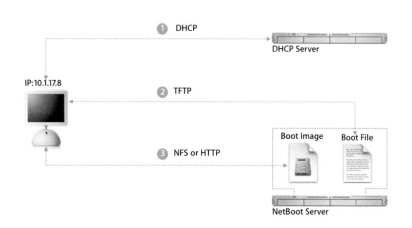

NOTE ▶ Previous versions of NetBoot server that used AFP to deliver network disk images could potentially run into AFP license restrictions. If you purchased the ten-client version of Mac OS X Server, your AFP license restricted you to supporting no more than ten AFP clients. This would limit the number of Mac OS 9 NetBoot clients to fewer than ten. This would not affect your Mac OS X NetBoot clients, since they use NFS or HTTP and are unrestricted even with the ten-client version of Mac OS X Server.

Using Home Folders With NetBoot

When you restart a client computer from a NetBoot image, the client computer receives a fresh copy of the system software and the startup volume. Users cannot store documents or preserve preferences on this startup volume, since it is a read-only image. If the administrator denies access to the local hard drive or removes the hard drive, users might not have any place to store documents. But if users log in using a network user account, they can store documents and preserve preferences in their network home folder.

When a user logs in to a NetBoot client computer using a network user account, the client computer retrieves their home folder from a share point. Typically, this share point resides on a server other than the NetBoot server, although it does not have to be.

TIP ▶ NetBoot service places high demands on a server. To prevent performance degradation, store home folders on a different server.

Creating Images With System Image Utility

System Image Utility is the tool you use to create Mac OS X NetBoot and Network Install images. It replaces the Network Image Utility of previous releases. Located in the /Applications/Server folder on your Mac OS X Server computer, System Image Utility uses files on a Mac OS X Install Disc, mounted volume, or disk image to create a NetBoot image.

Each image requires an image ID, which client computers use to identify similar images. When a client lists the available NetBoot images in the Startup Disk pane of System Preferences, if two images have the same ID, the client assumes that the images are identical, so it displays only one entry. If only one server will serve an image, assign it a value between 1 and 4095. If multiple servers will serve an image, assign it a value between 4096 and 65535.

When creating an image, you also specify where to store it. For the NetBoot service to recognize the image, it must be stored in /Library/NetBoot/NetBootSP*n*/ *imagename*.nbi, where *n* is the volume number and *imagename* is the image name you entered when you created the image. If you have already configured NetBoot service, the Save dialog includes a pop-up menu listing the available volumes. If you choose a volume from that pop-up menu, the save location changes to the NetBootSP*n* share point on that volume.

> **TIP** ▸ In a NetBoot environment, several clients booting from the same NetBoot server can place high demands on the server and slow down performance. To improve performance, you can set up additional NetBoot servers to serve the same images.

System Image Utility also enables you to customize your NetBoot or Network Install configurations by instituting the following:

▸ Use the *directory services feature* to copy the directory server settings from the server to each client image and to make unique CPU Directory Services settings. The user creating the image needs to authenticate locally to get a list of servers. If the system is not bound to any directory services servers, you can't make unique CPU settings.

▸ *Sharing preferences* help eliminate the common problem that all clients have the same hostname and Bonjour name. Currently this sharing preference is the same as on the image. The new feature allows you to add computer names to clients at runtime.

▸ You can also set *ByHost preferences* per client. In the past, host settings were clones of the system used to create the image. By matching the MAC addresses of the clients, you can install "clean" preferences.

▶ *Block Copy* is now the format for network image files. Older File Copy images may still be served, but only block image files will be created new. The disk image hierarchy is identical to the hierarchy of a bootable CD/DVD. However, this disk image does not contain any packages in System/Installation/Packages. Instead the Packages folder contains System.dmg, which is another disk image.

▶ You can set the image for automated operation for Network Install and Apple Software Restore (ASR) NetBoot images.

▶ Checksums are now supported in scripts. If acquired from the authentication panel, the checksum is compared against the tool with an md5 message digest.

> **NOTE ▶** Checksums validate an image by checking the files inside the image against a known list, thus making sure the files have not changed.

You can specify which model of hardware will be booted off of which image. For example, if you wanted to configure a portable or desktop image, you could choose those models from a list for each drive. The NetBoot service in Mac OS X Server v10.4 supports client computers with Macintosh firmware version 4.1.7 or later, and System Image Utility now contains a feature called Model Filter that enables you to determine which system the image will boot.

NetBoot Image Types

With System Image Utility, you can create two distinct types of NetBoot images:

▶ A *boot image* is a file that looks and acts like a mountable disk or volume. NetBoot boot images contain the system software needed to act as a startup disk for client computers on the network. When creating a boot image, you must specify a default user account that the client can use to access the network disk image. You must specify a user name, short name, and password.

▶ An *install image* is a special boot image that boots the client long enough to install software from the image, after which the client can boot from its own hard drive. Just as a boot image replaces the role of a hard drive, an install image is a replacement for an installation CD.

Types of Images

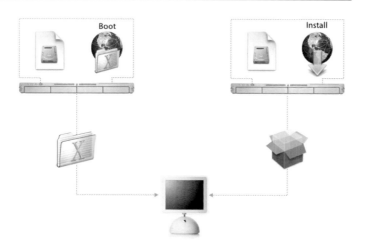

NOTE ▶ There is no real difference between the NetBoot and Network Install processes: A boot image starts up and runs either the Finder or the Installer. The distinction is how the image file is tagged. The tag allows the user to visually differentiate between image file types in utilities such as Startup Disk in System Preferences.

Using Network Install

Like a bootable CD-ROM, Network Install is a convenient way to reinstall the OS, applications, or other software onto local hard drives. For system administrators deploying large numbers of computers with the same version of Mac OS X, Network Install can prove very useful. Network Install does not require the insertion of a CD-ROM into each NetBoot client, because all startup and installation information is delivered over the network. You can perform software installations with Network Install using a collection of packages or an entire disk image (depending on the source used to create the image).

> **TIP** ▶ For installing small packages and not entire disks, using ARD to install the packages might be easier because not all packages require a restart. If NetInstall is chosen to deploy a package, the client system has already been restarted once to actually boot off the NetBoot server.

While creating an install image with System Image Utility, you have the option to automate the installation process to limit the amount of interaction from anyone at the client computer. Keep in mind that with this automation comes responsibility. Because an automatic network installation can be configured to erase the contents of the local hard drive before installation, data loss can occur. You must control access to this type of Network Install disk image and must communicate to those using these images the implications of using them. Always instruct users to back up critical data before using automatic network installations.

> **NOTE** ▶ Set the default NetBoot image on every server. Images that normal users can select should probably be NetBoot images, not Network Install images.

Creating NetBoot Images

When creating NetBoot images, specify a source for the image in System Image Utility. Prior to Mac OS X v10.3, only CDs or DVDs could be used as the source, but now System Image Utility can create images using hard drives or disk images as sources:

▶ CD or DVDs: You can use System Image Utility to build a new NetBoot image from a Mac OS X Install Disc. Startup images created using Install Discs contain a "clean" version of the operating system and require minimal configuration. Install images created using the Install Disc replicate the experience of starting from the Install Disc to install the OS. When using discs to create install images, you also have the option of creating application-only images, which install application software and documents but not the operating system. This is useful in certain situations where the entire image is not needed every time.

▶ Mounted volumes: When a mounted volume is selected as a source, the entire contents of the volume—including the operating system, configuration files, and applications—are copied to the image. When a client computer starts up from an image created from a mounted volume, the boot experience is similar to that of starting up from the original source volume. When a client computer starts up from an install image created from a mounted volume, a copy of the source volume is written to the client computer's disk drive. A benefit of using volumes for image sources is that the image creation is much faster than when using discs. Also, installations that use images created from volumes are faster than installations that use disc-created images.

▶ Disk images: Instead of using a configured hard drive as a source, you can use Disk Utility to create a disk image of a configured hard drive, and then use the disk image as a source for creating NetBoot images.

When creating the images, you have the option of adding additional software to the image. For example, you may need to include an update to the operating system with an image created from the Install Discs. You specify additional software to be installed, in the form of an installer package, in the Other Items field.

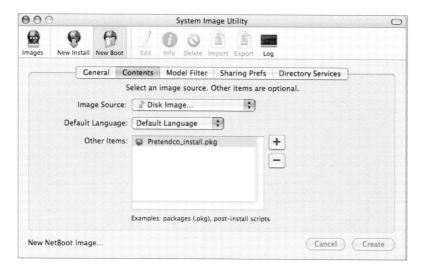

TIP Use the latest version of the operating system when creating NetBoot images, to ensure backward compatibility.

When adding new computers to the NetBoot environment, you may need to update the NetBoot image to support them. Check the OS software version that accompanied the new computer.

Specifying a Default Image and Protocol

The NetBoot service is configured in Server Admin, within which the Images pane lists the available NetBoot images on the server, which can host up to 25 different disk images. Each image can be enabled, allowing client computers to use the image to boot, or disabled, preventing client computers from accessing the image. While you can have several images, you must specify one of the NetBoot images as the default image. When you press the N key on a client computer at startup, and the client has never started up from that NetBoot server before, the server will provide the default image to start up the client.

For each image, you can also specify which protocol, NFS or HTTP, is used to serve the image. NFS continues to be the default and the preferred method. HTTP is an alternative that enables you to serve disk images without having to reconfigure your firewall to allow NFS traffic.

TIP Remember that image files can be very large and can take up a large amount of disk space on the server.

Understanding Shadow Files

Many clients can read from the same NetBoot image, but when a client needs to write anything (such as print jobs and other temporary files) back to its startup volume, NetBoot automatically redirects the written data to the client's *shadow files,* which are separate from regular system and application software. These shadow files preserve the unique identity of each client during the entire time the client is running off a NetBoot image. NetBoot also transparently maintains changed user data in the shadow files, while reading unchanged data from the shared system image. The shadow files are re-created at boot time, so any changes that the user makes to the startup volume are lost at restart.

This behavior has important implications. For example, if a user saves a document to the startup volume, after a restart that document is gone. This preserves the condition of the environment the administrator set up, but it also means that you should give users accounts on a network server if you want them to be able to save their documents.

For each image, you can specify where the shadow file is stored. When the Diskless option for an image is disabled, the shadow file is stored on the client computer's local hard drive at /private/var/netboot/.com.apple.NetBootX/Shadow. When the Diskless option is enabled, the shadow file is stored in a share point on the server named NetBootClients*n* in /Library/NetBoot, where *n* is the number of the client using the shadow file. With the Diskless option enabled, NetBoot enables you to operate client computers that are literally diskless.

Shadow Files

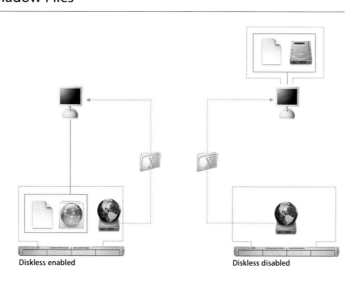

Diskless enabled   Diskless disabled

TIP Make sure you consider the storage need for shadow files when configuring your server. When running diskless, users may experience delays, since writes to the shadow files take place via the network and not locally.

Filtering NetBoot Clients

The NetBoot Filters pane permits you to allow or deny access to NetBoot services based on the client computer's hardware, or MAC, address. Once you enter a list of hardware addresses, you can either limit NetBoot access to just the listed computers or prevent the listed computers from using NetBoot (and allow all others to use it). This allows NetBoot and non-NetBoot clients to coexist in harmony. Filtering removes the risk of allowing non-NetBoot clients to access unlicensed applications or to accidentally perform a network installation. By maintaining accurate Filters settings, you can seamlessly integrate NetBoot into traditional network configurations.

NetBoot access is controlled through a list of hardware addresses. If you know a computer's hardware address, you can click the Add Hardware Address (+) button and type it in. Alternatively, if you enter a computer's DNS name in the Host Name field and click the search button (the magnifying glass), Server Admin retrieves the hardware address, which you can add by clicking the Add (+) button next to the Hardware Address field.

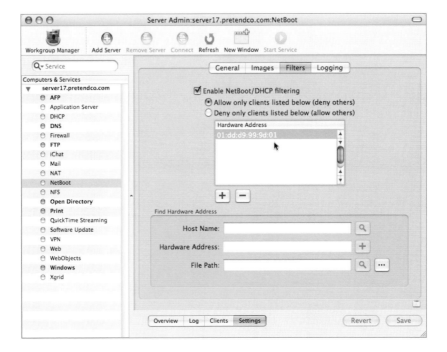

Configuring a NetBoot Client

The Open Firmware boot code contains the software used to boot a computer using a NetBoot image. As long as your client computer has the latest version of Open Firmware and is a supported client computer, you don't need to install any other special software.

There are three ways to cause a computer to use NetBoot at startup:

▶ Press the N key on the keyboard until the gray NetBoot globe appears in the center of the screen. This method allows you to use NetBoot for a single startup. Subsequent reboots return the computer to the previous startup state.

▶ Select the desired network disk image from the Startup Disk pane in System Preferences. The version of the Startup Disk pane included with Mac OS X v10.2 and later presents all available network disk images on the local network. Notice that NetBoot and Network Install disk images maintain unique icons to help users differentiate between the two types of images. With the desired network disk image selected, you can reboot the computer. The computer then attempts to use NetBoot on every subsequent startup.

▶ Hold down the Option key on the keyboard during startup. This invokes the Startup Manager, which presents an iconic list of available system folders as well as a globe icon for NetBoot. Click the globe icon and click the advance arrow to begin the NetBoot process.

Important to note are a couple of things that can upset the NetBoot process:

▶ If no network connection exists, a NetBoot client will eventually time out and look to a local drive to start up. You can prevent this by keeping local hard drives free of system software and denying users physical access to the Ethernet ports on a computer.

▶ Zapping the parameter RAM (PRAM) resets the configured startup disk, requiring you to reselect the NetBoot volume in the Startup Disk pane of System Preferences.

Monitoring NetBoot Clients

You can monitor NetBoot usage with Server Admin. The NetBoot Clients pane provides a list of client computers that have booted from the server. Note that this is a cumulative list—a list of all clients that have connected to the server—not a list of currently connected computers only. Each entry shows the last time the client booted.

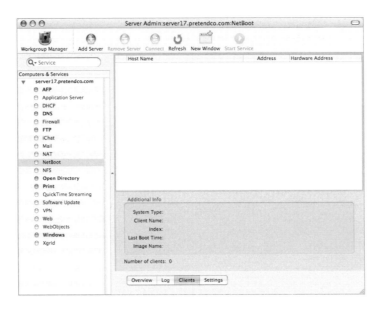

Troubleshooting NetBoot

NetBoot is a fairly straightforward process. If a client does not successfully start up from a NetBoot server, you can troubleshoot the issue by looking into the following areas:

▶ Check the network. The client needs an IP address, and DHCP and/or BootP must be running.

▶ Check the NetBoot server logs for BootP messages.

▶ Press and hold the Option key as you boot the client, and then choose NetBoot from the Open Firmware prompt.

▶ Check the disk space on the server. Shadow files and disk images may be filling the server's hard drive disk space. You may want to add bigger hard drives or more of them to accommodate these files.

▶ Check for server filters. Do you have filters enabled for IP address, hardware address, and model type? If you do, you should disable the filters to allow all computers on the network to NetBoot or NetInstall.

Creating and Delivering Custom Packages

Packages are Mac OS X constructs. They contain everything the Installer application needs to install groups of files. They can include application bundles, documentation files, scripts, and system resources, in addition to Installer-specific files directing the installation. Installation packages appear as single files in the Finder, as can application bundles. You can open both by Control-clicking the application icon and choosing Show Package Contents.

PackageMaker is an Apple Developer Tools application that enables you to create and edit package files. You can also use PackageMaker to develop *metapackages,* special packages that contain other packages or even other metapackages.

Creating and Populating Folders

To create a package, first reproduce the way you want the installed pieces to look on the target system when you are finished. The folders can be created in the Finder and should mirror the folder structure you want to install. The top-level folder is known as a *root folder* (called dstroot in the figure below), which contains the eventual contents of a package. You also need to create a *resources folder* if you want to customize the installation. The resources folder contains files that Installer can use during the installation of a package's contents. For example, it can hold a Read Me file that the user should read before installing the package.

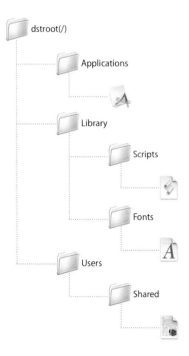

PackageMaker enables you to identify a package's contents. A package consists of the following:

▶ Bill of materials file: A binary file that describes the contents of the package.

▶ Information property list: An XML file that contains the information entered in the package definition file when the package is created.

▶ Archive file: The set of files to be installed, also known as *the payload.* The archive can be compressed to reduce the package's space requirements.

▶ Size-calculation file: A text file that contains the compressed and uncompressed sizes of the package's payload, which Installer uses to calculate the space required to install the payload.

▶ Resources: Optional files that Installer uses during an installation but doesn't install on the target computer. These include Read Me files, license-agreement files, and scripts.

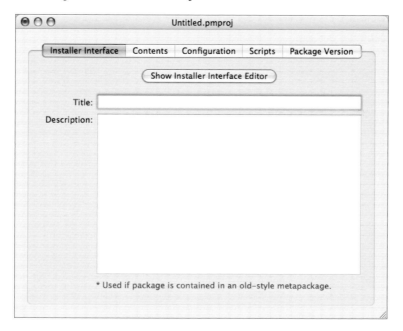

Understanding Metapackages

Metapackages—the concept of which was developed as software became more complicated—contain no files, but are groupings of either individual packages or other metapackages that you create in PackageMaker. You can group multiple packages into one package or share one package across multiple metapackages. The Mac OS X Install Disc is a primary example of a metapackage.

Metapackages may also contain any resources needed to display information to the user about the overall packages being installed. Metapackage custom install information (deciding exactly what to install from the metapackage) is created by using information about the package hierarchy.

The advantage of this method is that entire product packages can be placed within a metapackage with very little work. For example, the iTunes package is placed in the iLife metapackage.

Using Distribution Projects

PackageMaker for Mac OS X v10.4 introduces a new feature, *distribution projects*—single documents (usually within an Installer package) that describe the entire installation experience of a particular product. A *distribution script* contains all of the resources and logic necessary to provide the complete presentation of the Installer's user interface to the user. The result of interacting with the distribution script is a list of packages that will be passed to the installation engine.

Apple's original design of installer packages did not have the scale of the current Installer in mind. It was to make a package that describes the entire installation experience. As mentioned above, these packages contain various resources to display to the user in the Installer's user interface as well as all the files and information needed to actually install the software. You often need to change the configuration of a package that is placed within a metapackage so that it behaves as expected within its parent metapackage. By changing the subpackage, you are now making different packages for the same project—and keeping track of these different packages for the same files can get complicated.

To get around these limitations, the distribution document contains everything that the Installer needs to provide a consistent user experience. The same packages can be installed by different distribution projects without needing to change the contents to get the correct experience. Since the distribution project contains all the resources needed for the user experience, only the distribution project needs background pictures, Read Me text, licenses, and any other resources. (Of course a package can contain a license, but typically the distribution project will contain an overall license for all packages within.)

Adding Packages to a Network OS Install Image

As just explained, adding packages to other packages is best done using Package-Maker and metapackages. Yet modifying Network Install images is a separate process that entails adding packages to the existing Mac OS X Installer. If you need to edit a Network Install image, you will need to manually manipulate some of the special resource files that PackageMaker created. Adding single small packages to an already tested install may take less time than rebuilding a new Network Install image.

The info.plist file contains the package information. Since you are adding material to an existing package, use the Property List editor to edit the XML entries. Use Property List Editor to edit the package location and package selection entries in the info.plis. You must do this manually because the package was not created with PackageMaker.

Troubleshooting Packages

When creating packages, you should test them on as many different computers and versions of Mac OS X as you can. Keep a list of hardware and software limitations that you will support. Having this list handy will help you recall how the installations performed on various computers. Even with thorough testing, issues may arise. Initial troubleshooting of packages involves running the installations prior to rollout. Follow-up troubleshooting should involve the following:

▶ Verify that the files are copied to the appropriate locations.

▶ Make sure the file permissions are correct.

▶ Validate installation both as a normal user and as an administrator.

▶ Check to make sure there is enough disk space to install the package.

▶ Run install scripts separately to make sure they execute.

▶ Validate authorization if necessary.

▶ Add only pretested packages to metapackages.

Deploying and Updating With Apple Remote Desktop Admin

Apple Remote Desktop Admin provides a useful feature for deploying software: Install Packages. This feature enables you, the administrator, to send an Installer package to a computer or group of computers, and then run the installation without client intervention.

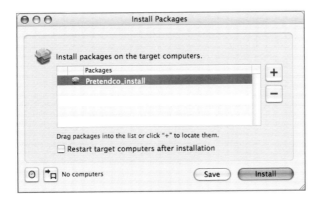

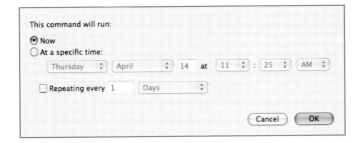

If you or the user has configured ARD correctly, the software will be installed with local admin privileges. This installation can be set to run at a specified time and need not be attended by the local user. A local user need not even be logged in. To qualify for use with the ARD Install Packages feature, the packages installed can be any Installer packages created by PackageMaker.

> **NOTE** ▶ The Remote Desktop application is a larger tool than just a remote package installer. It is not bundled with Mac OS X or Mac OS X Server, although the client software is part of the OS.

Configuring Network Startup With Apple Remote Desktop Admin

Apple Remote Desktop Admin can set the startup disk on any client computer, so you can choose between a volume on a local hard disk or any available NetBoot volume. Whichever you choose, the startup disk must have a valid system installed on it. To set the startup volume for multiple computers at once, the local volume name must be the same for all computers—something to consider when formatting the initial computers. As long as these requirements are met, you can set the startup disk to be a NetBoot volume provided by Mac OS X Server. This enables you to start up a number of clients from a NetBoot server, subsequently allowing for automated network installations.

TIP You can also use Screen Sharing and select the startup disk in System Preferences for each computer to change the startup disk preferences.

Creating Custom Packages

In this section, you will use PackageMaker to create a custom package, and then add files to the package. First you must install the Developer Tools on your Mac OS X server.

1 On your Mac OS X Server computer, double-click the Developer Tools package located in /Users/Shared/Student_Materials/MacOSX_Software and install the tools.

Before you configure your custom install package, you must create a folder to store the files you will be including in the package.

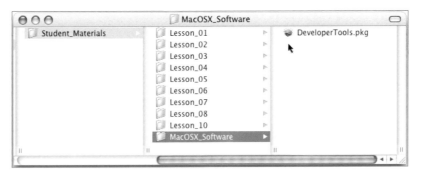

2 In the Finder on the server, navigate to the /Users/Shared folder, create a new folder, and name it *custompackage.*

3 Copy the contents of /Users/Shared/Student_Materials/Lesson10 into /Users/Shared/custompackage.

These are the files you will include in the package.

4 Create two subfolders, *Library* and *Users,* in custompackage.

This step is to mirror the /Library and /Users folders.

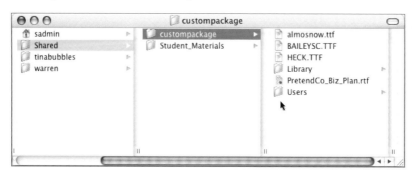

5   Create a subfolder in Library called *Fonts* and a subfolder in Users called *Shared*.

These folders will store the fonts you will install and PretendCo_Biz_Plan.rtf.

6   Copy the font files to the newly created /custompackage/Library/Fonts folder.

7   Copy PretendCo_Biz_Plan.rtf into the /custompackage/Users/Shared folder.

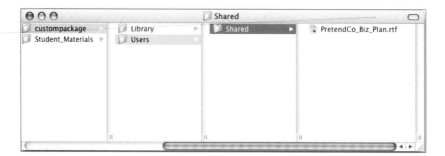

Next you will create a new PackageMaker file and point it to the newly created directory.

1   On your Mac OS X server, open the PackageMaker application, located in /Developer/Applications/Utilities.

2   Select Single Package Project and click OK.

3   In the Installer Interface, enter *Custom Software* in the Title field.

4   Click the Contents button and drag /Users/Shared/custompackage from the Finder into the Root field.

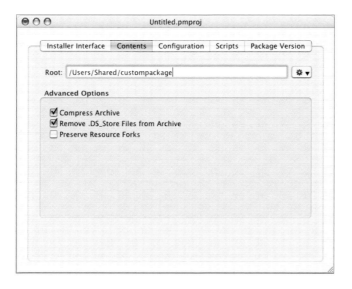

5   Click the Configuration button and choose Administrator from the
Authentication pop-up menu.

6   Click the Package Version button and enter the following values:

▶   Identifier: *com.student17.packagemaker*

▶   Get Info String: *1.0, PretendCo*

▶   Version: *1.0*

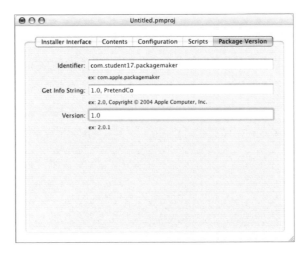

7 Choose Build from the Project menu, title the project *Custom Install*, save it to the desktop, and then quit PackageMaker without saving your document.

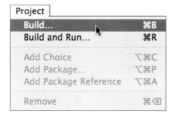

8 Copy the Custom Install package from your Mac OS X server to your Mac OS X computer via the file-sharing method of your choice.

9 Test the Custom Install package by double-clicking and installing it.

10 Confirm that there is a file called PretendCo_Biz_Plan.rtf now located in /Users/Shared and three new fonts—heck.ttf, baileysc.ttf, and almosnow.ttf—in your /Library/Fonts folder.

11 You can now remove these fonts and the PretendCo file from your Mac OS X computer.

What You've Learned

► Deployment options are available to keep multiple desktops up-to-date.

► NetBoot and Network Install is a server-based method of deploying.

► You can use PackageMaker to create custom installations.

► Administrators can use Apple Remote Desktop Admin to install custom packages.

References

The following documents provide more information about installing Mac OS X Server. (All of these and more are available at www.apple.com/server/documentation.)

Administration Guides

Mac OS X Server Getting Started (http://images.apple.com/server/pdfs/Getting_Started_v10.4.pdf)

System Imaging and Software Update Administration (http://images.apple.com/server/pdfs/System_Image_and_SW_Update_v10.4.pdf)

Apple Remote Desktop 2 Administration Guide (http://images.apple.com/server/pdfs/Apple_Remote_Desktop_Admin_Guide.pdf)

Deploying Mac OS X Computers for k-12 Education (http://images.apple.com/server/pdfs/Deploying_Mac_OS_X_for_K12_Education.pdf)

Apple Knowledge Base Documents

You can check for new and updated Knowledge Base documents at www.apple.com/support.

Books

Bartosh, Michael, and Haas, Jason. *Essential Mac OS X Panther Server Administration* (O'Reilly, 2005).

Regan, Schoun. *Mac OS X Server 10.4 Tiger: Visual QuickPro Guide* (Peachpit Press, 2005).

URLs

MacEnterprise: www.macenterprise.org

Iceberg: http://s.sudre.free.fr/Software/Iceberg.html

A Quick Look at PackageMaker and Installer: http://developer.apple.com/documentation/DeveloperTools/Conceptual/SoftwareDistribution/Concepts/sd_install_quick_look.html

Review Quiz

1. What are the advantages of using NetBoot?
2. What are three ways to configure the network startup disk?

3. What network protocols are used during the NetBoot startup sequence? What components are delivered over each of these protocols?

4. What is a NetBoot shadow file?

5. What is the difference between a package and a metapackage?

6. What tool must you use if you manually add packages to a metapackage, and why?

7. What is the Remote Desktop Admin feature you would use to install software, and are there any limitations?

Answers

1. Since NetBoot unifies and centralizes the system software that NetBoot clients use, software configuration and maintenance is reduced to a minimum. A single change to a NetBoot image propagates to all client computers on the next startup. NetBoot also decouples the system software from the computer, decreasing potential time invested in software troubleshooting.

2. A client must have selected a network disk image via the Startup pane within System Preferences, or the user must hold down the N key at startup to boot from the default NetBoot image or using Remote Desktop Admin.

3. NetBoot makes use of DHCP, TFTP, NFS, and HTTP during the NetBoot client startup sequence. DHCP provides the IP address, TFTP delivers the boot ROM ("booter") file, and NFS or HTTP is used to deliver the network disk image.

4. Since the NetBoot boot image is read-only, anything that the client computer writes to the volume is cached in the shadow file. This allows a user to make changes to the boot volume, including setting preferences and storing files; however, when the computer is restarted, all changes are erased.

5. A package is an Installer image file; a metapackage is a group file containing a number of packages or other metapackages.

6. Property List Editor, because the metapackage does not know about the additional packages.

7. You would use the Install Packages feature; must be a PackageMaker format file.

Introduction to Apple Remote Desktop

Apple Remote Desktop (ARD) 2 is Apple's desktop-management software, which enables administrators to manage Mac OS X systems quickly and easily. Completely redesigned to take advantage of the innovative technologies in Mac OS X, this powerful suite of tools facilitates a wide range of IT-management tasks. You can distribute software, create detailed software and hardware reports, control and configure systems, and offer live online help to end users—all without leaving your desk.

This appendix introduces you to ARD. You'll learn how to perform basic configuration of ARD client and administrator computers. You'll also find out what capabilities ARD provides for the management of computers, and how to maximize ARD's performance and security offerings.

What Is Apple Remote Desktop?

ARD is easy-to-use, powerful, open standards–based desktop-management software for all your networked Macintosh computers. IT professionals can remotely control and configure systems, install software, offer live online help to end users, and assemble detailed software and hardware reports for an entire Mac network.

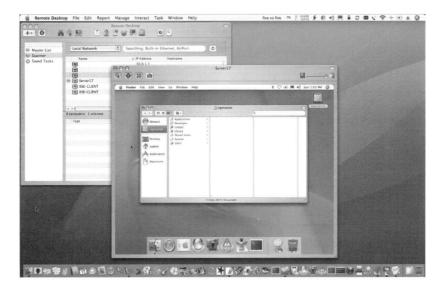

You can use ARD to:

▶ Manage client computers and maintain, upgrade, and distribute software.

▶ Collect more than 200 system-information attributes for any Macintosh computer on your network. Store the attributes in a Structured Query Language (SQL) database and view the information using one of several hardware or software reports.

▶ Provide help and remote assistance for users when they encounter problems.

▶ Interact with users by sending text messages, observing and controlling users' screens, and sharing their screens with other client users.

When used in a classroom, ARD enhances the learning experience and enables teachers to monitor and control students' computers. In corporate environments, it's the ideal solution for managing remote systems, reducing administration costs, and increasing productivity.

Installation and Configuration

There are two types of workstation in an ARD configuration: the administrator computer and the client computers. Each ARD configuration must have at least one administrator computer that controls the Apple Remote Desktop functions. The client computers are the recipients of the ARD actions that the administrator computer performs.

ARD has the same system requirements for both the administrator and client computers:

▶   Macintosh computer with PowerPC G3, G4, or G5 processor; or Xserve

▶   Mac OS X v10.2.8 or later

▶   Mac OS Extended (HFS+) formatted hard disk

▶   Ethernet (recommended), AirPort, FireWire, or other network connection

ARD can also be used to view and interact with non-Macintosh computers. Those systems must be running VNC-compatible server software.

Installing the Apple Remote Desktop Application

The first step in setting up an ARD configuration is to install the ARD software on the computer you plan to use to administer remote computers. The ARD install package installs the administration application, Remote Desktop, in the Applications folder.

After you have installed Remote Desktop, open it and create a main list of computers that you will manage. If ARD v1.2 was previously installed (or if you transferred computer lists from another administrator computer), all the existing computer lists are available in the new window. If no version of ARD was previously installed, you must enable and configure the client computers before Remote Desktop can administer them.

Updating the Client

Before you can use ARD to interact with a client computer, you must do one of the following:

▶ Install the ARD 2 client software.

▶ Update the client software.

For client computers running Mac OS X v10.2 or later, if ARD client software v1.2 or later is installed, you can use the Upgrade Client Software feature in the Remote Desktop application to update the client software.

> **NOTE** ▶ If the client computer is running Mac OS X v10.2 and does not have the ARD client software installed, or if the computer is not config-ured for ARD access, you will need to use Remote Desktop to create a client software install package. After you create the install package, you need the name and password of a user with administrator privileges on the client computer in order to install the package.

Configuring the Client

Once you have installed the ARD software on the client computers, you need to configure them to allow an ARD administrator computer to interact with them. Configuration of the ARD client software is done through the Sharing pane of System Preferences or through a custom client install package created with Remote Desktop. Additionally, directory services can be used to control ARD access. You must be able to authenticate as an administrator on the client computer to configure ARD locally.

Sharing Preference Pane Method

To enable ARD:

1 Open the Sharing pane of System Preferences and select ARD from the list of services.

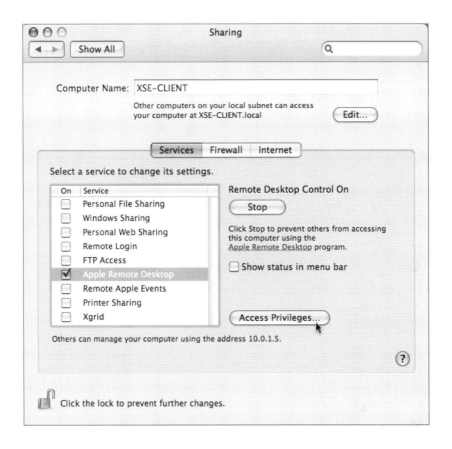

2   In the sheet that appears, specify access privileges, including which local
user accounts can interact with the ARD administrator.

For every user, you can specify which tasks the ARD administrator can
perform on the client computer. You can enable or disable individual preferences for each individual account, allowing different levels of control
for different user accounts. The lower portion of the sheet contains four
Computer Information fields. The information in these fields appears in
the reports that the administrator generates for the client. For example,

you can enter an inventory number, the computer's location, a serial number, and the name of the computer's owner.

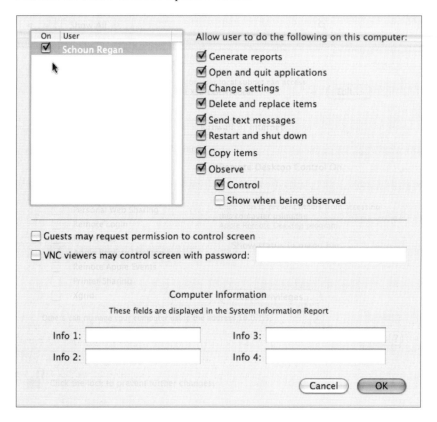

3   When you're done setting access privileges, click OK.

4   In the Sharing pane of System Preferences, select "Show status in menu bar" to add a menu to the right side of the menu bar on the client computer.

This menu shows status information and enables users to communicate with the administrator.

Custom Client Install Package Method

In addition to updating the ARD client software, the custom client install package created with the Remote Desktop application can also configure the client computer for ARD access. The custom client install package not only installs the ARD system software, but can also create users on the client computer with their ARD privileges already assigned.

The custom client install package is useful for configuring multiple computers to have the same ARD settings. Any values set in the custom install package will apply to all the computers that receive the installation. While creating a custom install package, you will have a chance to create new ARD administrator login names with passwords, and automatically set ARD access privileges and preferences.

Directory Services Method

You can also grant ARD administrative access without enabling any local users at all by enabling group-based authorization. When you use specially named groups from your directory services master domain, you don't have to add users and passwords to the client computers for ARD access. When directory services authorization is enabled on a client, the user name and password you supply when you authenticate to the computer is checked in the directory. If the name belongs to one of the ARD access groups (ard_admin, ard_reports, ard_manage, and ard_interact), you are granted the access privileges assigned to the group. These ARD groups are not preconfigured on Mac OS X Server so you must create them. When changing client settings or making a custom install packages, choose to enable directory services authorization on the clients, and specify these groups.

Remote Desktop List Configuration

Before you can audit, control, or maintain any client, you need to add it to an ARD computer list (explained in the next section). ARD has four methods of discovering possible clients. The first two are scanning a network or range and are often called *scanners:*

▶   Searching the local network

> ▶ Searching a range of IP addresses

> ▶ Using a specific IP address or domain name

> ▶ Importing a list of IP addresses

You can create as many scanners as you want. For instance, you can set up a scanner for doing computer name lookups, another that maps to the IP ranges in a remote building, and a third one that maps to the IP ranges of the floor upstairs.

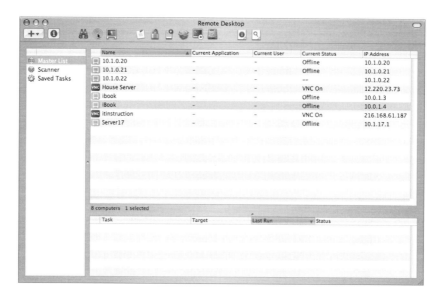

Finding Clients by Searching the Local Network

When you choose Local Network from the pop-up menu, ARD sends a subnet broadcast and Bonjour service broadcast to computers on the same subnet as the administrator computer. All possible clients on the local subnet appear in a list on the left side of the Remote Desktop window.

Finding Clients by Searching a Network Range

To locate computers by network range, you provide a beginning and ending IP address to scan; ARD queries each IP address between them in sequence, asking if the computer is a client computer. This method is best when searching for clients outside the local subnet, but on the local area network. To find computers that aren't on the local subnet, your local network's routers and firewalls must be properly configured to pass TCP and UDP packets on ports 3283 and 5900.

Finding Clients by Network Address

If you know the exact IP address or fully qualified domain name (FQDN) of a computer, you can use that IP address or domain name to add it to your master list.

Finding Clients by File Import

You can import a list of computers into Remote Desktop by importing a file listing the computers' IP addresses. The list can be in any compatible file format (text, spreadsheet, word processor) and must contain either IP addresses or FQDNs (such as mac-g5.myowndomain.com).

Managing Multiple Clients With Computer Lists

You can administer client computers individually, but most ARD features can be used to manage multiple computers at the same time. For example, you may want to install or update the same applications on all the computers in a particular department. Or you may want to share your computer screen to demonstrate a task to a group of users, such as students in a training room.

To manage multiple computers with a single action, you define ARD *computer lists,* groups of computers that you want to administer similarly. The default computer list is called Master List; this is a full list of all possible clients that you have located and authenticated to. You can create other lists to group the computers on your network in any way you want.

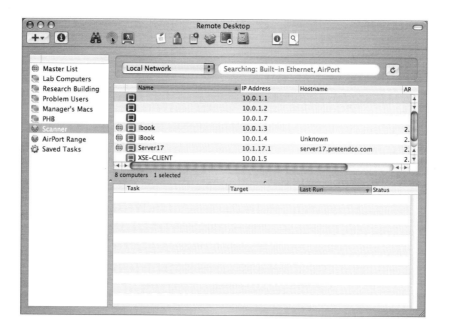

Setting up computer lists is easy—you simply import the identity of computers from files or from network scans. A particular computer can belong to more than one list, giving you a lot of flexibility for multicomputer management. A computer can be categorized by its type (laptop, desktop), its physical location (building 3, 4th floor), its use (marketing, engineering, computing), and so forth. The categorization of the computers is up to your discretion.

Apple Remote Desktop Capabilities

ARD provides a rich set of capabilities to enable administrators to remotely manage computers. ARD's functionality can be broken down into four key areas:

- ▶ Software distribution
- ▶ Asset management
- ▶ Remote administration
- ▶ Remote assistance

Software Distribution

With ARD you can install files, including applications and operating system updates, onto one or more remote computers. It can copy individual files or install software packages.

Copying Files

Remote Desktop provides administrators with the basic ability to manage computers over the network. With Remote Desktop, an administrator can distribute files to selected computers using the Copy Items command or install packages on selected computers using the Install Package command.

To copy items to the client computer:

1   From the main ARD window, select the location (one or more computers or a computer list) where you want the files to be copied.

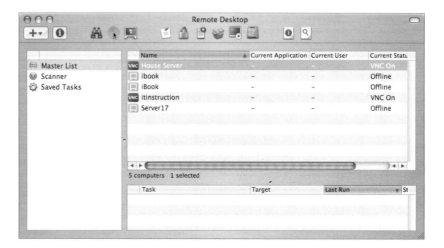

2   Under the Manage menu, choose Copy Items and add the files to the "Items to copy" list.

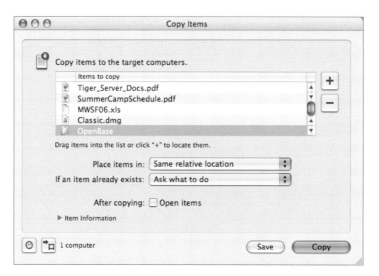

3   Select the destination location on the client computer from the "Place items in" pop-up menu.

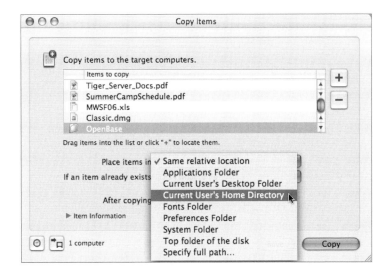

NOTE ▶ Be aware that if you choose "Same relative location" and the folder that contains the file on the administrator computer does not exist on the client computer, it will be created when the file is copied. Also, if you need to distribute files from a folder path that isn't common on all of the computers (such as the Documents folder in the administrator's home directory), you should choose "Specify full path" and provide the specific directory on the client computer in which to store the files.

4   Choose what to do if an item with the same name already exists (ask what to do or replace item).

5   Decide whether or not to place a checkmark in the Open Items checkbox.

Choosing to have all copied items open after being copied is useful for application installers being copied.

6   Click Copy to start the copying process.

Installing Packages

With ARD you can install software and software updates in PKG and MPKG formats on one or more client computers without user interaction or interruption, or even if no user is logged in. After installation, ARD erases the install package files and notifies you if the computers need to be restarted, as they do following an operating system update. You can also optionally restart the computers after the package has completed installation.

For example, you can use Apple Software Update to download an iTunes update or an operating system update to a test computer. If the update works as expected and introduces no compatibility issues, you copy the install package to the administrator computer to distribute to computers that need upgrading. Note that this approach conserves Internet bandwidth, because only one copy of the package needs to be downloaded. This also enables the administrator to upgrade multiple systems at the same time, so that all systems have the same versions of software installed. Before performing remote installations, you can send an ARD text message to notify users, perhaps letting them know that you'll be using ARD to lock their screens at a particular time before you start the installation.

You can also use ARD to deploy new versions of computational software to Xserve computers in a cluster node configuration. Additionally, you can use the PackageMaker tool from Apple's Developer Tools to create your own install packages, such as when you want to:

▶ Distribute school project materials or business forms and templates

▶ Automate the installation of multiple install packages

▶ Deploy custom applications

When you install software packages or metapackages using Remote Desktop, you will select the client computer from the Computer Status window and choose the Install Package command from the Manage menu. Select the package from the Install Package dialog or drag it into the window and click Install. The package will be copied and installed.

Asset Management

Through ARD's reporting capabilities, you can track the configurations of your networked computers. ARD's reports include system reports for identifying hardware configurations, as well as software reports for tracking installed applications, versions, and files.

Configuration Reports

ARD enables you to capture data describing the attributes of client computers, then generate reports based on the data. You specify how often you want to capture data, the data you want to capture, and the computers you want to profile. You can collect data just before generating a report, if you need up-to-the-minute information or you can schedule data to be collected by ARD at regular intervals and stored in its built-in SQL database for use on an as-needed basis. You can also specify where you want the database to reside—on the local administrator computer, or on a server where the ARD administration software is installed and always running, so data can be captured on an ongoing basis.

When you choose a type of report from the Report menu, a dialog prompts you for the name of the report and, in some cases, asks you to select the information items that you want the report to contain. When you click Get Report in the dialog, Remote Desktop displays a report window that lists the computers and their corresponding information items.

After you generate a report, you can save it in two ways: export it to a text file by choosing File > Export Report Window, or choose File > Save Report As to create a file in the Remote Desktop format. The Remote Desktop format can be viewed only from within the Remote Desktop application, so use that option if you want to ensure that only administrators can view the report.

You can use the results of a report to create a workflow. For example, you could perform a System Overview report on the computers you manage. If you sorted the report based upon the System Software column, you could then select all of the computers that have an out-of-date version of the operating system, create a new computer list, and perform an Install Package of a software update package to bring the computers up-to-date.

Remote Administration

With ARD you can configure multiple computers at the same time. For example, you can configure a lab full of computers to start up from a particular NetBoot image.

Running Scripts

You can use ARD to distribute and run UNIX shell scripts on client computers. For example, a script can mount an AFP server volume, from which it downloads a disk image to client computers. The script might also download an install package and then perform a command-line install. On an Xserve in a cluster node, you could also run a script that mounts an Xserve RAID disk designed for high throughput and then downloads large data sets for processing.

NOTE ▶ The ARD 2 client includes the systemsetup and networksetup command-line tools. With these you can configure Network, Energy Saver, and Date & Time System Preferences.

Setting Startup Disks

With ARD, you can manage the startup disk for your client computers from your own Macintosh. Set any number of your clients to boot from a network-based NetBoot or Network Install image, or have them start from a partition in their local hard drives. This feature is perfect for computer-lab managers or cluster-computing environments where the startup disk has to be switched from one to another frequently.

Another feature of ARD is the ability to set the network startup image of a client. When you select the Set Network Startup command, Remote Desktop searches the network for available NetBoot or Network Install images provided by a NetBoot server. You can either select the available image or specify a server and image. You can then set that image as the startup disk on the client and restart the client remotely.

> **NOTE ▶** If you set the network startup image of a client and the image does not have ARD client installed and configured, you will have to go to the computer and manually change the startup disk.

Locking Remote Computers

Using ARD, you can lock the screens of client computers for specified durations when you don't want the computers to be used. For example, you may need to perform network maintenance and want to make sure that computers don't use the network for a few hours. When you lock a client computer screen, users cannot see the desktop or use the mouse and keyboard on that computer.

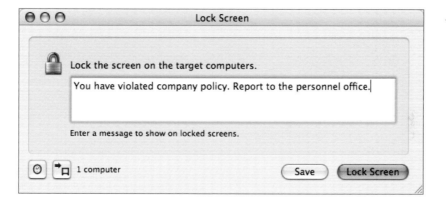

You can continue to work with computers using Remote Desktop after you've locked the users' screens. However, the screen becomes unlocked if you use the Observe, Control, or Share commands.

By default, ARD displays a picture of a padlock on locked screens, but you can display a custom picture or text messages to let users know when their computers will be available again. To use a custom image, make sure the image size fits on the client computer's screen. For example, if you have clients with 800 x 600 screens, a picture that is 1024 x 768 will be scaled down to fit the screen. Name the picture *Lock Screen Picture* and store it in the Preferences folder, which is inside the Library folder on the client computer.

Remote Assistance

ARD enables you to assist a user remotely. Through ARD's communication capabilities, you can send and receive messages to and from users. With ARD's interaction features, you can remotely observe or control a user's computer as if you were standing right in front of it.

Monitoring

In a classroom, a teacher may have 20 or more students using the computers to run instructional software or to use the Internet. ARD enables the teacher to monitor what is occurring on one or more client screens without having to

peer over the students' shoulders. Again, select which computers in the computer list you want to observe and choose Interact > Observe. If you select just
one computer, by default, the client computer will take over the administrator
screen. If you select more than one, then each screen will be displayed in part
of a window. Double-click a client screen in the window to magnify it to full
size. You can observe up to 250 clients at a time.

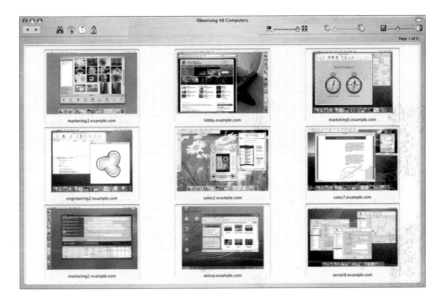

With ARD you can observe up to 50 screens simultaneously in a single window, so you can stay right on top of what's happening on your network and
offer your users the best remote assistance possible. You choose how many
screens you want to view in the Multi-Observe window. If you're monitoring
more screens than the number you have displayed in the window, ARD pages
through all the screens. You can set it to page automatically at a time interval
that you specify, or you can control the paging manually. You can control the
size of the Multi-Observe window and the color depth of the screens you're
observing—perfect for when you have limited bandwidth and want to optimize screen-sharing performance.

Controlling a Remote Computer

In addition to monitoring, you can use ARD to control a computer as if you were standing right in front of it. While you are controlling a computer, you have the option of choosing whether or not someone at the remote computer can also share control of the mouse and keyboard. If you are a teacher guiding a student through using a piece of software, you might want to allow the student to have control as well so that the student can perform some of the steps. If you are trying to quickly configure a computer, you might not want to allow someone locally to interrupt or get in the way.

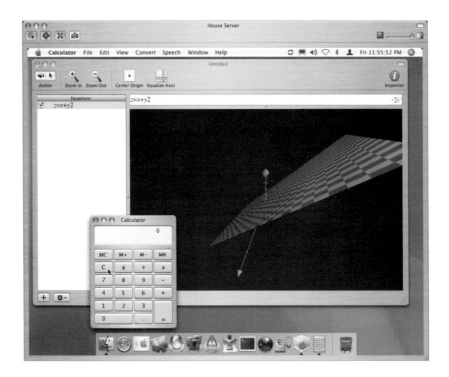

Resharing Screens

In a classroom or lab environment, you might find it useful to have one computer screen redisplayed on other computers. For example, if you were demonstrating an application, you might want to redisplay the demonstration on all the computers in the classroom to enable students to see the demonstration up close. ARD lets you share your screen or any one of your clients' screens with the other Mac OS X systems on your network.

Communicating Remotely

Easily accessible communication channels are essential to providing remote assistance. With ARD, if you need to make an announcement to everyone on your network, you can broadcast an instant text message. If your users ever need to talk to you, they can grab your attention by sending you a text message. Or if you need to engage in a private conversation with anyone, you can initiate a real-time, one-to-one text chat.

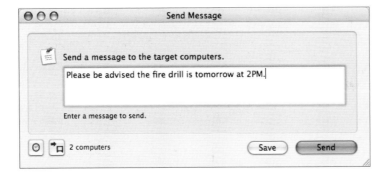

Getting the Best Performance

To get the best performance when using the Share Screen, Observe, and Control commands:

▶ Reduce the use of animation on remote computers. For example, you can simplify Dock preference settings by turning off animation, automatic hiding and showing, and magnification effects.

▶ View the client's screen in a smaller window when using the "Fit in window" option.

▶ View the client's screen with fewer colors.

▶ Use a solid color for the desktop of the screen you're sharing.

▶ Share screens only on local networks. If you share a screen with a computer connected across a router, screen changes happen more slowly.

▶ Organize computers you're administering with ARD into small groups, and close the administrator software when not in use. This helps reduce the number of status queries, thus reducing network traffic.

▶ Consider using switches instead of hubs.

If you are going through routers, ensure that you have a high maximum transmission unit (MTU) setting (typically 1200 or higher) and that the router isn't fragmenting packets.

Security

Remote Desktop can be a powerful tool for teaching, demonstrating, and performing maintenance tasks. For convenience, the administrator name and password used to access Remote Desktop can be stored in a keychain or can be required to be typed each time you open the application. However, the login name and password for each client computer are stored in the administrator's preferences and are strongly encrypted.

When using Remote Desktop, you should take the precautions described in the following table:

Task	Precaution
Administrator application security	If you leave the Remote Desktop password in your keychain, be sure to lock your keychain when you are not at your administrator computer.

Task	Precaution
	Consider limiting user accounts to disallow the use of Remote Desktop. Either in a Managed Client for Mac OS X environment or the Accounts pane in System Preferences, you can make sure only the users you designate can use Remote Desktop.
User privileges and permissions security	To disable or limit an administrator's access to an ARD client, open System Preferences on the client computer and make changes to settings in the Remote Desktop pane in the Sharing pane of System Preferences. The changes take effect after the current ARD session with the client computer ends.
	Remember that ARD keeps working on client computers, as long as the session remains open, even after the agent user password is changed.
Password access security	Never give the Remote Desktop password to anyone.
	Never give the administrator name or password to anyone.
	Use cryptographically sound passwords (no words found in a dictionary, eight characters or more, and include letters, numbers, and punctuation with no repeating patterns). You can use Password Assistant in the Accounts pane of System Preferences to help you choose strong passwords, then type them into Remote Desktop.

Task	Precaution
	Quit the Remote Desktop application when you have finished using it. If you have not stored the Remote Desktop password in your keychain, the application will prompt you to enter the administrator name and password when you open it again.
Physical access security	If you have stored the Remote Desktop password in your keychain, make sure the keychain is secured and the application isn't running while you are away from the Remote Desktop window.
	If you want to leave the Remote Desktop application open but need to be away from the computer, use a password-protected screen saver and select a hot corner so you can instantly activate the screen saver.

What You've Learned

▶ With Apple Remote Desktop you can remotely control and manage Macintosh desktops. It's your complete solution for remote desktop access, remote assistance, system management, and software distribution.

▶ ARD can run on a Macintosh computer with PowerPC G3, G4, or G5 processor; or an Xserve computer, with Mac OS X v10.2.8 or later installed and a Mac OS Extended (HFS+) formatted hard disk.

▶ The Remote Desktop application provides a rich set of commands to manage computers. With Remote Desktop you can control remote computers, share screens, communicate with users, copy files to client computers, and generate various reports on the state of the client computers.

▶ For best performance when using ARD, you should manage computers on the same local network. You should ensure that the size and resolution of the screens is not greater than the screen of the viewing computer. You should also organize computers into small lists.

References

The following documents provide more information about installing Mac OS X Server. (All of these and more are available at www.apple.com/server/documentation.)

Administration Guides

System Imaging and Software Update Administration (http://images.apple.com/server/pdfs/System_Image_and_SW_Update_v10.4.pdf)

Apple Remote Desktop 2 Administration Guide (http://images.apple.com/server/pdfs/Apple_Remote_Desktop_Admin_Guide.pdf)

Deploying Mac OS X Computers for k-12 Education (http://images.apple.com/server/pdfs/Deploying_Mac_OS_X_for_K12_Education.pdf)

Mac OS X Server Command-Line Administration (http://images.apple.com/server/pdfs/Command_Line_v10.4.pdf)

Knowledge Base Documents

You can check for new and updated Knowledge Base documents at www.apple.com/support.

Document 108024, "Apple Remote Desktop 2 Backing up the admin database"

Document 108030, "Apple Remote Desktop 2 Configuring remotely via command line (kickstart)"

Document 106847, "Apple Remote Desktop 2 Connecting through a firewall or NAT"

URLs

MacEnterprise: www.macenterprise.org

PostgreSQL: www.postgresql.org

Apple Remote Desktop Support: www.apple.com/supportremotedesktop

Apple Developer Connection, "A Quick Look at PackageMaker and Installer": http://developer.apple.com/documentation/DeveloperTools/Conceptual/Softw areDistribution/Concepts/sd_install_quick_look.html

Review Quiz

1. What is Apple Remote Desktop?

2. What are Apple Remote Desktop's system requirements for a client computer?

3. What are Apple Remote Desktop's system requirements for an administrator computer?

4. What are three things you can do to improve performance when you are using the Share Screen, Observe, or Control commands?

5. If you are unable to manage a computer on a remote network, what is one possible problem that needs to be resolved?

Answers

1. Apple Remote Desktop is software that enables an administrator to view screens of other computers, control remote computers, and generate reports about and install software onto remote computers.

2. Any Macintosh computer with PowerPC G3, G4, or G5 processor; or Xserve computer running Mac OS X v10.2.8 or later can run the Apple Remote Desktop client software.

3. The system requirements for an administrator computer are the same as those for a client computer.

4. Use fewer colors and a lower screen resolution on the screen you're shar-
    ing. Share screens only on local networks. Organize computers using
    Apple Remote Desktop into small groups.

5. Access to the computer through UDP port 3283 is probably blocked. If the
    router is providing addresses via NAT, you will need to set port forwarding
    to forward UDP port 3283 to the client computer.

Appendix **B**
Enterprise Solutions

This appendix provides a brief overview of other services and technologies offered by and sometimes involving Mac OS X Server. These services and technologies cover a wide range and are commonly known as Enterprise-level services. Many of these services have roots in the open-source community, while others are Apple's answer to technological issues. Although hundreds of pages could be written about each of these technologies, they are not the core focus of this book. We hope that introducing these technologies to you will help you ascertain which of them will fit within your organization and then embark on a journey to learn more. The services and technologies covered are:

▶ iChat Server

▶ QuickTime Streaming Server

▶ Mail services

▶ Web services

▶ Xgrid

▶ Xsan

iChat Server

Users and groups use Mac OS X Server iChat service to interact via chat from a secure server.

To use iChat service on a Mac OS X Server, users must be defined in the directories the server uses to authenticate. The iChat server uses SSL to provide for privacy of the chat data stream. It is based on the Jabber/XXMP protocol. Jabber is an open-source protocol that runs on a variety of operating systems. The iChat service is compatible with instant messaging applications from Mac OS X, Windows, Linux, and popular PDAs that work with the Jabber protocol.

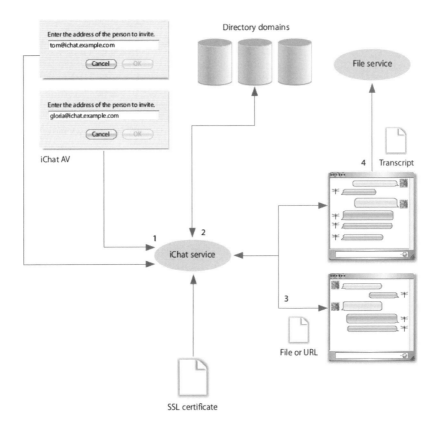

iChat Server Administration

To configure the iChat service, use Server Admin. You can configure the Host Domains, which are the domain names you want to work with. Host domains are used to construct screen names and these screen names identify the iChat service users.

You can designate a Welcome message, which is displayed when users log in to the iChat service, and you can designate the SSL certificate you want to use for the server.

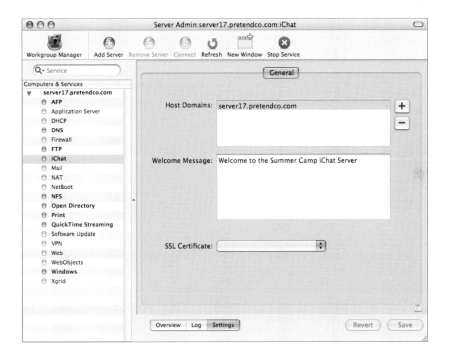

QuickTime Streaming Server

Mac OS X Server includes QuickTime Streaming Server (QTSS) version 5.0 in its suite of services.

QuickTime streaming is the delivery of QuickTime media, such as movies and live presentations, over a network in real time. A streaming server (a computer running QTSS) sends the media to a client computer, which plays the media as they are delivered. With streaming, no files are downloaded to the viewer's hard disk. You can stream media at various rates, from modem to broadband. With respect to protocols, QTSS uses the Real Time Protocol (RTP) and the Real Time Streaming Protocol (RTSP) to communicate with a client. QTSS is a standard RTP/RTSP server. With QTSS software, you can deliver video on demand, playlists of prerecorded content, or broadcasts of live events in real time using QuickTime Broadcaster or other third-party broadcasting applications.

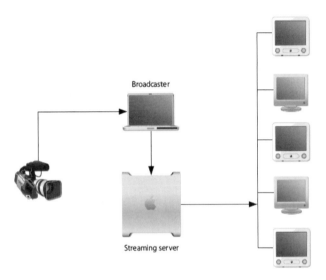

To use QTSS, you need to encode a QuickTime movie, typically by compressing it greatly for delivery over a network, and also hinting it. *Hinting* is a process that adds information to a movie to help the server break the movie into pieces to be sent over the network. You can both compress and hint movies with QuickTime Pro. Once hinted, QuickTime media can be delivered to any client that understands RTP and RTSP. Most commonly, this client is QuickTime Player. But any application that supports QuickTime playback has the capability to be a client for a streamed movie—this includes web browsers that use the QuickTime plug-in. The delivered medium can be a live broadcast, but it is more commonly a QuickTime file that has been hinted. When authoring RTSP streams, you can use QTSS to set the maximum streaming rate (maximum throughput) of the streaming server. Best performance occurs when the streams don't exceed 75 percent of available bandwidth. For example, for a 28 kilobits per second (Kbit/s) modem connection, don't use a rate higher than 21 Kbit/s. For a typical 56K modem connection, don't use a rate higher than 40 Kbit/s. For a T1 (1,500 Kbit/s) client connection, don't use a rate higher than 1,125 Kbit/s.

To access streaming content over a network via QuickTime Player, choose Open URL from the File menu, and then enter the URL, beginning with "rtsp://" (for example, rtsp://www.widgetmaster3000.com/product_highlights.mov).

You can administer and configure QTSS using Server Admin. To start QTSS, simply open Server Admin, click QuickTime Streaming in the Computers & Services pane, and click Start Service. To test the server and make sure it's running, open QuickTime Player on a client computer and enter the URL of one of the sample movies that are included with QTSS (sample movies are located in the folder /Library/QuickTimeStreaming/Movies). For example, to test whether QTSS is working at server17.pretendco.com, enter the following URL: *rtsp://server17.pretendco.com/sample_300kbit.mov*.

Server Admin provides five panes for administering QTSS:

▶ Overview—Provides a snapshot of current server activity.

▶ Logs—Displays error logs for troubleshooting purposes and lets you access logs that show information such as the number of times a media file has been accessed and when it was accessed.

▶ Connections—Provides information about connected users and active relays.

▶ Graphs—Displays a graph of the average number of connected users or a graph of throughput over time, from hours to days.

▶ Settings—Specify server settings, bind QTSS to specific IP addresses (if the server computer is multihomed, or has more than one IP address associated with it), enable relays, and change log settings.

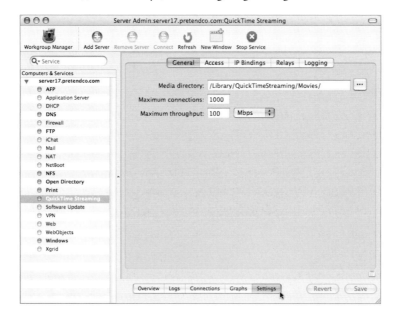

You can also administer QTSS using Web Admin, a Web-based application. Web Admin is useful for administering a streaming server remotely or from non-Mac OS X computers.

It's generally not a good idea to connect a streaming server to the Internet or local area network by digital subscriber line (DSL) or cable modem. The server will be severely limited by the relatively small bandwidth of DSL and cable modems for uploading data. In some cases, running a server on a DSL connection may break a DSL service agreement. Consult your DSL or cable modem service provider before setting up the server.

When setting up a QuickTime streaming solution, keep in mind the available bandwidth and how that affects the number of simultaneous connections that the streaming server can handle. While QTSS can handle about 4,000 simultaneous streaming connections, the bandwidth available to you might limit you to a small number of connections. For example, if you have a T1 line (1,500 Kbit/s) and you're streaming at 100 Kbit/s, the T1 bandwidth will limit you to a maximum of 15 simultaneous streams (1,500/100 = 15). Actually, in this scenario, you should not exceed 75 percent of the bandwidth (1,125 Kbit/s), which limits your streaming system to 11 simultaneous streams. But if you're streaming to a local network that runs at 100 Mbit/s, you can reliably accommodate approximately 750 connections.

Mail Services

Mac OS X Server v10.4 includes a mail server that is robust enough to provide mail services to a company or large workgroup, and secure enough to handle Internet mail. Mail server configuration is often complicated because the delivery of mail depends on the correct operation of a number of different services. Understanding this interdependence better equips you to track down problems and keep critical mail services running. You can configure these mail services through Server Admin.

Standards-based applications provide Mac OS X Server mail services. The mail transfer agent was developed by Postfix; it is used primarily to move mail between mail servers using the Simple Mail Transfer Protocol (SMTP). The local delivery agent, or incoming mail server, was developed by Cyrus, which is used for both Post Office Protocol (POP) and Internet Message Access Protocol (IMAP) services. Mac OS X Server WebMail was developed by SquirrelMail, and is a set of PHP scripts working within Mac OS X Server.

Web Services

Mac OS X Server provides you with a wealth of web services that are powered by the open-source, industry-standard Apache web server. Performance-optimized for Mac OS X Server, Apache gives you fast, reliable web hosting and an extensible architecture for delivering dynamic content and sophisticated web services, which you configure through Server Admin.

With Mac OS X Server, you can provide:

▶ Website hosting—A sample website comes preinstalled, and you can easily configure the server to host multiple websites that serve static and dynamic content.

▶ Web-based file access—You can set up Web-based Distributed Authoring and Versioning (WebDAV), with which you or your users can make changes to websites while the sites are running, and you can restrict access to your web documents by creating realms.

▶ Performance tuning and monitoring—You can use Server Admin to fine-tune and monitor the performance of your websites.

▶ Weblog—You can host a multiuser Weblog server that complies with the RSS standards.

▶ Proxy—You can set up a web proxy server to speed up response times and reduce network traffic.

Xgrid

In the most basic sense, a grid is a group of computers working together on a single problem. Although there is no canonical definition of a grid, the systems in a grid are most often loosely coupled, geographically dispersed, and to some extent, heterogeneous. One well-known example of a successful grid computing project is the University of California at Berkeley's SETI@Home project, in which computer users around the globe donate processing time for analyzing radio telescope data on behalf of the project team's search for extraterrestrial intelligence. This donated processing time would otherwise go unused during much of a typical day.

Xgrid has no real limitations on the amount of computing power it can support. The performance of the grid depends on the systems participating, the software running, and the network, among other factors.

You can participate in a large grid on many proprietary projects. Often these projects, as in cases such as SETI@Home and FightAIDS@home, are tied to a specific scientific purpose. They often have easy-to-install software packages that let any user participate in that particular project, and they often take the form of a screen saver or background process. But you don't need to think in terms of thousands or millions of rarely used computers to see the significance of a grid. For example, in a public computer lab in a university, or a company's office building full of desktop computers, the computers are used by students or employees for less time during the work day than the time they sit idle at night and on weekends.

Other grid projects such as the Globus Alliance are designed for large-scale computational grids with flexible resource-management tools and more intelligent grid-deployment methods. Instead of developing neatly packaged applications for a specific grid, such projects provide comprehensive frameworks for grid deployment.

With Xgrid users can easily install a client to participate in a computational grid of their choice, as in the SETI@Home model, while still providing the flexibility of a more generic framework to grid developers in deploying their grid applications, as in the Globus Alliance model. While some compromises are made when compared to either model, Xgrid provides the primary benefits of both:

▶ Ease of configuration—Xgrid is easier to set up than other enterprise clustering solutions.

▶ Versatility—Does not require clients to use the command line (but that capability is there for those who prefer it).

▶ Clean interface—Hides complex architecture for software and data distribution, job execution, and result aggregation.

▶ Better integration—Uses Bonjour for automatic discovery of available Xgrid controllers.

▶ Security—Xgrid is compatible with the UNIX security model.

▶ Extensibility—Provides a plug-in architecture with which developers can extend the functionality of Xgrid clusters.

▶ Broad applicability—Aims to support all grid computational needs, not just those of bioinformatics, fluid dynamics, or another specific science.

Xgrid Admin

Xgrid administration is handled by the Server Admin tool. Clicking the Xgrid service under the Computers & Services list will reveal the variables associated with managing an Xgrid deployment.

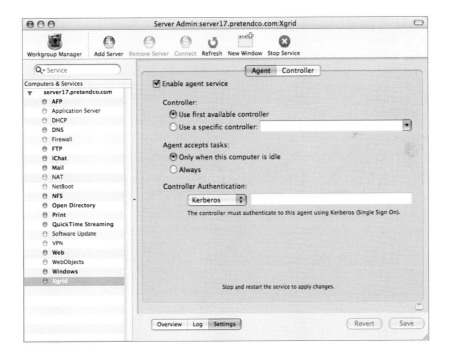

Managing a Grid

You can manage one or more computational grids with Xgrid Admin. In this context, a grid is a fixed group of agents with a dedicated queue. There can be multiple grids per controller, but at present any given agent can belong to only a single grid. You cannot move an agent between grids while a job (or a task) is running.

Connecting to a Controller

You use Xgrid Admin to connect to a controller, and that controller must be reachable on any network by the administrative computer running Xgrid Admin. Once Xgrid Admin is connected to the controller, you can view the status of its grid and manage its agents and jobs. To connect to an Xgrid controller:

1 Open Xgrid Admin and do one of the following:

▶ Choose the controller from the pop-up menu or type its name, and then click Connect.

▶ Select its name in the Controllers and Grids list and click Connect.

2 If necessary, select the appropriate authentication option, type a password, and click OK.

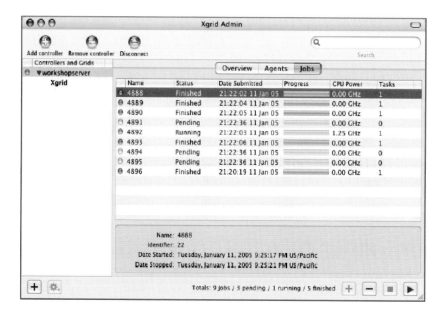

Adding a Controller to Xgrid Admin

You use Xgrid Admin to add a controller to the monitoring list. To add a controller to the monitoring list:

1   Open Xgrid Admin and click Add Controller.

2   Choose a controller from the pop-up menu or type its name, and then click Connect.

3   If necessary, select the appropriate authentication option, type a password, and click OK.

Removing a Controller

You can easily remove a controller from the monitoring list in Xgrid Admin. To remove a controller from the monitoring list:

1   Open Xgrid Admin and select a controller in the Controllers and Grids list.

2   Click Remove Controller.

Adding an Agent to a Grid

You can add an agent for a controller in Xgrid Admin. You can add agents that are currently offline and they will be available to the grid when their computers come online or their administrators make the agents active. To add an agent:

1   Open Xgrid Admin and select the controller in the Controllers and Grids list.

2   Click Agents in the button bar.

3   Click the Add (+) button below the list of agents.

4   Type a name for the agent and click OK.

Viewing a List of Agents in a Grid

You can see a list of agents for a controller in Xgrid Admin. To see a list of agents for a controller:

1   Open Xgrid Admin and select the grid in the Controllers and Grids list.

2   Click Agents in the button bar and select an agent in the list to display information about the CPU power and processors it uses.

The color bubble to the left of the name shows each agent's status.

Xsan

Xsan is Apple's *storage area network (SAN)* product offering. It is both a SAN file system and a cluster file system.

A SAN is a specialized network designed and optimized specifically for storage. In February 2003 Apple introduced the Xserve RAID, which supported Fibre Channel, the most popular storage-networking technology. With a Fibre Channel switch and Fibre Channel Host Bus Adaptor PCI cards, you were able to connect multiple computers and multiple Xserve RAIDs on a single Fibre Channel network.

What you could not do is share the Xserve RAID storage resources among many computers. Even though the network allowed any host to connect to any storage device, the multiple hosts had no way to coordinate access to a single storage device. Xsan is a cluster file system designed to work with hosts and storage connected together in a SAN. A SAN is a requirement for Xsan, but you can have Mac OS X connected to a SAN without Xsan. Xsan provides the ability for multiple hosts in a SAN to simultaneously connect to shared storage resources, such as Xserve RAID. Xsan gives you the ability to leverage the flexibility of storage networking for increased performance, improved management and scalability, and sharing data between hosts.

The process of creating a SAN with Xsan Admin is as follows:

1 Add a SAN.

2 Create at least one volume for the SAN.

3 Use pools (sets of RAID arrays, or LUNs) to make up the volumes.

4 Mount the volumes on the client computers so users can access the volume to store and retrieve data.

> **TIP** The key to implementing an Xsan deployment is planning the setup of the RAID arrays and the placement of those RAID arrays in storage pools.

The figure below shows a SAN called BASEMENT, with three volumes called, TOPSHELF, MIDDLESHELF, and BOTTOMSHELF. It further shows that the TOPSHELF volume is made up of storage pools called SQUASH and PICKLEJARA and that the pool SQUASH is made up of RAID arrays (or LUNs) called RADICLEVE1!A and RAIDCLEVEL1C.

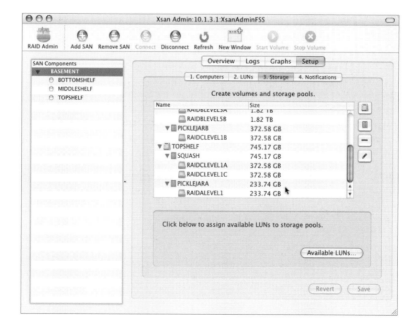

SANs Overview

Storage area networks are another solution to the limitations of Direct Attached Storage (DAS) and Networked Attached Storage (NAS). Using a network to access storage devices addresses the scalability limitations of DAS. Storage can be consolidated, addressing the issue of management of disks in DAS.

SAN uses disk block I/O, with no intermediate protocol and performance limitations of NAS. SAN removes the storage I/O from the LAN, improving both storage access performance and LAN messaging performance.

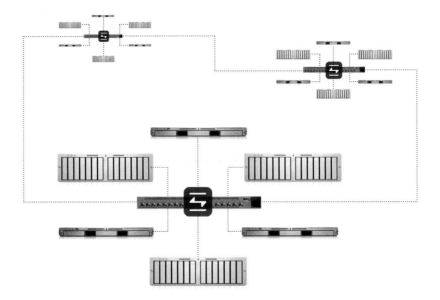

Using the Fibre Channel protocol for SAN is designed to optimize storage access. Typically a SAN uses Fibre Channel, a high-performance networking technology for connecting computers to storage devices. Using a SAN, multiple clients can connect directly to the storage network via a Fibre Channel switch, unlike a NAS system, which uses network file-sharing protocols to deliver stored data to network clients. Data is sent across the SAN network using high-speed SAN network connectivity. The SAN architecture physically and logically separates storage from servers and workstations so multiple hosts can be configured to access the same storage devices, and so servers and storage can scale independently. In a typical SAN configuration, a portion of the shared storage is allocated to each server for exclusive use by that computer. This is called *provisioning*, and is a logical extension of DAS. The host formats (partitions) the storage it has been enabled to see using a disk file system or volume manager and can share the storage (if desired) using a network file system. The host accesses the storage using block addressing, as it does with DAS.

Today, architectures are rarely pure NAS or pure SAN. Combinations are used to provide the optimal solution for application requirements. Application servers benefit from the scalable storage available through the SAN. These systems can then share their data with clients on the LAN network using network file systems such as AFP, SMB/CIFS, or NFS.

What You've Learned

▶ Mac OS X Server can host a Jabber server, to which clients from many different operating systems can connect.

▶ QuickTime Streaming Server (QTSS) is a robust service capable of streaming both live and prerecorded material.

▶ Apple uses Apache for its web-server software and includes Weblogs as a feature of Mac OS X Server v10.4.

▶ Xsan is Apple's answer to the SAN storage solution for Apple.

References

The following documents provide more information about installing Mac OS X Server. (All of these and more are available at www.apple.com/server/documentation.)

Administration Guides

Collaboration Services Administration (http://images.apple.com/server/pdfs/Collaboration_Services_v10.4.pdf)

QuickTime Streaming Server 5.5 Administration (http://images.apple.com/server/pdfs/QT_Streaming_Server_v10.4.pdf)

Mail Service Administration (http://images.apple.com/server/pdfs/Mail_Service_v10.4.pdf)

Web Technologies Administration (http://images.apple.com/server/pdfs/Web_Technologies_Admin_v10.4.pdf)

Xgrid Administration (http://images.apple.com/server/pdfs/Xgrid_Admin_v10.4.pdf)

Xsan 1.1 Administrator's Guide (http://images.apple.com/server/pdfs/20050603_Xsan_Admin_Guide.pdf)

Apple Knowledge Base Documents

You can check for new and updated Knowledge Base documents at www.apple.com/support.

Document 301581, "Services using SSL may not work properly on an upgraded server"

Document 301656, "Manually restoring mail databases when upgrading from 10.3"

Document 301508, "About the Mac OS X Server 10.4.1 Update"

Document 301782, "Xsan 1.1: How to install on a computer that has no keyboard or monitor"

Document 300634, "Xsan Help: Tips to avoid unexpected volume behavior"

Books

Green, Adam, and Geller, Matthew. *Xsan Quick Reference Guide* (Peachpit Press, 2005).

URLs

Jabber Server: www.jabber.org

Apache: www.apache.org

Postfix: www.postfix.com

Cyrus IMAP: asg.web.cmu.edu/cyrus

SquirrelMail: www.squirrelmail.org

Mailman: www.list.org

Storage Networking Industry Association: www.snia.org

Review Quiz

1. What application do you use to configure the host names for an iChat/Jabber server?

2. What must you do to a media file before you stream it?

3. What open-source projects comprise Apple's mail server?

4. What steps do you take to add a controller to Xgrid Admin?

5. Xsan is what type of file system?

Answers

1. Server Admin

2. The file must be hinted.

3. Postfix, Cyrus, SquirrelMail, and Mailman.

4. Open Xgrid Admin and click Add Controller, choose a controller from the pop-up menu or type its name, and click Connect. If necessary, select the appropriate authentication option, type a password, and click OK.

5. Xsan is a Storage Area Network file system and a cluster file system.

Appendix C
Additional Command-Line Interface Commands

The command-line interface has been around for a very long time. Its roots go back to the earliest computers. While there are literally hundreds of commands—and thousands of options within these commands—this appendix focuses on the commands that are an extension to the basic ones every administrator must know: cd, ls, and pwd. (Of course, the commands discussed here are by no means the only ones you should know.) You will get an overview of:

▶ Running commands to find files, manage processes, monitor usage, and manage disks and volumes

▶ Exchanging data between the Finder and the command line

Armed with this additional information, you should be able to better manage your Mac OS X server.

Finding Files Using locate and find

You can use both the find and locate commands in the Terminal to search the file system for files matching certain criteria. The locate command uses a database describing the known files on your system. The locate database is built and updated automatically as long as your system is running at the appropriate time. By default on Mac OS X and Mac OS X Server systems, the locate database is updated at 4:30 A.M. each Saturday. You can execute the script that updates the locate database using the command sudo /etc/weekly.

The locate command understands the wildcard characters used by the shell (wildcards are discussed later in this appendix). In order to pass the wildcard character on to the locate command, you must escape the character so that the shell doesn't process it. For example, the command locate "*.rtf" or locate *.rtf will print a list of all files with names ending in .rtf, while locate *.rtf results in an error.

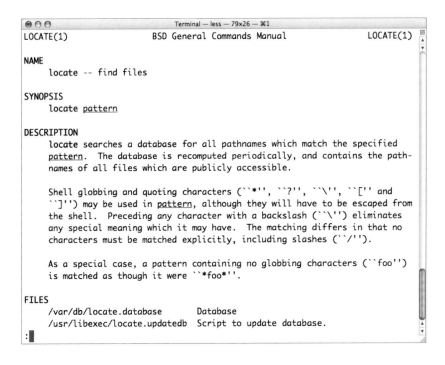

```
●○○                    Terminal — less — 79x26 — ⌘1
LOCATE(1)               BSD General Commands Manual               LOCATE(1)

NAME
     locate -- find files

SYNOPSIS
     locate pattern

DESCRIPTION
     locate searches a database for all pathnames which match the specified
     pattern.  The database is recomputed periodically, and contains the path-
     names of all files which are publicly accessible.

     Shell globbing and quoting characters (``*'', ``?'', ``\'', ``['' and
     ``]'') may be used in pattern, although they will have to be escaped from
     the shell.  Preceding any character with a backslash (``\'') eliminates
     any special meaning which it may have.  The matching differs in that no
     characters must be matched explicitly, including slashes (``/'').

     As a special case, a pattern containing no globbing characters (``foo'')
     is matched as though it were ``*foo*''.

FILES
     /var/db/locate.database        Database
     /usr/libexec/locate.updatedb   Script to update database.
:
```

The command find ~ -name *.rtf –print starts a search of the files in the user's home directory and prints on the screen all of the files with names ending in lowercase .rtf, while the command find ~ -iname *.rtf –print starts a search of the files in your home folder and lists all of the files with names ending in .rtf regardless if the rtf is in lowercase or uppercase.

File Locations

Mac OS X introduces a number of predefined folders intended to contain files of particular types. Since many applications depend on the name and location of these folders, they should not be renamed or moved. Most applications in the Mac OS X graphical user interface (GUI) reside in /Applications, and operating system files reside in /System.

By convention, UNIX programs store their configuration information in /etc while most command-line tools are installed in /bin, /sbin, /usr/bin, or /usr/sbin. Shells search these four folders to find the programs whose names you enter on the command line. Programs in other locations may be executed by specifying an absolute or relative path to the executable. For example, /Developer/Tools/GetFileInfo /Users executes the GetFileInfo command installed by the developer tools. The current folder is not part of the default search path on Mac OS X. This is important for Windows users, but it is a security risk to have a shell include the current folder in the search path, because it could allow unauthorized applications to execute.

Managing Processes From the Command Line

You can determine the currently running processes from the command line using the ps and top commands. Use top to see a regularly updated view of system utilization, including memory usage, page faults, and the set of currently executing processes.

```
● ○ ○                    Terminal — top — 79x26 — ⌘1
Processes:  74 total, 2 running, 72 sleeping... 261 threads           14:10:48
Load Avg:  0.16, 0.20, 0.23     CPU usage:  12.3% user, 14.9% sys, 72.8% idle
SharedLibs: num =  205, resident = 35.6M code, 4.41M data, 8.27M LinkEdit
MemRegions: num = 14742, resident =  553M + 9.50M private,  140M shared
PhysMem:   107M wired,  570M active,  285M inactive,  963M used, 60.2M free
VM: 10.0G +  130M   183496(0) pageins, 134812(0) pageouts

  PID COMMAND      %CPU   TIME    #TH #PRTS #MREGS RPRVT  RSHRD  RSIZE  VSIZE
 4744 top         10.8% 0:00.85   1    18    22    540K   336K   2.29M  26.9M
 4743 mdimport     0.0% 0:00.28   4    63    52    988K   3.36M  3.08M  41.2M
 4726 less         0.0% 0:00.01   1    13    19    132K   364K   944K   26.7M
 4723 sh           0.0% 0:00.00   1     8    17     48K   744K   368K   27.1M
 4722 sh           0.0% 0:00.00   1    13    17     48K   744K   564K   27.1M
 4721 man          0.0% 0:00.01   1    13    17    128K   336K   836K   26.6M
 4515 bash         0.0% 0:00.08   1    14    17    208K   692K   872K   27.1M
 4514 login        0.0% 0:00.02   1    16    36    132K   340K   556K   26.9M
 4512 Terminal     2.4% 0:07.70   7   195   243   3.77M  13.9M+ 12.7M- 229M
 4389 Mail         0.0% 0:14.75   8   146   334   10.7M  18.8M  21.8M  247M
 4258 Safari       0.0% 0:55.20   7   135   505   35.4M  18.6M  46.0M  263M
 4194 lookupd      0.0% 0:01.70   2    34    38    536K   724K   1.29M  28.5M
 3812 Microsoft    0.0% 0:04.70   3    70   154   1.62M  7.28M  3.29M  205M
 3811 Microsoft    1.2% 8:09.51   8   128   699   26.7M  26.1M+ 42.4M  325M
 3806 Keynote      0.6% 2:22.05   4   108   499   29.4M  19.3M+ 36.3M  303M
 3761 Image Capt   0.0% 0:00.80   3    75   144   996K   4.36M  2.40M  202M
 3759 GraphicCon   0.0% 0:23.62   5   114   331   5.43M  22.3M  9.36M  302M
 3758 Adobe Phot   0.5% 3:29.05   6   117  1734   264M   29.0M  275M   664M
```

In the leftmost column of the top tabular output, you will find the process identifier (PID) associated with that process. You can also use the ps command to determine the PID of a process. The PID is used to send a message to a particular process. For example, the command ps -auxww | grep TextEdit prints the PID# and other information for just the TextEdit process.

When you have the PID# for a process, you can send it the command kill -9 PID#. This command (where PID# is the number associated with the TextEdit process) asks the process with the given PID to terminate immediately. You can send a variety of commands to running processes, such as rereading a configuration file or logging additional information.

The killall command enables you to signal processes by name rather than by PID. The command killall -KILL TextEdit force-quits all processes that belong to you with the name TextEdit.

Monitoring System Usage

Many shell commands exist to help you monitor the system. The last command shows you which users have logged in most recently or when a specified user last logged in to your system.

```
●●●                    Terminal — bash — 74x26 — ⌘1
instructor:~ sregan$ last
sregan     ttyp2                    Sat Jul 16 12:47   still logged in
sregan     ttyp2                    Sat Jul 16 12:47 - 12:47  (00:00)
sregan     ttyp1                    Sat Jul 16 12:44   still logged in
sregan     ttyp1                    Sat Jul 16 12:44 - 12:44  (00:00)
sregan     console  instructor.local Fri Jul 15 09:35   still logged in
reboot     ~                        Fri Jul 15 09:35
shutdown   ~                        Fri Jul 15 09:19
sregan     console  instructor.local Fri Jul 15 01:50 - 09:19  (07:28)
reboot     ~                        Fri Jul 15 01:50
shutdown   ~                        Thu Jul 14 15:32
sregan     console  instructor.local Thu Jul 14 12:22 - 15:31  (03:08)
reboot     ~                        Thu Jul 14 12:22
shutdown   ~                        Thu Jul 14 12:21
sregan     ttyp1                    Thu Jul 14 12:09 - shutdown  (00:12)
sregan     ttyp1                    Thu Jul 14 12:09 - 12:09  (00:00)
test       console  instructor.local Thu Jul 14 10:14 - 12:21  (02:07)
sregan     ttyp1                    Thu Jul 14 09:36 - 12:09  (02:33)
sregan     ttyp1                    Thu Jul 14 09:36 - 09:36  (00:00)
sregan     console  instructor.local Thu Jul 14 08:40 - 10:14  (01:33)
reboot     ~                        Thu Jul 14 08:40
shutdown   ~                        Thu Jul 14 08:39
sregan     console  instructor.local Wed Jul 13 10:26 - 08:39  (22:13)
reboot     ~                        Wed Jul 13 10:25
shutdown   ~                        Wed Jul 13 09:57
sregan     console  instructor.local Wed Jul 13 09:35 - 09:57  (00:21)
```

The id command enables you to determine which groups a particular user has access to, or to determine the short name for a user given their user ID (UID).

Mac OS X systems maintain many log files. Viewing log files on your system or on another system using ssh can help you troubleshoot any number of problems. The command tail -n 10 /Library/Logs/Software\ Update.log displays the ten most recently installed software updates. The command tail -f /var/log/system.log displays the current contents of the system log, then continues to print new lines as they are added to the file.

Managing Disks and Volumes

You can get all of the functionality presently available in Disk Utility through two commands accessible from the command line. The first is hdiutil, which handles disk-image management. The second is diskutil, which includes the rest of the features. You can read the man pages to learn how to use the different features, or you can type the command at the command line, and the different options you can use will appear.

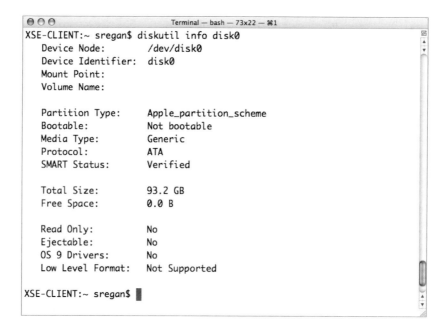

You can also use the df and du commands to determine free space and space utilization on a volume.

Working With the Command Line and the GUI

In Mac OS X, the command line and the GUI work hand-in-hand. Transferring data from one environment to the other and moving between the two environments is done very easily. You can select a group of files in the Finder and drag them to a Terminal window to add their paths to a command.

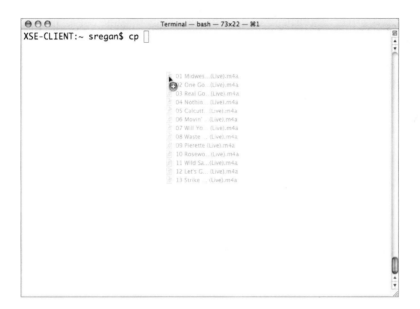

The open command enables you to open files and URLs as if you had double-clicked them in the Finder. For example, the command

open ~/Documents/ReadMe.rtf

launches TextEdit (or your preferred application for opening RTF files) and opens the specified ReadMe.rtf file. Similarly, the command

open http://www.apple.com

launches Safari (or your preferred web browser) and opens the Apple home page.

Searching Text Files Using pipe and grep

Use the grep command to search the contents of the listed text file or files. For example, in

grep domain /etc/resolv.conf

the file resolv.conf is searched for the word *domain* and the lines containing that word are displayed.

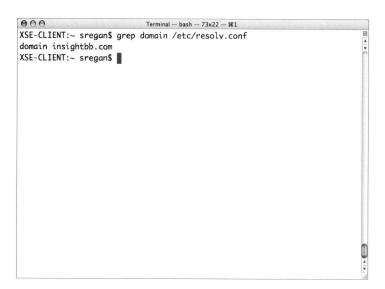

Often, the output of one command is used as input for another command. The UNIX pipe character (|) is used for this purpose. The command

    ps -auxww | grep Finder

executes the ps command and "pipes" its output (the process list) to the grep command. The grep command reads the process list as input, looking for the word *Finder,* and displays any lines containing *Finder* in the process list.

Additional Shell Filename Wildcards

Other wildcard characters enable you to specify more complex patterns than you can with the * character. The shell wildcards supported by UNIX shells are *, ?, and [ ].

```
● ○ ○                  Terminal — bash — 81x30 — ⌘1
ls: M*dd: No such file or directory
XSE-CLIENT:~/Music sregan$ ls -la M*d
Marshall Tucker Band:
total 0
drwxrwxrwx    3 sregan  sregan    102 May  2  2003 .
drwx------  674 sregan  sregan  22916 May 27 09:09 ..
drwxrwxrwx    3 sregan  sregan    102 Feb 14  2004 The Capricorn Years

Michael McDonald:
total 0
drwxrwxrwx    3 sregan  sregan    102 May 14  2003 .
drwx------  674 sregan  sregan  22916 May 27 09:09 ..
drwxrwxrwx    3 sregan  sregan    102 May 14  2003 Sweet Freedom

Michael Stanley Band:
total 16
drwxrwxrwx   14 sregan  sregan    476 Oct 25  2004 .
drwx------  674 sregan  sregan  22916 May 27 09:09 ..
-rw-rw-rw-    1 sregan  sregan   6148 May 26 00:05 .DS_Store
drwxrwxrwx    6 sregan  sregan    204 May  1  2003 Cabin Fever
drwxrwxrwx    6 sregan  sregan    204 Apr 30  2003 Greatest Hints
drwxrwxrwx    7 sregan  sregan    238 Apr 30  2003 Heartland
drwxrwxrwx    5 sregan  sregan    170 Feb 14  2004 Inside Moves
drwxrwxrwx    3 sregan  sregan    102 Apr 30  2003 Ladies' Choice
drwxr-xr-x    7 sregan  sregan    238 Feb 14  2004 MS-Live 2K
drwxrwxrwx    5 sregan  sregan    170 Apr 30  2003 MSB
drwxrwxrwx    4 sregan  sregan    136 Apr 30  2003 North Coast
drwxrwxrwx   15 sregan  sregan    510 Feb 14  2004 Stage Pass
drwxr-xr-x    3 sregan  sregan    102 Mar  8  2004 You Break It...You Bought It
drwxrwxrwx    3 sregan  sregan    102 Apr 30  2003 You Can't Fight Fashion
```

The ? wildcard matches any single character. The [ ] wildcard matches a single character in a list of characters appearing within square brackets. In the figure above, the list command is asked to only show those files whose names start with a capital M and end with a lowercase d, but can have any number of characters in between.

A few examples can help to build your understanding of wildcards. Consider a collection of five files with the names ReadMe.rtf, ReadMe.txt, read.rtf, read.txt, and It's All About Me.rtf:

▶   *.rtf matches ReadMe.rtf, read.rtf, and It's All About Me.rtf.

▶   ????.* matches read.rtf and read.txt.

▶   [Rr]*.rtf matches ReadMe.rtf and read.rtf.

▶   [A-Z]* matches ReadMe.rtf, ReadMe.txt, and It's All About Me.rtf.

Additional Mac OS X–Specific Commands

Additional Mac OS X–specific commands include:

▶   softwareupdate: Use to view the list of available updates and install updates that you specify.

▶   installer: Use to install certain packages and/or metapackages.

▶   pbcopy and pbpaste: Use to create data in one environment and use it in the other.

▶   atlookup: Use to view AppleTalk devices on your local network.

▶   plutil: Permits the conversion of binary files to XML style for editing.

▶   GetFileInfo and SetFile (both located in the Developer/Tools folder): Use to manipulate HFS files with resource forks, and to get and set file attributes (such as type and creator) associated with HFS files.

What You've Learned

▶   You can use locate and find to find files.

▶   The last command helps you keep track of user logins.

▶   The id command helps you keep track of user and group IDs.

▶   The tail command helps you view recent activity in a log file.

▶   The command-line interface gives you another way to force-quit applications and processes.

References

The following documents provide more information about installing Mac OS X Server. (All of these and more are available at www.apple.com/server/documentation.)

Administration Guides

Mac OS X Server Command-Line Administration (http://images.apple.com/server/pdfs/Command_Line_v10.4.pdf)

Apple Knowledge Base Documents

You can check for new and updated Knowledge Base documents at www.apple.com/support.

URLs

UNIX Home Page: www.unix.org

Review Quiz

1. The locate command is built into what script (and what is the location of the script) that runs automatically if the Mac OS X computer is on during that time period?

2. What does top show?

3. What command would you use to see a live continuous update of the system log file?

4. What does grep do?

Answers

1. /etc/weekly

2. The top command displays a regularly updated view of system utilization, including memory usage, page faults, and the set of currently executing processes.

3. tail –f /var/log/system.log

4. Searches the contents of the listed text files or items.

Index

A

A (address) DNS records, 82
access control entries (ACEs), 174
access control lists. *See* ACLs
account management, 354
    computer list accounts, 363–364
        creating, 364–366, 406–409
        creating guest lists, 366–367
        preferences, 409–414
    mobile user accounts, 357
        configuring, 430–432
        creating, 425–427
        deleting, 427
        synchronizing home folders,
            428–430
        verifying, 432–433
    network user accounts, 357
        home folders for all users, 360–361
        network home folder, 358–359
        views, 414
        views, Public, 415, 419–422
        views, testing, 422–425
    preferences, 369–373
        access restrictions to applications,
            378–381
        Dock, 388–390
        Finder, 390–392
        Login, 385–388
        precedence, 374–376
        preference manifests, 376–378
        print queue quotas, 394–395
        printers, 392–394
    troubleshooting, 433–434
    Workgroup Manager, 354–356
        Inspector, 356
    workgroups, 367–368
        group folders, 361–363, 402–404
        group folders, configuring, 404–406
        preferences, 361, 396–401
        preferences, checking against user
            preferences, 401
Account preferences (OS X), Login Options,
    12–13
ACEs (access control entries), 174
ACLs (access control lists). *See also* file-system
    ACLs (access control lists)
    Allow access permissions, 174, 175–176
    basics, 168–170
    Deny access permissions, 174, 176
    Effective Permissions Inspector, 170
        AFS setup, 285
    file-system, ACEs, 174
    file-system *versus* service ACLs, 163
        AFS, 288–289
    GUIDs, 170
    inheritance, *versus* POSIX permissions,
        282–284
    POSIX permissions, 170, 173–174
    workflow problems
        inheritance, 172–173
        multiple groups, 170–171
        nested groups, 171–172
Active Directory, 203
Activity pane, DNS, 93

administrator accounts
  configuring Mac OS X Server, 24, 32
  Workgroup Manager, 141–142
AFP (Apple Filing Protocol)
  accessing sharepoints, 25
  accessing through firewalls, 117
  authentication, 139
  case sensitivity, 346
  configuring, 294–296
  connection restrictions, 301–306
  file-sharing protocol comparison,
    347–348
  network user accounts, 358
  saving settings, 44–45
  share points, 282–283
  starting, 294–296
AFS (Apple File Service), 277
  access permissions setup, 280–281
  configuring, 279
  folders
    access restrictions, 296–298
    access setup, 284–285, 291–294
  inheritance, 280–281
  monitoring, 290
  server configuration, 29
  service access, 286–287
    adding users to groups, 298–301
    controlling, 287–288
  service ACLs versus file ACLs, 288–289
  share points, 280–281
    access setup, 284–285
    AFP, 282–283
    POSIX permissions versus
      inheritance, 282–284
  troubleshooting, 290, 345–346
aliases for clients, DNS, 89–91
  testing aliases, 92
Allow access permissions, 174, 175–176
Apache web server, 3510

Apple Developer Tools
  installing, 465–466
  PackageMaker, 458
Apple File Service. See AFS
Apple Filing Protocol. See AFP
Apple Remote Desktop. See ARD
Apple Software Restore (ASR) images, 448
Apple Software Update servers, 96
AppleTalk
  Name Binding Protocol, 258
  Open Directory discovery protocols, 203
  print queues, 250
    sharing, 251–252
    sharing versus creating, 252
ARD (Apple Remote Desktop)
  Admin
    configuring network startup, 464
    Install Packages, 440–441
  asset management, 487–489
  basics, 48–49
  capabilities, 274–275
  clients
    configuring, 276–279
    discovering, 479–481
    updating, 276
  installing, 275
  performance optimization, 495–496
  remote administration, 489–490
  remote computer assistance
    controlling computers, 494
    locks, 491–492
    monitoring, 492–493
    remote communication, 495
    resharing screens, 495
  security precautions, 496–498
  server configuration, 29
  software distribution
    copying files, 483–485
    installing packages, 486–487
  startup disk setup, 490–491

ASR (Apple Software Restore) images, 448
atlookup command, 532
authentication services
     AFP file services, 287
     authentication authority attributes,
          226–227
     crypt passwords, 226–228
     Kerberos, 130, 202, 226
     MS-CHAPv2, 130
     NFS clients, 321–322
     Open Directory, 202
          Password Server, 226
     password policies, 228
     PINs and tokens, 130
     SASL, 202
     server accounts, 138–139
     shadow passwords, 226–227
     verifying, LDAP over DHCP, 221
authorization
     server accounts, 161–162
          access *versus* user permissions, 162
          ACLs, file-system *versus* service
               ACLs, 163
          POSIX permissions, 162, 163–164
          POSIX permissions, limitations, 165
          POSIX permissions, setting with
               Workgroup Manager, 166–167
          Server Message Block print services, 264
          SMBs, 258

B

BDC (backup domain controller), Windows,
     202
Berkeley DB, Open Directory information,
     204
BIND (Berkeley Internet Name Domain), 78,
     79
Bonjour
     IP address assignment, 20
     Open Directory discovery protocols, 203
     without DHCP servers, 72

boot images, 448–449
BOOTP (Bootstrap Protocol), 60

C

case sensitivity
     file services protocols, 346
     SAMBA, 320
chmond +t command, 167
CIDR (Classless Inter-Domain Routing)
     netmasks, 117
CIFS (Common Internet File System). *See*
     SMB
CNAME (Canonical Name) DNS records, 82
command-line tools
     configuration information storage, 525
     and GUI, 529–530
     remote installation, Mac OS X Server, 19
comments, local user accounts, 145–148
computer list accounts, 363–364
     client management, 482–483
     computer lists
          creating, 364–366, 406–409
          guest lists, 366–367
     preferences, 409–414
Computers & Services list, 42–45
Confirm Settings screen, 30, 35
Control command (ARD), 495–496
CreateGroupFolder command, 402–404
CUPS logs, 266–267
custom installation
     client installation with ARF, 479
     deployment issues/solutions, 440–441
custom packages
     creating, 466–469
     deployment issues/solutions, 440–441,
          457–458
     folders
          creating/populating, 458–459
          resource folders, 458
          root folders, 458
     troubleshooting, 462

D

DAS (Direct Attached Storage), 518–519
date and time, configuring Mac OS X Server,
    30, 35
Deny access, all user accounts, 216
Deny access permissions, 174, 176, 195–197
deployment of Mac OS X Server
    ARD Admin
        basics, 463
        configuring network startup, 464
    issues/solutions, 440–441, 457–458
    server worksheet, 15–16
Developer Tools. *See* Apple Developer Tools
df command, 528
DHCP (Dynamic Host Configuration
    Protocol)
    basics, 53–56
    client IDs, 64, 69–71
    conflicts with other network services, 59
    DNS, 59, 67
    events, DORA, 63
    general information, 57–58
    IP address
        requests, 69–71
        static mapping, 60–61
    LDAP, 54, 59–60, 67–68
        binding clients to Open Directory
            master, 216–220
        verifying authentication, 221
    lease time, 58, 66–67
    logs, 69
        Clients pane in Server Admin,
            63–64
        Log pane in Server Admin, 62–63
    NetBoot, client startup, 444–445
    overview, 54–56
    overwriting with Gateway Setup
        Assistant, 106
    Service Backup Configurations folder, 108
        resetting DHCP from folder, 114
        saving to folder, 108

static IP address mapping, 60–61
subnets, 56–57, 65–69
troubleshooting
    for Mac OS X, 72
    for Mac OS X Server, 73
    turning off, 73–75
Direct Attached Storage (DAS), 518–519
Directory Access utility
    LDAP binding, 216–220
    NFS network home folders as home
        directory, 329
    Open Directory, 204
        connecting to existing systems, 206
directory services
    ARD client access, 479
    Open Directory authentication, 202
disk management, 528
Disk Utility, partitioning hard drives, 17
diskutil command, 528
distribution projects, 460–462
distribution scripts, 460
DNS (Domain Name System)
    aliases for clients, 89–91
    basics, 75–76
    BIND, 78, 79
    configuring, 78–79
    configuring DHCP, 59, 67
    isolating/resolving problems, 94–95
    lookups, 94
    monitoring activity, 92–93
    overwriting with Gateway Setup
        Assistant, 106
    process, 77–78
    search information, 88–89
    Service Backup Configurations folder
        resetting DNS from folder, 114
        saving to folder, 108
    troubleshooting, 94–95
    zones, 80–81
        records, 81–83
        records, adding, 84–87

Dock preferences, 388–390
Domain Name System. *See* DNS
DORA (Discover, Offer, Request,
    Acknowledge), DHCP events, 63
du command, 528
Dynamic Host Configuration Protocol.
    See DHCP
dynamic NAT maps, 125

E
eDirectory, Open Directory plug-ins, 203
Effective Permissions Inspector, 170
    AFS access-control settings, 285
    troubleshooting file services, 345
Energy Saver preferences (OS X), 13
Ethernet addresses, 61
Everyone permissions, 288
Export command, 148–151

F
Fibre Channel Host Bus Adaptor PCI cards,
    516
FightAIDS@home project, 512
file services. *See also* AFS; FTP; NFS; NFS
    resharing; Windows file services
    access permissions setup, 280–281
    case sensitivity, 346
    configuring, 279
    file sharing
        considerations, 276
        protocol comparison, 347–348
    Open Directory authentication, 202
    server configuration, 29
    setup, 278–280
file-system ACLs (access control lists)
    ACEs, 174
    folder structure, 177–180
        limiting users and groups, 195–197
        removing folders, 197

setting access and permissions for
    folders, 186–188
setting access control for folders,
    184–186
workflow results, 189–192
group accounts
    adding groups to groups, 192–194
    creating additional, 181–182
    deleting group members, 181–182
versus service ACLs, 163, 288–289
File Transfer Protocol. *See* FTP
find command, 524–525
Finder preferences, 390–392
firewalls/firewall service
    configuring
        advanced settings, 120–121
        basic settings, 116–118
    monitoring, 118–120
    overview, 114–116
    overwriting with Gateway Setup
        Assistant, 106
    Service Backup Configurations folder
        resetting DNS from folder, 114
        saving to folder, 108
    testing, 121–124
forked files, 335
forward lookups, 76
forward zones (DNS), 80
FQDN (fully qualified domain name), 84
    ARD client discovery, 481
    Kerberos authentication, 211
FTP (File Transfer Protocol) services, 277
    access permissions
        modifying, 339–340
        setup, 280–281
    accessing through firewalls, 117
    automatic file conversions, 335–336
    case sensitivity, 346
    configuring, 279, 334–339
    connecting client to server, 342–344

enabling, 333–335
file-sharing protocol comparison, 347–348
monitoring, 336–337
passive FTP, 335
server configuration, 29
starting, 340–342
troubleshooting, 345–346

G

Gateway Setup Assistant
  basics, 105–107
  configuring, 107–111
    timing for configuration, 107
    Service Backup Configurations folder
      resetting services, 114
      saving services, 108
  verifying setup, 111–113
GetFileInfo command, 525, 532
GIDs (group IDs), 153
  POSIX permissions, 164, 170
  searches by filtering, 208
Globus Alliance, 512
grep command, 530–531
group accounts, 151–152. *See also* mobile user accounts; network user accounts; user accounts
  ACLs, 176–177
    deleting group members, 181–182
  adding groups, 160–161
    to groups, 192–194
  adding users, 156–157
  creating, 153–155
  Deny access, 216
  exporting/importing, 148–151
  GIDs, 153
    POSIX permissions, 164, 170
    searches by filtering, 208
  POSIX permissions
    creating groups, 181–182

removing members from groups, 181–182
setting ownership and permissions, 182–184
versus workgroups, 361
GUIDs (globally unique IDs), 170

H

hardware addresses. *See* Ethernet addresses
hardware requirements, 13–15
hdiutil command, 528
hinting, 506
hostnames, 24–25
HTTP (HyperText Transfer Protocol) and NetBoot
  home folders, 446
  loading network disk images, 445
  specifying default image and protocol, 452

I

IANA (Internet Assigned Numbers Authority), 60
iChat service, 504–505
  server configuration, 29
ICMP (Internet Control Message Protocol), 128
id command, 527
Import command, 148–151
inheritance
  versus POSIX permissions, 282–284
  precedence of preferences, 374
Inspector, Workgroup Manager, 356
install images, 448–449
  automating installation process, 450
installer command, 532
installing. *See also* Network Install
  Apple Developer Tools, 465–466
  ARD, 275
  clients, custom installation, 479
  Mac OS X Server
    installation methods, 10
    locally, 17–19

on remote computers, 19–23
troubleshooting installation, 49
packages with ARD, 486–487
Server Admin Tools, 10
Internet Control Message Protocol (ICMP), 128
IP addresses
ARD client discovery, 480–481
CIDR netmasks, 117
DHCP
lease time, 58, 66–67
mapping addresses, 60–61
requests, 69–71
IP masquerading or aliasing. *See* NAT
(Network Address Translation)
IPP (Internet Printing Protocol), 249
configuring clients, 258
print queues, 250
sharing, 251–252
sharing *versus* creating, 252
print services, 249
ISPs (Internet service providers), 54

K

KDC (Kerberos Key Distribution Center)
Open Directory configuration, 211
Open Directory replica configuration, 224
single sign-on, 236–327
VPN configuration, 130
Kerberos authentication
AFP access controls, 287
FQDN, 211
lack of support by Finder/command-line
FTP, 334
Open Directory, 202
password policies, 228
single sign-on, 236–327
troubleshooting, 242–243
VPN configuration, 130
keyboard configuration, 23, 31
keywords, local user accounts, 145–148
killall command, 526

L

language configuration, 23, 31
last command, 527
Layer Two Tunneling Protocol (L2TP),
131–132
LDAP (Lightweight Directory Access
Protocol)
backup of directory files, 237–240
configuring DHCP, 54, 59, 67–68
directories, network user account setup,
212–214
Open Directory
binding clients to master, 216–220
connecting to existing directory
system, 206
troubleshooting services, 241–242
verifying authentication, 221
Open Directory replica, read-only copy
of LDAP directory, 224
lease time, 58, 66–67
license agreements, 21
Lightweight Directory Access Protocol. *See*
LDAP
Line Printer Daemon. *See* LPR
local hostnames, 25
locate command, 524–525
locking client computers, 491–492
Log pane, DNS, 93
lookups (DNS), 94
forward lookups, 76
LPR (Line Printer Daemon)
print queues, 250
default queues, 254–255
sharing, 251–252
sharing *versus* creating, 252
print services, 249
Bonjour, 258, 260
L2TP (Layer Two Tunneling Protocol), 131–132

M

MAC addresses, assigning IP addresses, 61
    NetBoot filtering, 454
Mac OS X Server
    configuring, 22–23
        administrator accounts, 24, 32
        Confirm Settings screen, 30, 35
        date and time, 30, 35
        destinatioin computer, 23, 31
        directory usage, 28–29, 34
        generating/saving data, 36–39
        keyboards, 23, 31
        languages, 23, 31
        network interfaces, 26, 33
        network names, 24–25, 32
        services, 29–30, 35
        software serial number, 23, 31
        TCP/IP connections, 27, 33–34
    deployment, server worksheet, 15–16
    installing
        installation methods, 10
        locally, 17–19
        on remote computers, 19–23
        troubleshooting installation, 49
    requirements, 13–15
    server daemons, 15
    watchdog process, 15
Macintosh Manager service, 43
Mail services
    basics, 509–510
    server configuration, 29
master zones (DNS), 80
    records, 82–83
metapackages, 458, 460
    adding packages to Network Install
        images, 462
    troubleshooting, 462
mobile user accounts, 357. *See also* group
    accounts; network user accounts;
    user accounts
    configuring, 430–432

    creating, 425–427
    deleting, 427
    synchronizing home folders, 428–430
    verifying, 432–433
MPKG format, 486
MS-CHAPv2 authentication, 130
MX (mail exchange) DNS records, 83

N

NAS (Networked Attached Storage), 518–519
NAT (Network Address Translation)
    configuring, 127–128
    dynamic NAT maps, 125
    monitoring, 128–129
    overview, 124–126
    overwriting with Gateway Setup
        Assistant, 106
    Port Address Translation maps, 125
    process, 126–127
    Service Backup Configurations folder
        resetting DNS from folder, 114
        saving to folder, 108
    static NAT maps, 125
NBNS (NetBIOS Name Service), 310
NetBIOS and SMB, 258
NetBoot service
    basics, 441–442
    clients
        configuring, 455–456
        filtering, 454
        monitoring, 456
        startup, 444–446, 464, 490
    deployment issues/solutions, 440–441
    images
        creating with System Image Utility,
            446–448, 450–452
        default image, 452
        NFS or HTTP protocols, 452
        shadow files, 452–453
    requirements, 443
    server configuration, 29

startup, 443–444
suitable computing environments, 443
troubleshooting, 457
NetInfo
backup of password databases, 237–240
Open Directory plug-ins, 204
netstat-rn command, 132–133
Network Address Translation. *See* NAT
Network File System. *See* NFS
Network Image Utility. *See* System Image
Utility
Network Install
deployment issues/solutions, 440
images
adding packages, 462
creating, 446–448
NetBoot startup, 444
startup disk setup with ARF, 490
using, 449–450
network interface amd name configuratin,
24–25, 26, 32–33
Network System Preferences (OS X)
built-in Ethernet, 70
DHCP client IDs, 64
DNS search information, 88–89
New Location, 12
Network System Preferences (OS X Server)
DNS search information, 88–89
link aggregate networking, 39–40
multiple settings for one interface,
27, 38–40
Network Time Protocol (NTP) services,
synchronizing clocks, 222, 237
Network Time service, 29
network user accounts, 357. *See also* group
accounts; mobile user accounts;
user accounts
authentication
configuring, 226–228
password policies, 228

binding clients to Open Directory
master, 216–220
verifying authentication, 221
Deny access, 216
home folders for all users, 360–361
logging in, 222–223
network home folder, 358–359
Open Directory passwords for LDAP
users, 228–229
enabling accounts, 232–234
importing/exporting user records,
229–232
local directory node cleanup,
235–236
resetting user passwords, 232–234
troubleshooting, 234
password policies, 215–216
setup, 212–214
network home folder, 358–359
views, 414
Public, 415, 419–422
testing, 422–425
Network Utility and DNS
Lookup pane, 94–95
testing aliases, 92
network-visible accounts, 140
networksetup command, 490
NFS (Network File System), 277
access permissions setup, 280–281
case sensitivity, 346
client authentication, 321–322
configuring, 279
file-sharing protocol comparison,
347–348
as home directories, 328–331
mapping, 322
NetBoot
loading network disk images, 445
specifying default image and
protocol, 452

network home folders, 324–326
  /Users folder configuration, 326–328
network user accounts, 358
overview, 320–321
share points
  Network Mount feature, 323–324,
    326–327, 331–332
  testing, 323–324, 331–332
troubleshooting, 345–346
NFS (Network File System) resharing, 277
  access permissions setup, 280–281
No Access permissions, 163
NTP (Network Time Protocol) services,
  synchronizing clocks, 222, 237

O

Observe command (ARD), 495–496
open command, 530
Open Directory
  authentication services, 202
  backup of directory files, 237–240
  configuring, 208–211
  discovery protocols, 203
  KDC, 211
    Kerberos single sign-on, 236–237
  LDAP, 203
  OpenLDAP implementation of
    LDAP, 203
  Password Server database, 211
    backup, 237–240
    Open Directory replica
      configuration, 224
    password policies, 228
  passwords for LDAP users, 228–229
    local directory node cleanup,
      235–236
    troubleshooting, 234
    user accounts, enabling, 232–234
    user accounts, importing/exporting
      records, 229–232

user accounts, resetting passwords,
  232–234
plug-ins, 203
print queues, 250
  sharing *versus* creating, 252
server connected to directory system,
  205, 206
standalone server, 204
synchronizing clocks with NTP
  services, 222
troubleshooting services, 240–241
  Kerberos, 242–243
  LDAP, 241–242
Open Directory master, 205, 207–208
  binding clients with LDAP
    configuration, 216–220
    verifying authentication, 221
  Kerberos single sign-on, 236–237
  synchronizing clocks with NTP
    services, 222
Open Directory replica, 205
  configuring, 223–225
  KDC, 224
  Password Server, 224
  read-only copy of LDAP directory, 224
  synchronizing clocks with NTP
    services, 222
Open Firmware boot code, 455
Overview pane, DNS, 92

P

PackageMaker
  adding packages to Network Install
    images, 462
  deployment issues/solutions, 440, 458
  distribution projects, 460–462
  metapackages, 458, 460
    troubleshooting, 462
passwords
  backup of Open Directory files, 237–240

network user accounts, logging in,
222–223
shared secret passphrases, 111
user authentication
crypt passwords, 226–228
password policies, 228
shadow passwords, 150–151,
226–227
PAT (Port Address Translation) maps, 125
pbcopy command, 532
pbpaste command, 532
PDC (primary domain controller),
Windows, 202
PIDs (process identifiers), 526
ping command, 92
PINs (personal identification numbers) in
authentication, 130
pipe character (|), 531
PKG format, 486
plutil command, 532
port-level multiplexed NAT. *See* PAT
port overloading. *See* PAT
POSIX permissions, 162, 163–164
ACLs, 170, 173–174
group accounts
creating, 181–182
removing members from groups,
181–182
versus inheritance, 282–284
limitations, 165
setting with Workgroup Manager,
166–167
Windows file service, 318
PPTP (Point-to-Point Tunneling Protocol),
131–132
preference manifests, 376–378
print services
access controls, 267–268
accessing through firewalls, 117
Apple Talk, Name Binding Protocol, 258

Internet Printing Protocol, 249
configuring clients, 258
Line Printer Daemon, 249
Bonjour, 258, 260
logging options, 255
monitoring, 266, 270–271
CUPS logs, 266–267
Open Directory authentication, 202
print queues, 249–251
creating and configuring, 259–261
default LPR queues, 254–255
managing, 265–266
printer pools, 252–254
quotas, 255–257, 394–395
troubleshooting, 269
printers
adding, 262–263
preferences, 392–394
testing, 263–264
server-based *versus* network-printer
sharing, 248
Server Message Block, 249
authorization, 258
Windows Network Neighborhood
using NetBIOS, 258
troubleshooting, 268–269
Printer Setup Utility, 262–263
process management, 525–526
ps command, 525–526, 531
PTR (pointer) DNS records, 83
pull and push echnology, 441

Q
QTSS (QuickTime Streaming Server),
505–509
QuickTime Streaming service, 29

R
RAID arrays, 516–517
RDA (Remote Directory Access), 116

Read & Write permissions, 163, 164, 166, 167
Read Only permissions, 163, 166, 167
Real Time Protocol (RTP), 506
Remote Desktop. *See* ARD (Apple Remote Desktop)
Remote Directory Access (RDA), 116
remote installation, Mac OS X Server, 18
    command-line tools, 19
    Server Assistant, 18, 19–23
RTP (Real Time Protocol), 506
RTSP (Real Time Streaming Protocol), 506, 507
Runscript *versus* runscript commands, 346–347

S

Samba 3, 202
SANs (storage area networks)
    overview, 518–519
    Xsan, 516–517
SASL (Simple Authenticatin and Security Layer), 202
scanners, 479
Secure Shell (SSH) protocol
    AFP access controls, 287
    filename wildcards, 531–532
    firewall configuration, 116
    system monitoring commands, 527
    zone records additions (DNS), 84–87
security overview, 104–105
server access
    controlling through server accounts, 161–162
    managing, 138
server accounts, 161–162
    access *versus* user permissions, 162
    ACLs, file-system *versus* service ACLs, 163
    authorization, 161–162
    POSIX permissions, 162, 163–164
        limitations, 165

    setting with Workgroup Manager, 166–167
Server Admin, 42–44
    firewall configuration, 116
Server Admin Tools installation, 10
Server Assistant
    configuring remotely, 23–35
        generating/saving data, 36–39
    installing Mac OS X Server
        on remote computers, 18, 19–23
        on Xserve systems, 18
server daemons, 15
server types, 54
server worksheet, 15–16
service ACLs (access control lists), 163
Service Location Protocol (SLP), 203
Set Network Startup command (ARD), 490
SetFile command, 532
SETI@Home project, 511–512
shadow files, NetBoot service, 452–453
shadow passwords, 150–151
    backup of databases, 237–240
    user authentication, 226–227
share points
    AFS, 280–281
        access setup, 284–285
        AFP, 282–283
        POSIX permissions *versus* inheritance, 282–284
        Windows file services, 306–307
        virtual share points, 310
Share Screen command (ARD), 495–496
shared secret passphrase, 111
Sharing System Preferences (OS X), 11, 276–279
Simple Authentication and Security Layer (SASL), 202
single address NAT. *See* PAT
single sign-on, Kerberos, 236–237
slave zones (DNS), 80

SLP (Service Location Protocol), 203
SMB (Server Message Block) protocol
    authentication, 139
    authorization, 258
    case sensitivity, 346
    file-sharing protocol comparison,
        347–348
    Open Directory discovery protocols, 203
    print queues, 250
        sharing, 251–252
        sharing *versus* creating, 252
    print services, 249
    troubleshooting, 345–346
    Windows file services, 277
        configuring services, 312–315
software serial numbers, 23, 31
Software Update Server, 41, 96–98
    server configuration, 30
softwareupdate command, 532
ssh command, 527
SSH (Secure Shell) protocol
    AFP access controls, 287
    filename wildcards, 531–532
    firewall configuration, 116
    system monitoring commands, 527
    zone records additions (DNS), 84–87
standalone server, Open Directory, 204, 208
static IP address mapping, configuring
    DHCP, 60–61
static NAT maps, 125
sticky bit, 167
subnets, DHCP
    configuring, 56–57
    creating, 65–69
System Image Utility image creation,
    446–448
    boot and install images, 448–449
System Preferences (OS X)
    Network pane
        built-in Ethernet, 70
        DHCP client IDs, 64
    Sharing, 11, 276–279

System preferences (OS X Server),
    Network pane
        link aggregate networking, 39–40
        multiple settings for one interface, 27,
          38–40
systemsetup command, 490

T

tail command, 527
TCP/IP connections
    configuring Mac OS X Server, 27, 33–34
    NAT-service monitoring, 128
Terminal utility
    viewing DHCP log files, 49
    zone records additions (DNS), 84–87
text file searches, 530
TFTP (Trivial File Transfer Protocol), 445
tokens, authentication, 130
top command, 525–526
troubleshooting
    account management, 433–434
    AFS, 290
    custom packages, 462
    DHCP
        for Mac OS X, 72
        for Mac OS X Server, 73
    DNS, 94–95
    Kerberos authentication, 242–243
    Mac OS X Server installation, 49
    metapackages, 462
    NetBoot, 457
    Open Directory services, 240–241
        LDAP user passwords, 234
        LDAP users, 241–242
    print services, 268–269
    VPNs, 132–133

U

UDP (User Datagram Protocol), 128
UIDs (user IDs), 141–142
    POSIX permissions, 164, 170
    searches by filtering, 208

UNIX hostnames. *See* hostnames
user accounts, 139–141. *See also* group
    accounts; mobile user accounts; network
    user accounts
    adding group membership, 158–160
    Deny access, 216
    exporting/importing, 148–151
    GIDs, 153
    local user accounts
        adding users, 142–145, 189
        configuring comments and
            keywords, 145–148
    print quotas, 256–257
    UIDs, 141–142
        POSIX permissions, 164, 170
    UIDs (user IDs)
        POSIX permissions, 164, 170
        searches by filtering, 208

V

volume management, 528
VPNs (virtual private networks), 129–130
    authentication methods, 130
    configuring, 131–132
        clients, 132
    overwriting with Gateway Setup
        Assistant, 106
    Service Backup Configurations folder
        resetting DNS from folder, 114
        saving to folder, 108
    shared secret passphrase, 111
    troubleshooting, 132–133

W

watchdog process, 15
Web Admin, QTSS administration, 508
Web Services
    accessing through firewalls, 117
    basics, 510–511

WebDAV (Web-based Distributed Authoring
    and Versioning), 511
wildcard characters, 531–532
Windows
    ACL compatibility, 162
    primary or backup domain
        controllers, 202
Windows file services, 258, 277
    access permissions
        restrictions, 317–320
        setup, 280–281
    accessing through firewalls, 117
    browsing from clients, 311
    Code Page, 309
    configuring, 279, 312–315
        access, 315–316
    domain master browsers, 309
    monitoring, 311–312
    NetBIOS
        server discovery, 307–308
        workgroups, 307, 308
    oplocks, 306
    server configuration, 30
    share points, 306–307
        virtual share points, 310
    SMB protocol, 277
        configuring services, 312–315
    starting services, 315–316
    WINS, 310
Windows services, Open Directory
    authentication, 202
WINS (Windows Internet Name
    Service), 310
Workgroup Manager, 354–356
    basics, 45–47
    Inspector, 356
    preferences, 47, 369–373
        access restrictions to applications,
            378–381
        Dock, 388–390

Finder, 390–392
Login, 385–388
precedence, 374–376
preference manifests, 376–378
print queue quotas, 394–395
printers, 392–394
workgroups, 367–368
group folders, 361–363, 402–404
configuring, 404–406
versus groups, 361
preferences, 361, 396–401
checking against user preferences, 401
Write Only permissions, 163, 167

X
Xgrid Admin, 513–516
Xgrid Agent services, 511–513
server configuration, 30
Xgrid Controller services, server
configuration, 30
Xsan, 516–517
Xserve systems
installing Mac OS X Server, 18
NAT service for private networks, 126
RAID arrays, 516–517

Z
zones/zone files (DNS), 79, 80–81
records (DNS), 81–87

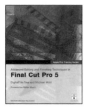